Alfred Hardaker

A Brief History of Pawnbroking

With Full Narrative of How the Act of 1872 was Fought for and Obtained...

Alfred Hardaker

A Brief History of Pawnbroking
With Full Narrative of How the Act of 1872 was Fought for and Obtained...

ISBN/EAN: 9783337141097

Printed in Europe, USA, Canada, Australia, Japan

Cover: Foto ©ninafisch / pixelio.de

More available books at **www.hansebooks.com**

A BRIEF HISTORY

OF

PAWNBROKING

A BRIEF HISTORY

OF

PAWNBROKING

WITH FULL NARRATIVE OF

HOW THE ACT OF 1872 WAS FOUGHT FOR AND
OBTAINED AND THE
STOLEN GOODS BILL OPPOSED AND DEFEATED

BY

ALFRED HARDAKER

Liverpool

SECRETARY TO THE NATIONAL ASSOCIATION
IN EACH STRUGGLE

LONDON
JACKSON RUSTON AND KEESON
EAGLE COURT DEAN STREET
HIGH HOLBORN W.C.
1892

CONTENTS

INTRODUCTORY.

I know of no attempt having previously been made to compile a complete History of Pawnbroking, with the one exception of that written by Mr. W. A. H. Hows, as long ago as 1847. A valuable contribution, so far as ancient money-lending may have been interesting, was made by the late Francis Turner, Esq., Barrister-at-Law, in his introduction to the "Contract of Pawn," published anterior to the present Act becoming law.

Neither of these authors—although both lived to see its accomplishment—dreamt that the idea had taken possession of men's minds, that the time had come for thorough Pawnbroking Reform being attempted, nor that it would be successful. The great struggle made, lasting from 1868 to 1872, and culminating with the passing of the present Act, has therefore never previously been recorded. Neither, again, has the fierce, protracted, bold and successful Defence made against the "Stolen Goods Bill," extending as it did from 1881 to 1884, been chronicled by any Historian.

As both the events now mentioned were, without doubt, the most momentous since the Pawnbroking Trade became regulated by statute—if not, indeed, throughout its whole existence—it has been considered desirable by many, that, while the documents are available, and a few of those gentlemen who took leading parts in both attack and defence, still live, some authentic, reliable, and detailed chronicle should, in a brief space, be compiled.

A

In undertaking this duty, I feel that I accept a work
of no small labour; for being in possession of abundant
material, difficulties of arrangement and selection
present themselves, so that the narrative, as far as it
may be called original, entails much consideration, in
order that it may be connected, lucid, and interesting.

For the rest, I lay no claim to originality, as I am
entirely dependent upon the works before mentioned,
with the addition of a few contributions to periodical
literature; but the purpose of the present History is
not mainly to speculate on the Origin or Antiquity of
the Trade, and its difficult and irregular progress
through the middle ages: therefore those sections of
the subject will be briefly treated. The main object,
as has been previously intimated, is to give a detailed
compilation of the History of the two memorable campaigns through Parliament; showing the preparations
necessary; the labour involved, and the obstacles to be
surmounted; the friends made and the enemies dis-
comfited; methods employed, and oppositions baffled.

It is believed that this information, concisely collated,
will prove of great value to future leaders of the Trade
who may undertake the arduous duties of champion-
ship, in the places of those veterans who have "borne
the heat and burthen of the day," in past exciting
times.

                              ALFRED HARDAKER.
Liverpool, 1891.

CHAPTER I

Commercial necessities appear to have invented a system of money lending in the most remote ages, and in all countries. In China, the reputed oldest of civilized nations, some form of Pawnbroking existed, and trade was done in advances on commodities, even before money was coined. The late Mr. Francis Turner* informs us that pledging was well known to the roving Arabs, one of whom finely remarked: "The life of a man is no more than a pledge in the hands of destiny." Amongst ancient decisions, Sir William Jones on Bailments, quoted by Mr. Turner, gives one by the Mufti of Constantinople, which is recorded in an ancient M.S. Sir William Jones discovered at Cambridge. It states that one "Zaid had left with Amoa divers goods in pledge for a certain sum of money, and some ruffians having entered the house of Amoa, took away his own goods, together with those pawned by Zaid." The enquiry made was whether, since the debt became extinct by the loss of the pledge, and since the goods pawned exceeded in value the amount of the debt, Zaid could legally demand the balance of Amoa? To which question the great law officer of the Othman Court

* *Contract of Pawn.*

A 2

answered: "Olzman, it cannot be." So that in those
early days was understood the principle of non-liability,
where the holder of the pledge had taken as much care
of it as of his own property.

"Thrice," says a modern writer, "within the forty-two
chapters of the Book of Job allusion is made to the
deposit of pledges as a security for money. The allusions
in question (Job xxii. v. 6; xxiv. 3-7.), are all uncompli-
mentary to the lender and seem to imply that the
advance should have been made in charity and not with
a view to getting a living."* This opinion has by no
means been confined to Job's era or country.

Some quarter of a century ago a lecture was delivered
on the "Three gilt balls," and the lecturer boldly stated
—on what authority we know not—that the Pawnbroker was of very ancient lineage. "He was known in
Nineveh; was understood in Babylon, existed in Pom-
peii, and flourished when Greece was in its zenith."
This may be all true, but there is a suspicious taint
about these bold assertions, as if facts had been
sacrificed to epigram. That the Trade did flourish in
Greece and Rome, we have abundant proof, and that
lending money on goods was of daily occurrence, for
the Roman law contains many enactments upon
the subject.† "Herodotus relates how the ancient
Egyptians pawned the dead and embalmed bodies
of their friends. In Rome, when Vitellius was
appointed General by the Emperor Galba, he pawned
his mother's ear-rings to support his family during
his absence. In India money dealers' benches may

* *Quarterly Review.*

† As to immovable property, and there was only an agreement
that it should be security for a debt, it was called both in Greek
and Roman law *Hypotheca.* When the thing pledged was
put in possession of the lender it was named by the Romans
Pignus.—Quarterly Review.

be seen in every bazaar."* It was known also in very remote times among the Hindoos. "In short," says the modern author we have before quoted, "without delving further in the dust of antiquity, we may assume that borrowers and lenders have existed from the dim dawn of man's history, and that the plan of getting a loan upon the security of a material deposit was so obvious, as to have occurred to the impecunious from the very earliest times."

The conclusion we must come to is that the universal mother called "necessity," had early in the development of the human family a son called "invention," and money lending was one of his earliest works.

* Essay on Pawnbroking, by Mr. Phillips, in 1864.

CHAPTER II

Although it is our intention to deal as briefly as possible with all matters connected with the subject which may be considered mythical or legendary, no sketch of the History of Pawnbroking could approach completeness which did not record some account of the various theories which have been expounded, as to why the money lending fraternity should have adopted as their Trade emblem the "three golden balls."

The most poetic and pleasing, if not most ancient, is the legend which Mr. Turner* quotes from "Sacred and Legendary Art." by Mrs. Jameson. The Pawnbrokers' badge and cognizance has been properly enough referred to the Lombard merchants who carried on business in England in the 13th and 14th centuries. But the Lombards had merely assumed the emblem which had been applied to St. Nicholas as their charitable predecessor in the same line. The good Saint was Bishop of Panthera, in Lycia. Mrs. Jameson gives the fable as follows: "Now in that city there dwelt a certain nobleman who had three daughters, and from being very rich he became poor; so poor that there remained no means of obtaining food for his

* *Contract of Pawn.*

daughters but by sacrificing them to an infamous life;
and often times it came into his mind to tell them so,
but shame and sorrow held him dumb. Meantime the
maidens wept continually, not knowing what to do,
and not having bread to eat, and their father became
more and more desperate. When Nicholas heard of
this, he thought it a shame that such a thing should
happen in a Christian land; therefore one night, when
the maidens were asleep, and their father alone sat
watching and weeping, he took a handful of gold, and
tying it up in an handkerchief, he repaired to the
dwelling of the poor man. He considered how he might
bestow it without making himself known, and while he
stood irresolute, the moon coming from behind a cloud,
showed him a window open, so he threw it in and it fell
at the feet of the father, who, when he found it,
returned thanks, and with it he portioned his eldest
daughter. The second time Nicholas provided a similar
sum, and again he threw it in by night, and with it the
nobleman married his second daughter. But he greatly
desired to know who it was that came to his aid;
therefore, he determined to watch, and when the good
Saint came for the third time, he was discovered, for
the nobleman seized him by the skirt of his robe, and
flung himself at his feet, saying, "Oh, Nicholas, servant
of God, why seek to hide thyself?" and he kissed his
feet and hands. But Nicholas made him promise that
he would tell no man.

"In the engraving which accompanies the story,"
wrote Mr. Turner, "the saint is represented standing
on tip toe, and about to throw a bell shaped purse into
the window of the house. The merchant is seen
through an open doorway, sitting sorrowfully in the
nearest room, while his three daughters are sleeping in
a room beyond. The three purses of gold, or as they
are more commonly figured, the three golden balls,
disposed in exact Pawnbroker fashion, are to this day

the recognised and special emblem of the charitable
Nicholas."

All other speculations as to the origin of the Pawnbrokers' insignia are prosaic and common place compared with the foregoing. Mr. Alchin, who was long
custodian of the Corporation Library at Guildhall, held
that the signs suspended over the doors of the Lombards were originally three flat yellow effigies of
byzants, or gold coins, laid heraldically upon a sable
field. These flat discs were afterwards converted into
spherical gilt balls, which could be seen glittering in
the light.*

When Antwerp was in its commercial splendour, we
are told the inhabitants erected a Bourse, and adopted
the sign of Three Purses, the coat of arms of the family
of La Bourse.†

Cobbett who wrote a work on " Pawns and Pledges,"
traces the three balls to the escutcheon of the noble
family of the *Medici.* He also says that extravagant
joke had converted the three spheres into a bunch of
golden apples from the gardens of Hesperides, and the
fabled wearers were descendants of Perseus.

Beckman, in his " History of Inventions," intimates
that the founder of the Medici family was a physician,
and that the three balls were either three boluses, or
three cupping-glasses.

When the South Sea Bubble burst in 1731, Hogarth
expressed his belief that it was in a spirit of derision
that three *blue*, or sometimes golden, balls were hung
after this time, and represented gilt or painted
bubbles.

Dr. Brewer, in " Phrase and Fable," gives the St.
Nicholas legend, and says also that the three balls were
the cognisance of the Medici family. Be this, however,
as it may, it is from the Lombard family (the first

* Hows' *History*, p. 48.   † *Ibid.*

great money-lenders in England), that the sign has been appropriated by Pawnbrokers.*

By some Members of the Trade it is regretted that the ancient symbol of money-lending cannot be registered as a " Trade mark," as it is often misappropriated in seaport towns by outfitters to sailors and others, and under its shadow rascaldom has made a victim of poor Jack. There is no law in existence, at present, which could enable this desire to be accomplished.

The largest Pawnbroker in the world, we suppose, is happy in his ability to append the legend, "*Sub hoc signo floresco,*" beneath the three balls; and it is hoped other members can echo the sentiment, and that beneath the glittering trio the Trade may flourish for many generations yet to come.

* Hows' *History*, page 61.

CHAPTER III

From the few available sources open to us, we learn
that there can be little doubt that the early English
money-lenders were the Jews, who emigrated to this
country early in the reign of William the Conqueror.
Then, as now, they seemed to command the "liquid
capital" of the world, and were intensely hated in
consequence. They held the monopoly of the business
from 1066, to the reign of Edward I., in 1272, simply,
we suppose, because such other wealth as the country
could boast would be in land, and houses, and stock,
with very little of any circulating medium. How it is
that the purse strings of the world should be under the
control of this wonderful and energetic race, it is not
our purpose to enquire here; but as far as history has
any record, it appears the genius of these people was
generally concentrated on making and amassing money.

The interest generally charged during the period
from 1060 to 1290 was from 2d. to 3d. in the £1 *per
week,* so that there is little wonder there should arise
great outcries against usury. The sum of threepence
would represent nearly as much as half-a-crown in the
present time, but as the pound would also possess the
same proportion of purchasing power, we can see that
the per centage rate would vary from 45 to 65 per

cent., and we have no information as to the kind or
quality of the security offered; likely enough in many
cases it would be of the slenderest.

After this oppression of usury, unsparingly exercised
by the Jews, there came, in retaliation, many and bitter
persecutions in the exercise of their hazardous calling.
The tortures suffered by Izaac of York as depicted in
"Ivanhoe," were equalled by those inflicted on one
Aaron of York, whom Henry III. compelled to pay
40,000 marks to clear himself of a false accusation of
forgery.   King John, the father of Henry, compelled a
Jew of Bristol to pay 10,000 marks or to lose a tooth
a-day until he complied.   The Jew suffered the loss of
seven teeth and then paid the sum demanded.

Besides these monetary losses, cruelty, and the
uncertainty of life, with no hope of justice, drove
great numbers out of England, and obliged those who
remained to close their money bags.   In this way,
opportunity was opened for other usurers, so the
Lombards made their appearance, and were assisted
by native Englishmen of an equally remorseless type.
Where the Jews had scourged borrowers with whips,
the Lombards scourged with scorpions; and at length
Henry III. determined that laws should be passed
forbidding any persons, *except himself*, to prey upon his
subjects.*

Richard I. however, was so oppressed with necessities, that he was more lenient, as the financiers
accommodated him with considerable amounts of
money on loan.   It is curious also to learn that his
successor gave a written guarantee to pay the debt;
and this document is supposed to be the earliest
known instance of a letter of credit, afterwards the
great factor in commercial life now known as a
Bill of Exchange.

* Turner.

Several edicts were fulminated against the usury practised by the Lombards, but by their union, and being much richer, together with their cunning, they were always able to beat their English rivals. And "as it is impossible," says Hume, "for a nation to subsist without lenders of money, and as none will lend without compensation, the practice of usury was secretly carried on by the English themselves upon their fellow subjects, or by the Lombards."

CHAPTER IV

It is established beyond dispute that, whatever high and admirable attributes our former Rulers were possessed of, they seemed to be generally in a state of impecuniosity. When the country was sparcely populated and contained no such gigantic manufacturing centres as now, taxes were difficult to collect, and the people earned little and spent less.

In our researches, we have found many records of Royal pawning. It is said that Henry III. of England pledged a valuable "Image of the Virgin" to obtain money to pay his officers. The famous Cid Campeador pawned a locked chest, supposed to contain his jewels, but which only contained his honour, and which the founder of Spanish royalty was fortunate enough to redeem, which proves that there were confiding money lenders even in those days. Edward I. pawned the customs dues, Edward III. having no dues to pawn, deposited his crown on three separate occasions; once it remained "up the spout" eight years. Well might Shakespere say

" Redeem from broking pawn the blemished crown."

In 1339 this "regular customer" pledged both his own and his Queen's crown at the same time, and in

1340 the whole of his jewels followed. Henry V. pawned his crown to his "uncle" the Bishop of Winchester for 100,000 marks, and his jewels to various other persons, authorizing them to sell them in *twelve months*. Henry VI., we are told, pledged one of the crown jewels called the "Rich Collar," in three pieces, to different persons, to pay the expenses of his wedding with Margaret of Anjou, and never redeemed it ; while his bride was obliged to pawn her plate at Rouen to pay the expenses of her journey to England. When Richard II. married Queen Anne of Bohemia, he pawned a large quantity of jewels with the citizens of London, for the same purpose. In 1485 the Earl of Richmond (afterwards Henry VII.), borrowed money from the French King, leaving two live pledges, in the persons of the Marquis of Dorset, and Sir Thomas Boucher. Having "marched thus far into the bowels of the land," he won the crown at Bosworth Field, and on this borrowed 6,000 marks of the citizens of London, and *redeemed the gentlemen*.

Peter, the cruel King of Castile, being attacked by the Duke of Anjou, in 1387, and being deserted by his subjects, was compelled to fly. He offered 60,000 florins to the Black Prince, to restore him to his throne; but, not having the ready money, he put his two daughters in pawn until he could procure it. Whether, or not, he kept his word and redeemed the ladies, the chronicler does not relate.

In 1508, the Archduke Charles of Austria pawned "the rich fleur-de-lys" to Henry VII., for 50,000 crowns. The jewel weighed in gold and precious stones, 21lozs. 10dwts., and was given by Henry VIII. to Francis I. of France, he having the right (but not the money) to redeem it. This transaction rather detracts from the splendour of the "Field of the Cloth of Gold."

The great Isabella, who, when Columbus vainly begged to be permitted to find a new world for Spain,

and, when wearied and repulsed, had turned his back
upon the Court, nobly avowed her determination to
pawn her jewels in the cause. "I undertook the enterprise for my own crown of Castile," said the Queen,
"and will pledge my jewels to raise the necessary
funds." "The Queen," says the historian, "despatched
a messenger on horseback with all speed to call back
Columbus. He was overtaken at the bridge of Pinos,
a pass of the mountains. When the courier delivered
his message, Columbus hesitated to subject himself
again to the delay and equivocations of the Court.
When he was informed, however, of the ardour expressed by the Queen, and the positive promise she
had given, he returned immediately to Santa Fé, confiding in the noble probity of that princess. If the
Americans had duly reflected on this incident, they
certainly, with the stars and stripes, had quartered the
three balls in their national flag.*

In 1361, Northbury, Bishop of London, bequeathed
1,000 marks to be placed in the Treasury of St. Paul's
to be lent on pledges, without interest, directing that
if the money was not repaid in *twelve months*, the
preacher should give notice from the Cross of St.
Paul's on the next Sunday, that if the pledge was not
redeemed in fourteen days (of grace we presume), it
should be sold. He ordered that a layman might
borrow £10; a dean or canon, £20; a citizen or nobleman, £20; a bishop, £40. Imagine a bishop of modern
times condescending to borrow so paltry a sum.

In threading these interesting legends together, it
occurs to us as curious how early in the history of
money-lending the twelve months' forfeiture was
thought of, and how firmly fixed it is in the popular
mind to this day.

* *"The Pawnbroker,"* from *"Heads of the People,"* by
Douglas Jerrold.

CHAPTER V

About the middle of the 16th century, Pawnbroking, in some shape or other, had become so much of a settled business, that attempts began to be made to regulate it by Act of Parliament. In 1546 a legal rate of interest was fixed at ten per cent., by 57th Henry VIII., cap. 9, apparently in the hope of putting down usury. The attempt was, however, ineffectual, as this law was repealed in 1552, but re-enacted in 1571 by 13th Elizabeth, cap. 8, the preamble of which recites that the Act for repressing usury "had not done so much good as was hoped it would."

The most comprehensive legislation occurred in 1603, when an Act as passed 1st Jac. I., cap. 21, intituled "An Act Againste Brokers." The preamble is a tirade against the iniquitous practices "as of long and ancient tyme, by divers hundred years," of persons who were called Brokers. It is much too long to give here in full. Its meaning may be gathered by a few quotations and a summary of the clauses. The first clause said :—"Be it enacted and declared by our Sovraigne Lorde the Kinge, with the assent of the Lords spirituall and temporall, and Commons in the present Parliament assembled, and by the authoritie of the same, that no sale, exchange, pawne, or mortgage of any jewells, plate, apparell, household stuffe, or other goods of what kinde, nature, or qualitie the same shall be of, and that shall be wrongfullie or unjustlie purloyned, taken, robbed, or stollen from any person or persons or bodies politicke, and which at any time hereafter shall be sold, altered, delivered, exchanged, pawned, or done awaye with in the citie of London," Westminster, Middlesex, Southwark, and Surrey included, "to any broker or brokers, or pawne-takers, by any meanes whatsoever, directlie or indirectlie, shall worke or make any change or alteration of the propertie or interest of and from any person or persons, or bodies politicke, from whom the same jewells, plate, &c., &c., any law, usage, or custome to the contrarie notwithstandinge."

The second clause states that, "for the better maintayninge of true and honest dealinge, and for the eschewinge and avoydinge of falsehood, fraude, and deceits in such kinde of Brokers and Pawn-takers : Be it furthermore enacted" that any goods stolen may be demanded by the owners, and may require the pawntaker to declare whether such goods have come into "their possessions," and shall declare, show and manifest the same, and say how and by what means he had them or came by the same. If the Pawn-taker refuse to disclose such information, he shall forfeit unto the true owner double the value of the things stolen. The third clause simply provides that such Brokers, Pawntakers or Fripperers, shall not be confounded with the ancient trade of Brokers within the City of London, and the act shall not be "prejudiciall or hurtfull" to those gentlemen who are supposed to be legitimate and industrious traders ; while the others are "Fripperers and no brokers, nor exercising of any honeste and lawfull trade, and within the memory of many yet livinge such kinde of persons tradesmen were verie few

and of small number." They are also styled "upstart
brokers," and they "daylie do leave and give over
their handie and manual occupations, and have and
daylie do set up a trade of buyinge and sellinge, and
sellinge and takinge to pawne of all kinde of worne
apparell * * * findinge therebie that the same is a
more idle and easier kinde of trade of livinge, and
that there riseth and groweth to them a more readie,
more great, more profitable, and speedier advantage
and gaine than by their former manuall labours and
trades did or could bringe them."

The "Notes to the Act" are—First—Ancient mode
of allowance and business of Broker in London.

Section 1.—"Origin of Pawnbrokers, or dealers in
apparell, &c.

"Evils resulting from their traffic.

"No sale or pawne of any stollen jewells, plate, or
other goods, to any Pawnbroker in London, &c.,
shall alter the propertie therein."

Section 2.—"Pawnbrokers refusinge to produce
goods to the owner from whom stollen, shall
forfeite double the value."

Section 3.—"Not to affect Brokers between Merchants, &c."

Frippery imports the trade or traffic of old or
secondhand clothes and goods. The Company of
Frippiers, or Fripperers, at Paris, are a regular
Corporation of ancient standing.*

This description of Pawnbroking as it then existed
cannot by any stretch of the imagination be called
flattering, and it has been frequently used, we are told,
by hostile writers as showing the low estimation in
which the business was held. But we have no proof
that the description is a true one, as the Act may have

* Hows.

been drafted by some Orr-Ewing of the period, whose prejudices have blinded him to the truth.

It will hardly be believed that the Act just quoted was in operation up to the year 1872, and was only repealed by our Act passed in that year, and known as 35 and 36 Vict., c. 93.

CHAPTER VI

In the year 1638 King Charles I. granted the citizens of London a Charter. Amongst a great variety of matters was the following:—"And whereas divers burglaries, felonies, robberies, clandestine stealings, and thefts of goods, jewels, apparel, and household stuff and other things, are daily committed within our City of London, and liberties of the same, to the grievous damage of some of our subjects inhabiting there, or in parts adjoining. We, for the better discovery of such like offenders, and of things so lost, with, and for us, our heirs and successors, by these presents do ordain, grant, and constitute, that from henceforth and for ever, within the said City of London, and the liberties of the same, there be, and shall be, a certain office of register of all, and for all sales and pawns made, or to be made, to retailing Brokers within the said city, and liberties of the same, and for any goods, jewels, apparel, household stuff, and other things so to be sold or pawned by any persons.

"And further, we do give and grant to the said Mayor and Commonalty and citizens of the said city, and their successors, that it may and shall be lawful to the citizens of the said city, and any of them, for the time being, to expose and hang in and over the streets and ways and alleys of the said city, and suburbs of the same, signs and posts of signs affixed to their houses and shops, for the better finding out such citizens' dwellings, shops, arts, and occupations without impediment, molestation or interruption of us, our heirs and successors, or by any officers or ministers whatsoever of us, our heirs or successors."

It appears a matter of regret that the modern and practical spirit of Bumbledom should permeate our local Governments, so that they vigorously discourage the quaint and picturesome custom here sanctioned by Royal Charter, of hanging out signs symbolical of, or indicating a tradesman's business.

There was a schedule attached to the Charter, defining the fees to be charged for registration, as follows:—

" *Fees to be taken by the Register for Brokers.*

" For the bond to be entered into by every Broaker, Brogger, and Huckster to the Chamber,—Eightpence.

" For every bargain, contract, and pawn, for and upon which shall be lent or given One Shilling or above, and under Five Shillings,—One Farthing.

" For every the like for which shall be lent Five Shillings or more, and under Twenty Shillings,—One Halfpenny.

" For every the like on which shall be lent Twenty Shillings or more, and under Forty Shillings,—One Penny.

" For every the like on which shall be lent Forty Shillings or more,—Twopence."

During the reign of Charles II. two Acts were passed, 13 and 14 Car. II., cap. 15, and 20 Car. II., cap. 6, both containing clauses against unlawfully pawning by " silk throwsters."

The 8 and 9 William III., cap. 36, and 9 Geo. I., cap. 27, also contained other regulations for the conduct of the Trade.

Mr. Hows quotes a handbill of the period he assumes of either William III., or Anne, of a system of registration said to have been agreed to by the Pawnbrokers of the time.

It is prefaced by a preamble of anything but a flattering nature :—

"Great mischiefs daily arising by the common practice of Pawnbrokers and their accomplices in and about the City of London, thieves and other dishonest persons being thereby encouraged to steal, purloin, or imbezel goods and chattells, for want of some good law to prevent the frauds and concealment of Pawnbrokers. It is therefore humbly proposed that an Act should pass to the effect following :—

"1st.—That all Pawnbrokers within the bills of mortality, and within ten reputed miles of the same, now using that trade, shall, by a certain day, enter their names and descriptions, and the goods in their possession or power in an office, with the names and descriptions of the persons from whom they have the same.

"2nd.—That all Pawnbrokers who shall begin that trade, shall within   days enter their names and descriptions, and both they and other Pawnbrokers who before so traded or sought a livelihood, shall, within   days after receiving any goods, distinctly and separately enter, or cause to be entered, every particular on parcels, with the quality, quantity, and respected value, and the money lent thereon, together with the names and descriptions of the persons from whom the said goods, &c. were received, with a register to be appointed by commission from the Crown * * * keeping an office within the said limits, and shall keep the same affixed to every distinct particular or parcel, when and as often as the goods are redeemed or sold.

" 3rd.—The copies from the register to be returned to the office within certain time.

"4th.—Every offender against the Act to forfeit an amount, two-thirds to the use of the poor, and one to the informer.

"5th.—A searcher to be appointed by the register *to have free access to the house* of the Pawnbroker, and on complaint to a Justice of the Peace, he may grant a warrant to the searcher, *with a constable*, to break open doors, &c. The Act not to extend to goldsmiths, known merchants, or exchange brokers, or packers ' of cloath.' "

Even as we read these crude attempts at legislation, we perceive faint glimmerings of the formation of public opinion on the subject tending to the principles which culminated in the greatest Act of the time, our old Geo. III. cap. 99, passed in the year 1800.

CHAPTER VII

THREATENED EXTINCTION

Accustomed, as Pawnbrokers have become, to unjust and bitter attacks being made upon them and their Trade, they would be disinclined to believe that any reasonable person should have had the audacity to meditate their utter extinction. Yet such open and avowed hostility manifested itself in the year 1746, by the introduction of a Bill into the House of Commons, for suppressing the Pawnbroking business and rendering it illegal. We have not been able to trace the names of the authors and promoters of the Bill, but fortunately there is a speech extant delivered in defence of the Trade by a statesman of that day—Mr. Robert Hicks; and we think it would be impossible to plead the cause of the Trade in diction more eloquent, or logic more convincing. He commenced as follows :—"Mr. Speaker, —I hope gentlemen will not be so thoughtless in their care for the property of private men, or in their resentment against offenders, and those who intentionally receive stolen goods, as to put an end to trade, and to the transferring of property from man to man, by bargain and sale; for as long as you allow of any trade or transfer of property, there will be thefts committed and offenders will make out receivers. If you should make an end of Pawnbrokers, or lending money on goods, this would not diminish such offences. They were known before the establishment of the business —much more so I am informed. If there were none to lend money on goods privately, there would be more persons set up to be purchasers of secondhand goods, and among such—those who came dishonestly by any articles—would always find ready purchasers, without asking questions as Pawnbrokers are obliged to as to their names, places of abode, &c., and how they came by such goods." The hon. gentleman then described brokers and secondhand dealers, and how notorious it was that they took little trouble in making inquiries when they could get cheap bargains. He then resumed as follows :—"There can be no inducement to a Pawnbroker to become dishonest and knowingly receive goods improperly come by, because he cannot conceal such things ; he must answer for his duplicates, and he must have all the goods taken forthcoming for a twelvemonth, and they could be traced out from him even longer than that; whereas a receiver, if he suspects the goods will be immediately sought after, he can in a moment send them on shipboard and have them disposed of abroad, which is the reason that numerous stolen articles could never be recovered." The hon. gentleman does not appear to have been aware of the existence of the melting-pot and the re-setter. He proceeded with his argument as follows :— "The Pawnbroker keeps his goods openly in his ware-house, in hourly expectation of their being redeemed ; the receiver, if he suspects them to be stolen, conceals them and sends them to a foreign market. If you should be mad enough to abolish the Pawnbroking business, let me also observe, it is to such dishonest dealers you send poor honest people to sell their property, to answer their necessities, and you must allow very bad would be the terms they would get, cheating, cozening, and every advantage would be taken by such

dealers, and no redemption ever afterwards for them,
as in the case of only lending money on articles; and
were you, I say, mad enough to abolish this Act, you
would multiply the number of such harpies. We find,
Sir, Pawnbrokers are more cautious of receiving stolen
goods, and accordingly we find more thieves stopped
and apprehended by Pawnbrokers than by any other
trade whatsoever, notwithstanding the risk a Pawnbroker runs of being sued and put to great expense,
in case he happens to stop an innocent person.* If it
were not for this risk, I am persuaded all our Pawnbrokers would be so diligent, and so ready to stop
suspected persons offering to pawn goods with them,
that no thief, nor any one concerned with a thief,
would ever apply to them for getting money upon
anything they had stolen; therefore, if you intend to
make any law for the more efficiently preventing its
being in the power of thieves to raise money upon their
stolen goods, instead of putting an end to that, so
useful to tradesmen and the poor, you should make a
law for enabling Pawnbrokers to stop suspected
persons who came to pawn or sell, till they gave a
satisfactory account of themselves. If you should do
this, it would be dangerous for thieves to offer their
stolen goods to any but such as they know to be
receivers and purchasers of stolen goods. This, Sir, in
my opinion is the most proper method for putting an
end to, or at least for lessening, the evil which is now
made a pretence for putting an end to the business
of Pawnbroking; but I have shown that Pawnbroking
is neither the cause of the evil complained of, nor
would the evil be removed or lessened by putting an
end to the business."

The hon. gentleman then dealt with charges that
Pawnbrokers placed temptation in the way of appren-

* Did at that period.—A. H.

tices, journeymen, and servants, and the easy access
caused many to rob their masters and pawn the goods.
He also defended the Trade against allegations that
they encouraged and assisted fraudulent Bankrupts,
which he stoutly denied. "The goods of unfortunate
bankrupts are often, it is true," said the hon. gentleman,
"found in the hands of Pawnbrokers, but such men
never designed to fly beyond the seas, or cheat their
creditors; they pawn with the sincere intention to
redeem, and their not redeeming proceeded not from
any fraudulent design, but from their being disappointed in their hopes of recovering their circumstances. * * * * If, by pawning a parcel of goods to
answer an immediate pressing demand, many are
preserved from ruin, and enabled by change of fortune,
or by getting payment of some of their outstanding
debts, not only to redeem their goods they pawned, but
to carry on for the future a prosperous trade, and
perhaps enrich their families; I say, to abolish entirely
the business of Pawnbroking, or to put it under such
regulations as would have that effect, would certainly
be the cause of ruin to many, who might otherwise
save themselves, and would no way prevent those
frauds which are carried on by persons who take up
goods upon credit, with the villainous design of turning
them into ready money, in order to fly and carry such
along with them beyond the seas."

The hon. gentleman then showed his wonderful and
extensive knowledge of his subject by taking up the
question of interest. He drew the attention of the
House to the fact that other traders made far larger
profits than the Pawnbroker, for, he instanced, any
shopkeeper might lay in a stock that day and sell
it next, or in a week or a month hence, and it
would not be thought unreasonable for him to sell in
that time what he paid five shillings for, for six, and
if hon. members made a calculation they would find

it at least 240 per cent.; but if a Pawnbroker charged 25 per cent. within the same period in the transaction he would only get 2½ per cent. for the month. To show, however, how thoroughly conversant the hon. gentleman was with his subject we must use his own words. "What they then take," speaking of Pawnbrokers, "ought not to be wholly looked upon as an interest for their money, but as a reward for their time and trouble, as well as interest; and if we consider the trouble they must be at, we cannot reckon either the one or the other extravagant. If a Pawnbroker lends but five shillings for a week, he must unfold and examine the pledge offered; he must write and put a bill upon it, with the person's name that brought it, the sum lent upon it, and the day of the month the property was pledged; he must fold it up again carefully, and carry it and lay it up in his warehouse, and he must make an entry of it in his day book; then when the pledger comes to redeem, he must go and fetch it from his warehouse, and he must make a new entry in his day book; after all this trouble, besides paying and receiving money, he gets but three halfpence, which is the highest interest. reward, or profit. * * * * Twenty-five per cent, is therefore no extravagant demand upon small sums for a short time."

Of course there is nothing new, it may be said, in all this, for in the various movements which have been commenced in the present generation, the same arguments have been used till they are worn threadbare, but it is surely surprising to find them marshalled by a statesman in the last century. But with all our copious quotations we cannot find space for more than a seventh of the entire speech. We must therefore be content to conclude with the peroration and the result.

"By this Bill, therefore, you will only add to the oppression of the poor. * * * * I hope I have

now shown, sir, that if this Bill produce any effect
it will be a bad one, and that it will not cure any of
the evils complained of; therefore I hope the hon.
gentlemen who have brought it in, will either drop it
or agree to its being amended; for, though I am
against this Bill, I am far from being against our
passing a proper Bill for regulating the business of
Pawnbroking, and for encouraging men of good
character and plentiful fortunes to follow that business; which, in my opinion, is the only method we can
take for rendering it useful and respectable."

The question being put the Bill was negatived
without a division.

After which Mr. Hicks moved for leave to bring in
a Bill to regulate the business of a Pawnbroker, which
was unanimously agreed to.

The usefulness of the foregoing statements and
arguments in favour of the Trade may be appreciated
by many Members when they are unexpectedly
attacked by the press or individuals. It is partly
on this account we have thought them worthy
of being placed in permanent record, and it cannot
but be gratifying to all interested that so determined
and able a champion should have espoused our cause
as long as 145 years ago.

CHAPTER VIII

We have no means of ascertaining the result of Mr. Robert Hicks' passionate appeal to the House of Commons, or of the leave given him to introduce a Bill to amend the Pawnbroking laws. There appears, however, to have been an Act passed in 1757, 30 Geo. II., cap. 24, but it is said to have been insufficient in its provisions. Sir John Fielding—brother to the celebrated Henry Fielding, novelist, author of "Tom Jones," &c.—a Magistrate for Middlesex, having had much experience of Pawnbrokers appearing before him, thought he could assist the legislature by writing his opinions and offering practical suggestions, somewhat in the style of Mr. C. E. Howard Vincent, of later date, but with the additional advantage that the Magistrate's "Regulations" were the result of practical experience, and were not founded on garbled and unsupported reports compiled by ignorant and not altogether unbiased policemen. Sir John wrote a work entitled "*Extracts from the penal laws*," wherein the Pawnbrokers' Acts are severely commented on. It was in this book that his suggestions appeared, and it will be perceived that many of them have since become law.

This portion of the work is entitled, "*Observations, Suggestions, and Regulations made by Sir John Fielding, one of his Majesty's Justices of the Peace, concerning Act* 30, *Geo. II., cap.* 24."

"It is recommended to all persons who pledge goods of any kind to take duplicates, as they will find many conveniences and advantages from so doing, as the remaining part of the Act will show.

"Where there is sufficient cause of suspicion for Pawnbrokers to stop goods, they shall always, if possible, stop the party; as the contrary will appear to the disadvantage of the Pawnbroker.

"Advises not to require Bills of Sale on pledges under £10.

"Besides the restraints laid upon the Pawnbrokers by this Act, the reputable part of them agreed, for the more easy detection of frauds and felonies, to observe several rules that have been recommended to them as follows :—*

"1st. Some one newspaper to be fixed on by them to be taken in, and public notice to be given of the same. This will save expenses to the Pawnbrokers of different papers, and show the public where to advertise things lost, stolen, or fraudulently obtained. The *Public Advertiser* was then fixed on to be the paper to be taken in.

"2nd. A correct list of the Pawnbrokers' names and places of abode to be given to Sir John Fielding, that handbills may be sent; which, as they make no noise, may often detect in cases of consequence. These bills may be numbered, so that if any Pawnbroker finds himself neglected by their not being brought regularly, he may complain to that Magistrate.

* It appears that Pawnbrokers of repute had agreed to the regulations.—A. H.

"3rd. It would be useful to distinguish the time of day in which every pledge is received. *Ex. gra.*, for morning, 'M;' for the afternoon, 'A;' as this may often prove material evidence.

"4th. To advertise, at the Pawnbroker's expense, the clauses relating to the punishment of persons pawning goods without the consent of the owners; and the Pawnbroker's power of stopping persons suspected.

"5th. Pawnbrokers to shut up at Nine, from Michaelmas (30th September), to Lady Day (25th March); and at Ten from Lady-Day to Michaelmas, Saturday excepted; and to exclude from their Select Society* all those that will not comply therewith.

"6th, This Select Body to use their best endeavours to convict offenders against the Sabbath; and likewise to convict persons offending against the late Act of Parliament, in not making proper enquiries and such entries in their books as is thereby required. This, vigorously executed, will destroy petty Pawnbrokers who keep chandlers' shops and ale houses, by whom it has been too common for stolen goods to be received.

"7th. To take nothing of a strange messenger, that may not be supposed to be their own, unless you take down the name of the real owner, their place of abode, &c.; and, in pledges of consequence, such as plate, jewels, &c., to send to the owner.

"8th. To keep a book on purpose for watches, in which all watches advertised to be lost or stolen, should be entered.

"9th. To take no goods whatever of any soldier in his regimentals.

---

* Even in those early days Protection, or *Select* Societies, were advantageous.—A. H.

"10th. No person to be admitted a Member of the Select Body who has not served a regular apprenticeship to the business, unless ballotted in by the Society.

"11th. Never to send a boy before a Magistrate or Court of Justice, when the master can attend and give the same evidence.

"12th. To be particularly careful in receiving piece-goods, as an error or mistake of that kind may bring a stronger imputation.

"13th. To receive no pledges from children unless their parents or masters or mistresses are well known to the Pawnbroker; and in general to avoid so doing as much as possible.

"14th. Great care should be taken to keep books with the utmost regularity, as they may come under the cognizance of the Magistrates.

"15th. That every Member of the Select Society should have the name of the constable nearest to him, and that his servants should know the same, and to have a by-word to his servants to go for the constable."

Eminently practicable as many of the foregoing regulations are—and some have become law and others common practice in the Trade—there is a strong smack of the Dogberry style in giving the Pawnbrokers "their charge." But Pawnbrokers were not held in very high esteem at this period, and there appears to have existed that inevitable connection in the public mind between thieves and Pawnbrokers. Henry Fielding—himself also a magistrate—in his novel of "Amelia," gives the following sketch of a scene in a police-court:—

"'Indeed, and please your majesty,' said she (the prisoner), 'I took no more than two shifts of madame's, and I pawned them for five shillings, which I gave for the gown that's upon my back; and as for the money in my pocket, it is every farthing of it my own. I am sure I intended to carry back the articles as soon as ever I could get the money to take them out.'

"The girl having told where the Pawnbroker lived, the justice sent to him to produce the articles, which he presently did; for he expected that a warrant to search his house would be the consequence of his refusal.

"The articles being produced, on which the honest Pawnbroker had lent five shillings, appeared plainly to be worth thirty; so that by their goodness, as well as by their size, it was certain they could not have belonged to the girl. Booth, her master, grew very warm against the Pawnbroker. 'I hope, sir,' said he to the justice, 'there is some punishment for this fellow likewise, who so plainly appears to have known that these goods were stolen. The shops of these fellows may indeed be called the fountains of theft; for it is in reality the encouragement which they meet with from these receivers of their goods which induces men very often to become thieves; so that these deserve equal, if not severer punishment than the thieves themselves.'" It is no uncommon thing to meet with "Mr. Booth's" in the present day, who express their indignation at the Pawnbroker's conduct, when likely enough, their own wilful carelessness is little less than contributory negligence.

The reference to Chandlers in the 6th rule, is amusingly illustrated in an old pamphlet entitled "*Pawnbrokers detected and dissected.*" The chandlers it states took in pledges without license, the greater part of the money being laid out in the same shops. The following is the illustration which the author stated may be relied on :—

"A hard working carpenter whose wages did not exceed £1 a week, possessed a large tin kettle; his wife in the course of the week pledged the kettle for sixpence, on Saturday evening the husband brought home a leg of mutton and a half-peck loaf, out of his wages; and as the mutton was to be boiled, the wife, at the

chandler's shop, on Sunday morning, pledged the loaf
and paid a halfpenny, and released the kettle, she then
boiled the mutton and took it up, wiped the kettle out
and paid a halfpenny and released the loaf; after
which the husband and wife sat down and eat a hearty
dinner."*

At one time it was legal for publicans to take in
pledges; but this was prohibited by law in 1751.

In 1784 Pawnbrokers obtained a new Act for the
regulation of the Trade, and the preamble stated ;—
"And whereas several tenders of money, for principal
and interest of money lent and warehouse-room of
goods pledged, latterly made for the redemption of goods
pledged to Pawnbrokers, the amount of which interest
and charges so tendered hath been much below the
amount of the usual and customary interest and charges
taken by Pawnbrokers in the said trade, and at a rate
much below the necessary expenses thereof, &c."

Mr. Hows says the rates of profit by this Act were
greater than those allowed by the Act of 1800, but
does not inform us what they were. He also states
that there were eight new Acts passed in sixteen
years, but leaves us in ignorance of their purport.
He opines, however, that there must have existed a
state of uncertainty which would be prejudicial to the
welfare of the Trade. Few persons, who understand
the subject, will be inclined to disagree with him.

* Hows' *History.*

CHAPTER IX

In the year 1785, so thoroughly impregnated had the public mind become with the illusion that a Pawnbroker's profits were enormous, that it was thought reasonable he should dispense some of them for the benefit of the State. Consequently an Act was passed in that year (25 Geo. III., cap 48) imposing stamp duties on licences; but whether or not it was discovered that the amount was insufficient, the Act was repealed by 55 Geo. III., cap. 184, which fixed the rate existing up to 1872, namely, £15 for London, and £7 10s. for the country.

The former of the two Acts, writes Mr. Turner, is remarkable as containing the first attempt at the statutory definition of the term Pawnbroker. It provided, "That all persons who shall receive or take, by way of pawn, pledge, or exchange, of, or from any person or persons whomsoever, any goods or chattels for the repayment of money lent thereon, shall respectively be deemed Pawnbrokers within the intent and meaning of this Act and shall take out a licence accordingly."

Before the Usury Laws were abrogated, the popular idea existed that Five per cent. was the natural interest which should be paid for all money held on loan; all other and higher interest was considered usury.   In the 6th section of the Act already quoted, it "provided always, that nothing in this Act contained shall extend, or be construed to extend to any person or persons, who shall lend money upon pawn or pledge, at, or *under* the rate of £5 per centum per annum interest, without taking any further or greater profit for the loan or forbearance of such money lent on any pretence whatever."   The act 55 Geo. III., cap. 184, was repealed by the Act of 1872, as described in the First Schedule, in part, "As far as the Act relates to licences to Pawnbrokers."

Usury is derived from the Latin *usura*, which signifies money paid for the use of money lent. The old term in use in England to signify what we call interest, seems to have been usury, and even in the present day there are uneducated people, who, when applying to renew a pledge, will say they wish to pay the "use," so that in some parts of the country—especially Ireland—the term has originally meant interest or money paid for the "use" of money lent, and has doubtless come down orally through many generations.   Lord Bacon, in his Essay on Usury, says, "The commodities of usury are, first, that however usury in some respects hindereth merchandising, yet in some other it advanceth it, for it is certain that the greatest part of trade is driven by young merchants upon borrowing at interest; so as if the usurer either call in or keep back his money, there will ensue presently a great stand of trade: the second is, that, were it not for this easy borrowing upon interest, men's necessities would draw upon them a most sudden undoing, in that they would be forced to sell their means (be it land or goods) far under foot, and so, whereas usury doth but gnaw upon them, bad markets would swallow them quite up.   As for mortgaging, or pawning, it will little mend the matter;

for either men will not take pawns without *use*,* or if
they do, they will look precisely for the forfeiture."
After the maximum rate of interest had been fixed by
law the word was used to signify the taking of more
interest than the law allowed, while at the present day
it is usually applied only to exorbitant rates of interest.

In early times it was considered a great moral wrong
for one who lent money to require in payment anything
more than the money lent.   The laws of Menu allow
interest even to the extent of 18 or 24 per cent., but
the ancient laws of Egypt restricted the practice, and
the Koran absolutely forbids it.

At the present day the old prejudice against interest
has almost died out, and it is no longer considered
wrong to pay for the use of money, any more than for
the use of a house, a horse, a boat, or any other property.   The fact however, that the nature of money
makes it easier for the lender to oppress the borrower,
has at various times, and among most nations, caused
the maximum rate of interest to be fixed by law.   In
England in the reign of Henry VIII., this rate was fixed
at 10 per cent.; in the time of James it was reduced to
8 per cent; during the period of the Commonwealth
it was 6 per cent.; and this was the rate during the
reign of Charles II.; and by the statute 12 Anne, s. 2,
c. 16, passed in 1713, it was reduced to 5 per. cent.,
beyond which rate, with certain exceptions—Pawnbrokers for instance—it was illegal to charge interest
for over a century.   Subsequently the opinion that
money should be borrowed and repaid, or bought and
sold, upon whatever terms the parties should agree to,
like any other property, gained ground, " in deference
to unanswerable arguments," † so that various Acts
modifying the terms of the Usury Laws were passed,

* Footnote by Whately : " Use." Interest.

† *Quarterly Review.*

until by the 17 and 18 Vic. cap. 90, the whole of these laws were repealed, and it is now lawful, with certain exceptions, to contract for any amount of interest. The law, however, still restricts the amount of interest which may be charged by Pawnbrokers upon loans of £2 and under, and the courts under special circumstances frequently relieve persons who have undertaken to pay exorbitant rates of interest to unconscionable money lenders.*

The law does not recognise the charge of interest upon interest, or, as it is called, compound interest. This, however, is a rule easily evaded by the borrower granting a further acknowledgment of the interest as though it were principal : such new contract changes the interest already due into a principal sum.

The Act for the repeal of the Usury Laws, 17 and 18 Vict., is a model of conciseness, consisting only of four clauses. The first states :—"The several Acts and parts of Acts made in the parliaments of *England* and *Scotland, Great Britain,* and *Ireland,* mentioned in the schedule hereto, and all existing laws against usury, *shall be repealed.*" The fourth clause is :—" Provided always, that nothing herein contained shall extend or be construed to extend to repeal or affect any statute relating to Pawnbrokers, but that all laws touching and concerning Pawnbrokers shall remain in full force and effect, to all intents and purposes whatsoever, as if this Act had not been passed." ·

The schedule referred to repeals "Acts and parts of Acts" to the following extent.—37 Hen. 8. c. 9.— 13 Eliz. c. 8.—21 Jas. 1. c. 17, made perpetual by 3 Car. 1. c. 4. sec. 5.—12 Car. 2. c. 13.—Confirmed by 13 Car. 2. stat. 1 c. 14.—12 Anne, stat. 2. c. 16.—53 Geo. 3. c.

* *National Encyclopedia,* vol. XIV.

141.—3 Geo. 4. c. 92.—7 Geo. 4. c. 75.—5 and 6 W. 4. c. 41.—13 and 14 Vict. c. 56. The following Acts of the Scottish Parliament, "An Act of the eleventh parliament of King James the VI., chapter fifty-two, 'It is not lesum to take ane greater annual rent for the 100 pounds nor ten pounds, or five bolls Victual.'

"An Act of the fourteenth parliament of King James the VI., chapter two hundred and twenty-two, 'For punishment of committers of usury.'

"An Act of the fifteenth parliament of King James the VI., chapter two hundred and fifty-one, 'It is not leasum to take mair annuall rent or profit nor ten for the hundreth.'

"An Act of the sixteenth parliament of King James the VI., chapter seven, 'Explanations of the Acts of Parliament anent Ocker and Usury.'

"An Act of the twenty-third parliament of King James the VI., chapter twenty-eight, 'Anent taking of annual rent beforehand to be usury.'"

Acts of parliament of Ireland. "An Act of the tenth year of King Charles the I., session two, chapter twenty-two, intituled 'An Act against Usury.'

"An Act of the second year of Queen Anne, chapter sixteen, intituled, 'An Act for reducing interest of money to eight per cent. for the future.'

"An Act of the eighth year of King George the I., chapter thirteen, intituled 'An Act for reducing the interest of money to seven per cent.'

"An Act of the fifth year of King George the II., chapter seven, intituled 'An Act for reducing the interest of money to six per cent.'"

Thus after the battle against usury had been carried on for centuries, it was allowed to die peacefully by a repeal Act of four clauses, and a schedule repealing twenty-one different enactments, which had attempted to regulate it.

CHAPTER X

We have now arrived at an important stage in our journey, that of the passing of the Act, which, with few alterations, ruled the destinies of the Trade for seventy-two years. This was the 39 and 40 Geo. III., cap. 99, intituled "An Act for better regulating the Business of Pawnbrokers," and was passed on the 28th July, in the year 1800. It was not a consolidation Act, and did not repeal any of the tinkering legislation which had been going on during previous centuries. It took the place of a tentative measure, 36 Geo. III., cap. 87, with the same title, which had been passed for "Three whole Years," and then expired; so it was considered "expedient that provision should be made for more effectually regulating the Trade or Business of Pawnbrokers." And the regulations were as stringent and drastic as they could well be made, the Act itself being crowded with pains, penalties, and pitfalls, that one is lost in amazement that so numerous a body of intelligent Tradesmen, could, for nearly three-quarters of a century, endure its intolerable thraldom.

The Act consisted of thirty-six sections, but some of them were of so diffuse a nature that a few of them would occupy nearly as much space in print as the whole of the present Act itself. The first section is of

the character of a preamble, setting out the reasons for
a new Act as quoted.

The Second Section defines the rates to be taken,
"over and above the Principal Sum, or Sums which
shall have been lent and advanced upon the respective
Pledge, or Pledges (*videlicet*).

"For every pledge on which not more than two
shillings and sixpence shall have been lent the sum of
one halfpenny for any time during which the said
pledge shall remain in pawn not exceeding one
calendar month."   Five shillings, one penny; seven
and sixpence, "one penny halfpenny"; ten shillings
two pence, and so on at the rate of fourpence in the
pound per month up to and not exceeding forty-two
shillings, the interest of which was eight pence. Exceeding forty-two shillings and not exceeding ten pounds,
at and after the rate of threepence and no more, for
the loan of every twenty shillings so lent, by the
calendar month.   These charges were to be made in
lieu of and as full satisfaction for all interest due and
warehouse room.

Section 3 enacted that in all cases where any intermediate sum lent should exceed the sum of two shillings
and sixpence and not exceed forty shillings the Pawnbroker should take by way of profit at and after the rate
of fourpence and no more for the loan of twenty shillings
by the calendar month including the current month.

This section, it will be perceived, introduced the
percentage system of calculation for all sums lent, not
being complete half-crowns, thus producing fractional
sums, which, in a large business it was impossible to
take.   This was the favourite section of the informers,
and led to more penalties being inflicted, and constant
harassing of Members of the Trade than all the other
sections of the Act.

The fourth section lays down that if the profit upon
any sum lent, or as part principal and part profit shall

amount to a total sum of which the piece of money of the lowest denomination shall be one farthing, and the person redeeming shall pay the principal and profit except the last remaining farthing, "and shall not be able to produce and pay to such Pawnbroker or Pawnbrokers, his, her, or their servant or agent, a current farthing, and which shall be to the satisfaction and liking of such person or persons but shall in lieu thereof tender to such person or persons to receive the same one halfpenny in order to discharge the said remaining farthing so due as aforesaid, the said Pawnbroker, or Pawnbrokers, his, her, or their servant or agent, to whom such tender of a halfpenny for such purpose as aforesaid shall be made, shall in exchange thereof deliver unto such person or persons so redeeming goods as aforesaid *one good and lawful farthing of the current coin of this kingdom, or in default thereof shall wholly abate the said remaining farthing* from the total sum to be received by him or them of such person or persons so redeeming goods or chattels as aforesaid."

The drawing of the foregoing clause is a fair specimen of the exact and prolix language employed throughout the entire Act, which also displays the same attention to every petty detail, in every clause. But for prolixity and exactitude, the sixth section, which is entitled "Pawns to be entered in Books" beats every other in the compilation, though nearly equalled in length by one or two that follow. We pass over section five, which is a labyrinth of repetition and relates to "Limiting the profits for part of a month," to summarise section six, which set one of the most difficult tasks, or rather, series of tasks, for a Pawnbroker, or his assistant to perform, that human ingenuity could invent so far as the regulation of any business is concerned. To give an idea of the length of this section and the involved impositions it exacted, it consisted of no less than 975 words, all relating to booking the pledges, and writing the duplicates. It began by stating "that all and every person or persons," who shall take by way of pawn or pledge, any goods or chattels and whereon shall be lent any sum of money exceeding five shillings should "forthwith and before he, she, or they shall or may advance or lend any money, enter or cause to be entered *in a fair and regular manner* in a book or books to be kept for that purpose, a description of the goods or chattels which they shall receive in pawn, pledge or exchange; the sum of money to be lent thereon with the day of the month and year on which, and the name of the person by whom such goods and chattels were so pawned."

Then must be entered the name of the street and number of the house where such person "shall abide," and whether such person is a lodger or the keeper of a house, "by using the letter 'L' if a lodger, and the letter 'H' if a housekeeper, and also the name and place of abode of the owner or owners of such goods, &c." Then it is provided that goods pledged for sums not exceeding five shillings, shall be entered in the same exact manner, not "forthwith," but within four hours next after the goods have been pledged. This established what were known in the Trade as "lows" and "mediums." The "auctions" were for sums exceeding ten shillings, and must be entered in the manner aforesaid, but in books kept expressly for that purpose, and apart from all other pledges whatever. They were too to be numbered in such book progressively as they were received in pawn, "in the manner following; *(videlicet)*, the first pledge that is received in pawn in the month of *September* next, shall be numbered No. 1, the second No. 2, and so on progressively to the end of the month," and the like regulation was to be observed for every month in the year.

Next, this inexhaustible clause deals with the writing of the ticket, here called a note or memorandum, which

THE "OLD ACT"

was to be fairly and legibly written, or in part written and in part printed, and must contain all the previous particulars as were taken for entry in the books, including a full description of the goods, name and address of the pledger, with number of the house and whether a lodger or housekeeper, and the name and address of the owner in the same full manner. The Pawnbroker was prohibited from receiving or retaining any pledge unless the pawner accepted the ticket.

The clause then concluded by stating the charges to be made for the duplicate. For sums less than five shillings the ticket should be given gratis; above five shillings and less than ten, one halfpenny; ten shillings and less than twenty, one penny; twenty shillings and up to five pounds, twopence; for five pounds and upwards, the fee was fourpence "and no more."

In giving a compressed account of this prosy section, it will not be easy for such Members of the Trade who have commenced business under the Act of 1872, to comprehend the difficulty in carrying out all the provisions of the complex section under consideration. For the omission of any one of the directions—even the "H" or "L" in book or duplicate—the Pawnbroker was liable to a penalty of *ten pounds,* and we have known such penalties to be inflicted.

To proceed, section 7 enacted that the amount of profits should be indorsed on duplicates, on pledges redeemed, such duplicates to be kept in "his custody" for one year then next following.

Section 8 inflicted penalties against unlawfully pawning goods the property of others. The fines were to be not exceeding five pounds nor less than twenty shillings, and if forfeiture was not paid *forthwith* the justices " shall commit the party or parties so convicted to the House of Correction or some other public prison, of the county, there to remain and be kept to *hard labour,* for the space of three calendar months; and if

within three days before the expiration of the term of
commitment the forfeiture should remain unpaid, the
justices might order the persons so convicted to be
publicly whipped. In the case of any overplus arising
after the claim of the party aggrieved, the balance
should be paid for the use of the poor of the parish.

Section 9 inflicted the penalty of imprisonment not
exceeding three calendar months upon any person who
forged, counterfeited, altered, or caused such forgery
&c., of any duplicate, and who should utter, lend or
sell, such document with intent to defraud.

Section 10 gave power to justices to inflict a similar
term of imprisonment on any persons not giving a good
account of themselves on offering to pawn goods, and
the Pawnbroker had reason to suspect such goods were
stolen or otherwise illegally or clandestinely obtained.

Section 11 enacted that persons buying or taking in
pledge unfinished goods, linen, or apparel, intrusted to
wash or mend, should forfeit double sum lent, and restore
the goods. This is much the same as the law now existing,
without the interminable verbiage of the old section.

The 12th section empowered peace officers to search
Pawnbrokers' premises under a search warrant, for unfinished goods unlawfully come by. It was a long prosy
section, full of repetition, especially as to the jurisdiction of the justices of the peace "for the County,
Riding, Division, City, Liberty, Town or Place," where
the Pawnbroker's house might be situated.

Section 13 enacted that where goods were unlawfully
pawned the justices could order the Pawnbroker to
restore them to the true owner.

The 14th section, a long and complex one, gave
power to punish the Pawnbroker who would not
deliver up goods when ordered. The penalty was a
sum not exceeding £10, and in default committal to
prison there to remain, "without bail or mainprize,"
until the goods were delivered up.

By section 15 persons producing the duplicate deemed to be the owners, unless the Pawnbroker should have had previous notice from the real owner, *not* to deliver the same.   Section 16 regulated giving declarations, much the same as now, but not requiring a witness.   Section 17 defines the term of forfeiture to be 12 months, and might be sold.   Those of ten shillings and under did not become the *absolute* property of the Pawnbroker, but were redeemable so long as they remained in the Pawnbroker's possession and within the period defined by the statute of limitations.   Goods above ten shillings to be sold by auction under similar regulations as at present, but no privilege was given to the Pawnbroker to bid for and buy goods which would afterwards become his own property.   Section 18 provides for the quarterly sales; 19, that pledges should be kept three months longer than twelve months on notice being given (*i.e.*—"backing"). Section 20, account of sales to be entered in books, open for inspection of pledger for three years, and who might demand overplus; sec. 21, Pawnbroker not to purchase goods in pledge; pledges not to be taken from persons under 12 years of age, or intoxicated, and fixing the hours of business; sec. 22, table of the rates of profit to be placed in view; sec. 23, names and business to be painted over door; sec. 24, penalty for selling goods before the time of forfeiture or injuring them; sec. 25, Pawnbrokers to produce books when necessary; and sec. 26, penalties for offences against the Act not to be less than forty shillings and not exceeding £10.   The sting in this section from which the Trade suffered severely was in the words, "and the Justices *shall* award one moiety of the said penalties to the party complaining" (not aggrieved) *i.e.*—the Informer; and the remainder to the overseers of the poor of the parish.

The clauses following to the conclusion, state that churchwardens must prosecute ; *convicted persons* not

to be allowed to prosecute or inform ; act not applicable
to persons lending money at £5 per cent., but to extend
to exors., &c., of Pawnbrokers ; persons sued to plead
general issue ; persons in the place where the offence
occurs to be competent witnesses ; form of conviction ;
and appeal.   The last section declared the Act to be a
public one.

We have here given as copious a delineation of
the Act of 1800, as the space at disposal will permit ;
and it is hoped that it is sufficiently lucid to enable
younger generations to form an accurate conception of
the intricate and perplexing legal restrictions and
regulations which harassed their predecessors in the
conduct of so difficult a business as Pawnbroking.
That ardent aspirations for delivery from this bondage
should have animated the minds of many at a comparatively early date, is not surprising ; but that
practical alleviation from such oppression was not
consummated for nearly three-quarters of a century,
seems inexplicable.   Want of *unity* in numbers, money,
and motive, doubtless will account for the delay.

CHAPTER XI

We are told in classical legends that one Cadmus, son of Agenor, King of Phœnicia, went forth, at the bidding of the gods, into a strange country there to build a city. Being in want of water he sent his men to search, and they found a fountain, but it was guarded by a fierce dragon, which the men dare not approach. Cadmus, however, slew the dragon, and sowed the ground with its teeth, when behold, they grew up and took the form of armed men.

The dissemination of the sections of the Act of 1800, had a somewhat similarly magic effect, for at once there sprung into being a body of infamous and un-scrupulous pests, known as informers, who levied black mail, and issued informations against Pawnbrokers for the most trivial offences or omissions. These men had been in fair positions as lawyer's clerks, auctioneer's assistants, and one a police serjeant. Their *modus operandi* consisted in employing confederates to pledge articles of sufficient value, and if there was any infor-mality in the writing of the ticket—even as we have said to the omission of the "H" or "L" or the number of the house—or if a fraction of interest too much should be taken, an information would be issued against the offending Pawnbroker. As the penalty

D

could not be less than forty shillings, and might be
anything up to £10, the informer getting one-half the
amount inflicted, a very profitable business was carried
on.   We have it on good authority that some London
Pawnbrokers, early in the century, rather than be
brought before Magistrates, or live in a state of uncertainty, actually paid the villains a certain sum per
annum to be allowed to carry on their business in
peace and security.

Nor were their depredations confined to the Metropolis; for they found a pleasant and lucrative change
in taking a "provincial tour" periodically, and did
well in such places as Bristol, Sheffield, Manchester,
Liverpool, and other large towns.

The best known of these conspiring wretches were
Calligan, or O'Callaghan alias M'Callan, who had been
in both the London and Birmingham police forces; a
man named Birch who sometimes varied his occupation
by laying information against keepers of "Dolly shops,"
or illegal Pawnbrokers.   Then there were, Atkinson,
Stowell, Moore, Carter, Wyatt, and an active and
daring fellow named Martin.   This man died at
Birmingham, in January 1841, and a local paper inserted a short obituary notice.   It stated that Martin
died at his house in Pope-street.   He had existed for
many years upon the produce of informations against
Pawnbrokers, and it was a remarkable saying of his,
that had it not been for what he termed the *persecution*
of the press, he should have made an independent
fortune.

In the same year Callaghan had the impudence to
propose to the Birmingham Pawnbrokers, that for the
modest bonus of £20, he would undertake to lay no informations for twelve months.   But his audacity and
greed met with no response, for the Birmingham
Association unanimously passed a resolution, greatly
to their credit, and the satisfaction of the whole Trade,

"That this Society will take Callaghan's proposal into consideration that day twelve months."

We cannot more forcibly convey the operations of these pests to society than to give an illustration of their proceedings in a police court, and so select a day, over fifty years ago, at Northampton, where M'Callan laid informations against a Mr. Negus, Pawnbroker, whom it was alleged in one case had taken illegal interest to the amount of *one farthing and a-half.*

Before the opening of the case, M'Callan stated that on a previous occasion Mr. Dennis, solicitor for the Pawnbrokers, had thrown out insinuations against his character and competency to prefer those informations. (It will be remembered that we pointed out in the previous chapter that section 29 debarred *convicted persons* from laying informations, and this was what the Informer referred to.) M'Callan said he wished to know whether or not Mr. Dennis was prepared to sustain those charges? Mr. Dennis then handed in a document to the Bench, of which the following is a copy:—

"Extract from the Commissioner's book. Charles O'Callaghan. Police Serjeant, joined the force October 15th, 1839, and was dismissed January 8th, 1840, for most improper conduct in procuring articles under false pretences, and frequenting public-houses when on duty. The result—dismissed by Francis Burgess, Esqr., Commissioner of Birmingham Police.

"Charles O'Callaghan, *alias* Charles M'Cullen, *alias* Charles Cullen, late of the London and Birmingham Police, lived at 7, Bartlett-buildings, East-street, Shoreditch; aged about 32 to 35; tall person about 6 feet 1 or 2 inches; respectable appearance, long features, dark complexion. True Copy, R. H. Stephens, Chief Supt. of the Birmingham Police."

M'Callan here defied any person breathing the vital air, to prove that he had ever been convicted of a felonious offence.

The Court decided that the document was no bar to the competency of the informer, so the case proceeded.

Martha Hazeldean, a witness, then stated that she went to Mr. Negus's, in St. Giles-square, and tendered a duplicate for a blue jacket which had been pledged for 3s. Three shillings and a penny was the sum demanded, which she paid. The ticket was not endorsed in her presence. The penny interest was *a farthing and a-half more* than the legal interest. Had often received half-a-farthing from a Pawnbroker.

M'Callan: Have you one here ?—Witness: Yes.—M'Callan: Produce it for these gentlemen.—Witness did so.

On the cross-examination by Mr. Dennis, the witness admitted that the jacket belonged to M'Callan, and that she had received it from him for the purpose of pledging it to ascertain the rate of interest the Pawnbroker would take. She had been employed in the same way at Bedford, where M'Callan had been laying informations, and in several other places in the country and London. She had been employed in this way for *three years* at 14s. per week and travelling expenses.

Mr. Dennis addressed the bench for the defence that the Magistrates had seen no proclamation that made the half-farthing current; it was not known by Act of Parliament unless the proclamation was produced. He also objected to the information as it ought to have stated the precise fraction of legal interest to which the Pawnbroker was entitled, namely, *one-tenth of a farthing more.*

Evidence was then given by persons employed by the defendant, after which the Magistrates dismissed the information without assigning any reason.

M'Callan, however, nothing daunted, proceeded with a second information for a similar offence, and called his retained witness Hazeldean, who deposed to

having been charged 3s. 1d. by Mr. Negus for the
redemption of a shirt and handkerchief, on the 28th
June.   In defence the unsupported evidence of the
Pawnbroker only was offered, and he stated that the
interest charged was ¾d.   The Bench considered the
case proved, and inflicted the lowest penalty of forty
shillings and costs.

Another case was then proceeded with, being a charge
against Mr. Cavit, that he had advanced 4s. upon a
wedding ring, and on redemption he had taken as
interest one penny instead of three farthings and one-
tenth of a penny, which was the legal interest.   The
informer confined the charge to the excess of half-a-
farthing.   The same paid retainer appeared to give
evidence and the information was dismissed.

M'Callan had yet another case but he declined to
proceed as he thought the Magistrates had made up
their minds against him.   The result of this day's
work for the informer was that he had to pay £1 2s.
costs in cases dismissed, while he received £1, the
moiety of the penalty inflicted: result, informer 2s. out
of pocket.   This is but one example, showing one day's
proceedings originated by these vile imposters, whose
nefarious transactions instituted by one or other of
them, extended over nearly half-a-century.   They
were not always allowed so much latitude as was extended to M'Callan, at Northampton.   In a case which
Birch brought forward at the Thames Police Court, in
London, he was proceeding to examine a witness with
the *sang froid* of a practising solicitor, when the
Magistrate asked, "Are you a professional man?"
Birch replied, "No; I am in the informing line."   The
Magistrate said, "Then I cannot permit you to address
the witness;" after which Mr. Birch subsided.

This man found a lucrative employment in laying
informations against keepers of "Dolly Shops," or
unlicensed Pawnbrokers, which were very common at

one time all over the country.   He would send one of
his paid creatures to sell some article, on the
understanding that it could be re-purchased
in a day or two on the payment of a small profit.   In
one day at the Thames Police Court, Birch succeeded
in getting one fine of £10 inflicted, and two others of
£5 each, so that his share of the profits would be £10.

An Act was subsequently passed (19 and 20 Vict.),
further defining Pawnbrokers, which put an end to
illegal lending or buying "with or under any agreement or understanding, express or implied," that the
goods were to be redeemed or repurchased on any
terms whatever.   This clause was imported bodily into
the Act of 1872, and now stands therein as section 4.

In the Act 2 and 3 Vict., c. 71, sec. 34, a blow was
dealt at the professional informer.   It recites ; " And
whereas by divers acts, the moiety or other fixed
portion of the penalties to be thereby recovered, is
adjudged to the informer, and the same has been found
to encourage the corrupt practices of common informers ; for prevention thereof be it enacted, that
where by any Act now in force, or hereafter to be
passed, a moiety or other fixed portion of the penalty or
penalties thereby imposed is or shall be directed to be
paid to the informer *not being the party aggrieved*, it
shall be lawful for any one of the said magistrates
before whom the conviction shall be had to adjudge
that no part or such part only of the penalty as he
shall think fit, shall be paid to the informer."

This discretionary power was for some years confined
to the Metropolitan police district, but the Act 22 and
23 Vict. c. 14, extended sections of 2 and 3 Vict., cap.
71, to all parts of England.   These sections were
32, 33, 34 and 35, and were known when passed as the
"four clauses," but before being made general they
had in many large cities and towns been engrafted
into local Acts.

Section 32 prescribed another grip on the informer's freedom, by awarding amends for the laying of frivolous informations.   They had then to proceed with great caution, for the section stated that if "it shall appear to the Magistrate by whom the case shall be heard that there was no sufficient ground for making the charge, the Magistrate shall have power to award such amends, not more than the sum of five pounds, *to be paid by the informer* to the party informed or complained against for his loss of time and expenses in the matter as to the Magistrate shall seem meet."

Yet another blow, and the informer lay scotched, but not killed outright.   As we have shown, one of his methods was to extort black-mail by laying, or threatening to lay, informations against a Pawnbroker.   The latter, in many instances, would rather pay some amount than waste time in the precincts of a frowsy police court—in those times considerably worse than now,—and as any terms were profits to the informer, he would gladly accept the money.   Another of the "four clauses," however, stepped in, and no doubt, to the mind of the informer, *persecuted* him unmercifully.   Section 33 said :—" That in case any person shall lodge any information * * for any offence alleged to have been committed by which he was not personally aggrieved, * * and shall afterwards directly or indirectly receive * * any sum of money or other reward for compounding, delaying, or withdrawing the information, it shall be lawful for any one of the said Magistrates to issue his warrant or summons for bringing before him the party charged with the offence of so compounding &c., and if such offence be proved * * such informer shall be liable to a penalty of not more than *ten pounds*."

And so, gradually but surely, the professional informer was hunted down; his "honourable and legal calling" was beset with risks, and the fun and profit were no longer on the one side only.   Many long

weary, harassing years elapsed ere relief came to the
Pawnbroker, and he could breathe freely and without
the fear that any pledge he might take was being
planted by the restless lynx-eyed informer. The
wretches sank lower and lower, and after an occa-
sional and fitful appearance in some provincial town,
with but poor success, they were reduced to offering
for sale printed cards containing calculations of the
legal interest for the guide and information of Pawnbrokers. For these publications, about the size of an
ordinary penny multiplication table, the modest sum of
half-a-crown was solicited. The demand was so small,
however, that the results did not pay travelling expenses.

To the present generation the informer is unknown;
he was the "Bogey-man" of the past. Enlightened
legislation slowly hurried him to his doom, and the
substitution of the step-rate, instead of a percentage one,
in the Act of 1872, killed him outright, and the species
has happily become extinct.

CHAPTER XII

PAWNBROKERS' ASSOCIATIONS: PROTECTIVE AND DEFENSIVE

Suffering from the incessant attacks of the professional Informer, who ofttimes blended his occupation with that of the ingenious "duffer," the conditions under which Pawnbrokers carried on the business, after the passing of the old Act, were uncertain, unsafe, and almost intolerable. The instinct of self-defence, as against an enemy always in ambush, as it were, was slow in development, and, to be effective, required united forces in capital and numbers. London, spreading over a wide area, with no such means of locomotion, ninety-one years ago, as exist now, was, comparatively speaking, like an extensive sea studded with islands; as the East had little commerce with the West, the North with the South, and the Central not much with any. Thus in the latter district the venerable but still stalwart Bouverie Society, now over a century old, flourished in a small way and provided a common meeting place for a few tradesmen resident in the neighbourhood. But the entertainments were more of a social order than of stern dry business, although, then as now, Trade topics were discussed, advice sought and given, but no defence or legal assistance was rendered. The same may be said of the Northern

Friendly Society, which has come far enough South as
to meet in Holborn.   Other small coteries no doubt
existed whose members mutually assisted each other in
counsel and advice.   But it should not be forgotten
that in those days—now apparently as remote as the
middle ages—there was no penny post; the electric
telegraph but lay embryo in the inventor's brain,
who had not been troubled with wild dreams of such a
means of intercommunication as the telephone.   Thus
the Trade were lying in clusters, as it were, with few
means of meeting to arrange any common plan of action
in their troubles.

It was not until the year 1821 that a regular Trade
Society was organized under the title of the " Pawnbrokers' Institution," and having for its objects the
protection of its members by imparting early information of frauds and deceptions on the Trade, and to
guard against the practices of common informers and
other designing persons.   The terms of membership
for some years were five guineas for the entrance fee,
and an annual subscription of one guinea.   These
excessive terms were resisted by a large number of the
Trade in London, who succeeded in 1836 in establishing
a new Society under the title of the " Pawnbrokers'
Association," to which the late William Nathan acted
as Honorary Secretary.   It was not, however, until
February, 1842, that the inaugural dinner took place,
and on that occasion Mr. Nathan explained the reasons
for objecting to the older Institution.   In reply to the
toast of his health, he is reported to have said, " Next
to your approbation, nothing cheers me so much as to
feel that the Association is prospering.   I little thought
in the year 1836, to see it what it is now.   Informers
then dragged us up to be fined every day, they had
but to sue on a writ for some attorney as bad as themselves, and the Pawnbroker found it better to pay all
expenses and pocket the affront.   There was certainly

another Society, but the conditions which had to be gone through were very disagreeable; there was first to be black balled; when that ordeal was passed there was an enormous sum to be paid as an entrance fee, and to know that at least one-half was spent in eating and drinking; and, in addition, there was no chance of getting on the Committee unless by paying £3 or £4 to make up the deficiency of the dinner bills."

This description of the parent Society is certainly not one to inspire us with confidence and admiration, as being a beneficial organization likely to promote or protect the interests of the Trade. But the strong opposition of the new Association brought about gradual reforms; the entrance fee was reduced to a guinea, and the expenditure was correspondingly mitigated. Then a splendid rivalry ensued for the acquisition of new members. This went on to the year 1847, when after considerable negociation and persuasion the two Societies became one under the present title of the "Metropolitan United Pawnbrokers' Protection Society."

In the provinces the idea of unity for mutual defence, appears to have taken root earlier even than in London. The Manchester and Salford Association is probably the oldest in the kingdom, for it has attained its 82nd or 83rd year of existence. It has always been a stalwart, flourishing, and energetic combination, generally to be found in the van of progress. The Liverpool Association is perhaps not many years its junior, but no record is to be found in its archives of the date of its establishment. It seems to have been the cradle of reform, for nearly 50 years ago we find addresses issued to the Trade, and emanating from this Association, urging an amendment of the Act, then existing. Many of the Country Associations are of considerable age, as Bristol, Nottingham, Sheffield, Newcastle, Birmingham, Glasgow, and numerous

others. In these later days, they exist in every
important town in the kingdom, and many of them
find useful work to do, although the common Informer has been obliterated.

Although in many crises through which the Trade
has passed the advantages of unity throughout the land
for the common cause, have been frequently demon-
strated, all attempts to found a National Society or
Federation of Societies have ignominiously failed. As
long ago as 1835, a Parliamentary Committee was
formed in London to oppose some measures introduced
into the House of Commons, and to champion the cause
of the Trade generally. It is a curious fact that this
Committee did not think it necessary to report to their
constituents until December 1842. They then called a
meeting of the Trade to which they read their report.
Their Parliamentary experience had convinced them that
a union of the Pawnbrokers of Great Britain was very
desirable. National defence had been thought necessary, they said, in consequence of the Foreman of the
Grand Jury at the Session of the Central Criminal
Court having made a presentment containing a most
sweeping denunciation of Pawnbrokers as guilty of
receiving stolen property and promoting juvenile de-
linquency. A meeting was called, and a deputation
waited upon the offending foreman, and the result of
the interview was described in the report as having
been "most perfectly satisfactory."

This Committee next thought an amendment of the
Act was desirable, and made application to Lord John
Russell, then the Home Secretary, asking him to receive a deputation on the subject. This his Lordship
refused, and sent a curt message to the effect that
he "could not undertake any measure relative to the
Pawnbrokers' Act." This, adds the report, set the
matter completely at rest, and induced the Committee
to suspend all further proceedings.

They were however called back to life in consequence of Lord Clements moving for a Committee of Inquiry into the Pawnbroking Laws in Ireland, and a Bill was brought into the House of Commons, intituled a Bill to establish a British Pledge Society. They succeeded in getting this Bill withdrawn, and again suspended operations. When animation returned in 1842, they had become convinced, as a result of correspondence with the Provincial Trade, that the interests of all would be best served by a union of the whole of the existing Associations, and expressed themselves that such an organization was a consummation devoutly to be wished. The basis of such a General Association they thought would be (1st) To obtain full and particular information concerning all measures affecting Pawnbrokers, whether of a local or a general character ; 2nd. to gather information on all cases from local Societies ; and 3rd. to promote measures for the suppression of " Dolly-shops," " Wee pawns," or " Little Goes," &c.

The report was adopted, and a resolution passed " That in the opinion of this meeting an Association of the Pawnbrokers of Great Britain should be formed." A vote of thanks to the Committee closed the proceedings, and the idea of a National Association seemed to have been successfully launched. It was not however until October 10th, 1843—nearly a year after the former proceedings—that the Committee issued another report, which was of a remarkable, if not unique nature. It commenced by stating that the provisional Committee appointed in the previous December to draw up rules and regulations for the government of " An Association of the Pawnbrokers of Great Britain for the purpose of obtaining information concerning all measures legislative or otherwise, affecting Pawnbrokers, and to promote or oppose the same, to collect all cases and opinions relating to the Trade; for mutual advice and protection ; and generally to promote the

interest and respectability of Pawnbrokers, without interfering in the conduct of the case of any individual,"
begged to report that a few days after their appointment they were deprived, by a serious accident, of the
assistance of an active member; during many months
therefore the Committee "were from various circumstances, dormant." Further, that at the time they
should have resumed their labours, the Charitable Pawn
Offices Bill was introduced into Parliament, and all
their energies and funds were required, and successfully
used, as the Bill was withdrawn. They could only
report therefore that during the long period of ten
months *they had done nothing* for the object for which
they were appointed, so were *prepared to receive such
censure*, as the Members might be pleased to visit them
with. They begged to resign "from a sure conviction
that you would deservedly deprive them" of the
positions they had held. They suggested, however,
that a new provisional Committee should be appointed,
who should send a circular to every Pawnbroker, requesting him to state his opinion, and what amount he
would contribute.

This curiosity of " report " literature was adopted by
the meeting, but no other Committee was appointed to
succeed the invertebrate one just before dissolved.
Several speakers regretted the unexpected result, as
they felt the Trade would practically be left entirely
defenceless, and there seemed to be Parliamentary
and other attacks made upon them daily.

The defunct Committee commenced under bright
auspices, and possessed funds to the amount of £83,
wherewith to endow the new National Society. Other
money had been contributed too, there being 350 London
Pawnbrokers who subscribed £227. The provinces
made a lamentably beggarly show; for 1,600 Pawnbrokers in all other parts of England and Scotland,
only raised £80 19s. Well might one of the Members

present exclaim, "It is a thankless task, working for the Trade!" However, in the ten months all this money had been frittered away on Parliamentary agents, other expensive and somewhat useless luxuries, so that the balance sheet showed there was £7 owing to the Treasurer. A speaker, in very sarcastic language, characterized the conduct of the Country Trade as anything but creditable, for, he said, the London Trade had contributed something like 15s. per head, while the Country Pawnbrokers had only subscribed about *one shilling each*.

And thus ended the first attempt to form a National Association. Promising from its inception every hope of a strong and useful organization, it cannot but be regretted that such an ineffectual and flaccid effort was made that the whole scheme sank into miserable and complete failure. The cause of this lamentable collapse was not, however, to be laid only at the threshold of that limp and lifeless Committee, which so meekly desired to be gently kicked out of office, but mostly to the hopelessly indifferent attitude of the country. From the earliest years in which the writer took an interested and active part in Trade movements, it has always been current gossip that London, at heart, was always dead against any reform in the Act of Parliament; that the action of the Metropolitan Trade had always been to create obstacles and impede all the avenues that led to alteration. But it appears, from the experience of the dejected and rejected Committee, that the apathy of the Country Pawnbrokers was the real cause of the first effort to effect national unity being abandoned. The credit, so long withheld, to achieve this desirable consummation, evidently belongs to London.

It may perhaps, be permitted to the author to state, that in the year 1866, two years after being elected Secretary of the Liverpool Pawnbrokers' Association, he proposed a National Union of the Defence Associations throughout Great Britain. The proposal

was in the first instance received with every expression
of approval, and a largely attended meeting was held in
Liverpool attended by representatives from London (Mr.
Geo. Attenborough, Hon. Sec.), Nottingham, Leeds (3),
Manchester (3); Bolton, Bradford (2); Birmingham,
Sheffield (3); St. Helens, Bury, Blackburn and Macclesfield. Resolutions all in favour of the scheme were
enthusiastically carried, and a prosperous and successful voyage appeared assured. Obstructions not expected
to be encountered were created, and so protracted and
harassing was the opposition, that the author and all
the Committee resigned, and the National Association
remains unaccomplished to this day.

While this volume was passing through the press,
we were favoured, through the kindness of a friend,
with some further information relative to the London
Societies. We had assigned, it appears, greater antiquity to the Northern Friendly Society than it
was entitled to, its origin being only 1837. The
author was, through the same kindly authority, informed that the earliest Metropolitan Pawnbroking
Societies of which records have been preserved are—
The Local Society of Pawnbrokers of Southwark and
its environs, which held its meetings at the Half Moon
Inn, Borough, in 1812; the Eastern Society, which
held its first meeting at the Laurel Tree, Brick-lane,
on the 13th of April, 1813; and the Bouverie Society,
which was also frequently spoken of as the Queen's
Head or Holborn Society. The Southwark Society, in
December, 1812, issued a circular to the Trade at large,
recommending them to form themselves into one
Society, which should be entitled—"The Society of
Pawnbrokers to Protect themselves against the Frauds
of Swindlers and Sharpers." Nothing, however, resulted
from this effort until September, 1821, when what is now
known as "The Metropolitan Pawnbrokers' Protection
Society" was started under the above quaint title.

CHAPTER XIII

In preceding chapters, we have narrated how Kings, Queens, and other potentates, were, in the earlier ages, driven by their necessities to seek the aid of the Pawnbroker, but the story has yet to be related how an English King was himself near becoming a Pawnbroker—or rather the head of a Pawnbroking establishment. This was no other than Charles I. of pious, but impecunious memory. Some person living during the reign of that monarch, being aware, doubtless, that all the ingenious methods that could be devised for raising money were nearly exhausted, projected a scheme for the establishment of a gigantic Pawn House. Mr. Hows tells us that he saw the veritable MSS. in the British Museum, and that he quoted verbatim from the originals. The first is called the "M.S. Hargrave, No. 321, page 697." Hargrave, we presume, was the loyal patriot who desired to elevate his royal master, in the social scale, by making him a Pawnbroker. At any rate he proceeds to inform the citizens of London, that he proposes what he calls " A project declaring howe the intollerable injuries done to the poore subject by brokers and usurers, that take 30, 40, 50, 60, and more in the hundreth, maye be

E

remided and redressed, the subjectes thereby greatly
relieved and eased, and his Majesty much beneffitted;
which is thus to be effected."

"That the cittie of London wilbe pleased of the
moneyes of the Chamber of Orphanes porçons, (which
we presume means trust money), or of their owne
moneys, to make a bank of ready money amounting to
£100,000, and that the samebe placed in a Pawnhouse
for that purpose to be provided, and to be governed
or directed and disposed of by a Treasurer, 4 Aldermen,
and other inferriour officers by them to be chosed as is
hereafter expressed.

"And what moneyes more shalbe required for that
purpose of the same Pawnhouse maybe had as before,
or elles of the perticuler citizens, for which shalbe
paied 7 in the hundreth per annum: And it is to be
thought that by the cittie of London there wilbe
borrowed yearely from the Pawnehouse uppon pawnes,
£300,000; and if a man consider what may be borrowed
upon houschold stuffe, what upon clothes, jewels,
houses, and lands, and howe many doe noweadayes in
and about London live uppon brokery and usury,
perhaps *ten or twelve thousand*, and how much they
have to doe, noebodie will doubt at it, and indeed I
have heard by credible report that one citizen onlie in
London, putting out his money to brokers, winnith by
it most every yeare 10 or 13 thousand pounds; soe
that 1 gesse there wilbe borrowed more rather than
lesser than (as is aforesaid) £300,000; which at 15 in
the hundreth per annum is £45,000."

Having, to his own mind satisfactorily, earned this
large profit, he disposes of it in the following liberal
manner:—

" For interest to the proprietaries at seven   £   s.   d.
    in the hundred per annum   21,000   0   0
" For that some money nowe and then lyeth
    dead and unemployed and soe looseing 9,000   0   0

	£	s.	d.
"For his Majestic for two-third parts of the profits	10,000	0	0
"For the pawnehouse for one third part of the profit	5,000	0	0
	45,000	0	0

"The £5,000 for the pawnehouse are in this manner to be employed:—

	£	s.	d.
"To a Treasurer at £1,000 per annum	1,000	0	0
"Four Aldermen or overseers of the pawne-house, at £500 le peece per annum	2,000	0	0
"Two clerkes for the house, to keep the lidger-booke, register-booke, and accompts, both of principal, stock increase, money taken upon interest, and to observe the dayes when the pawnes be taken in, at £100 le peece per ann.	200	0	0
"Two auditors for the Kinge, to looke the truth of passing the accompts	200	0	0
"Two clerkes more for the re-delivery of the pawnes and keepeing the accompts of the interest money, one for the King, and one for the house, at £100 le peece	200	0	0
"Two goldsmiths, at £60 le peece	120	0	0
"Two brokers for merchants at £60 le peece	120	0	0
"Four common brokers at £50 le peece	200	0	0
"Eight servants for their diet and waiges at £20 le peece	160	0	0
"Three women servants, for their diet and waiges at £20 le peece	60	0	0
"For house-rente, fyre, inke, paper and other charges	300	0	0
	4,560	0	0

" For remaine £440 which may be put as a stock in the pawne house, being the revenue for his Majestie	£	s.	d.
	440	0	0
	5,000	0	0

" Or elles it may be agreed that if the one-third part of the profit for the Pawnehouse will not suffice to supplie the said charges of the Pawnehouse, then the said charges shalbe defalketh out of his Majesties part, and soe likewise what shalbe more amounting of the said one-third part the said benefitt shalbe for his Majestie."

It is hardly necessary to record that this ambitious and impracticable scheme was a dismal failure. The " Cittie of London " would have none of it, nor would it spare any money, as they, the Merchants, " being constrained to keep it in readiness against all charges and suddaine eventes." Likewise " the cittie will not have their wealth or state knowne." Also, " that it would be a great danger to the cittie to putt her money into a Pawnehouse," for " the cittie is rich enough, and neede not to put out her money for to gett by it any more."

Then the projector answered all these and other objections at great length, but although the M.S. is very quaint and ancient, we have not space for lengthened quotations. One curious matter in the way of protection of the stock and premises may be named as being ingenious if not inconvenient. It is suggested " that noeboddy should robbe the Pawnehouse by digging under it, it may be procured that there should runne water under it, and soe, nocbody may by digging gett any goods out of it."

The golden dream of this devoted Royalist vanished into incorporeal air, when the light of the experienced London merchant was thrown upon it; the King never became a Pawnbroker, nor drew his handsome annual stipend of £10,000.

The earliest Charitable Pawnbroking, indeed, the earliest Pawnbroking Establishments of any kind, in England, were the Charitable Loan Funds, known as "the Oxford Chests." The earliest example of these Institutions, is one established by Robert Grossteste, the Chancellor of the University in 1240, who issued an ordinance to provide for the proper maintenance of certain funds which had previously been subject to some maladministrations. The immediate effect of this ordinance was the creation of the first "chest," called the *Frideswyde Chest.* It runs somewhat to this effect: The money paid by the townsmen of Oxford as a kind of fine on account of a certain injury inflicted by them upon the University, not having been hitherto regularly applied to the use of poor scholars, Robert Grossteste, as diocesan, issues an ordinance to regulate the same. The money, with additions thereto from bequests or otherwise, shall be deposited in St. Frideswydes Priory: and one of the brethren of that Priory, appointed by the Priors and approved by the Chancellor, along with two distinct persons to be elected by the University, shall have the custody thereof: It shall be lent to poor scholars upon proper pledges being given for the same: such scholars must not hold a benefice of the value of ten marks. If the pledge be not redeemed within a year, it may be sold. Any scholar thus borrowing shall sign a writing by which he shall bind himself not to go to law or appeal against the above conditions, and that he will submit himself to the Chancellor in everything relating to the transaction. The aforesaid Guardians of this money shall annually render an account before Auditors appointed by the University for this purpose.

It appears that many of the old City companies were sometimes in the habit of advancing money on pledges. The Drapers' Company had an entry, as follows:—
"1528 Thomas Pykkes brought into this house as a

pledge a stand nutt and cover, all sylv', and p'cell gylt."
The Merchant Tailors' Company have an entry to this
effect:—"1563. William Hector deliverd in pledge, for
his fine of 40s., a Ring of Gold, for calling Thomas
Wilford a prating boy."*

In 1657, one Samuel Lambe, merchant, addressed a
letter to Oliver Cromwell, "the Lord Protector." It
was printed in pamphlet form and advocated the
establishment of a Bank for the Nation, and the
following paragraph will illustrate its purport:—"That
the same Bankes may also furnish another Banke with
a competent stock, to let out any sum of money under
five or ten pounds, at reasonable rates upon pawne or
other security; whereas now many poor people, to
raise a small stock to get a living by, are forced to give
intolerable rates, as about 6d. per week for the use
of 20s."

The pamphlet was said to be " printed at the Author's
charge, for the benefit of the English Nation, and to be
considered of, and put in execution, as the High Court
of Parliament, in their great wisdoms, shall think
meet." Their "great wisdoms," however, neither
thought nor acted in the matter. About this period
other similar schemes were advocated by a Dr.
Chamberlayne, a Mr. Murray, and others, but none of
them were ever carried out.

At last, in 1707-8, was established the afterwards
notorious " Charitable Corporation, for lending money to
the industrious, but necessitous poor," and the public
were led to believe that Charitable Pawnbroking had
been started on a sound basis. In the preliminary
announcements it was stated that the ostensible motives
in forming the Company were to defeat the extortionate
and extravagant usury made by the Pawnbrokers, which
often amounted to from 30 to 60 per cent. It obtained

---

* Hows: from Herbert's *History of the Twelve Great
Companies.*

its Act in 1708, but did not commence its business of
lending to the "industrious, but necessitous poor,"
till 1719.   The capital was at first £30,000, and the
Corporation paid for some years, dividends at the rate
of 10 per cent.   In 1722 its capital was enlarged to
£100,000, which, it was soon discovered, could not be
invested in legitimate Pawnbroking.   Having still to
pay a dividend that should not exhibit any falling off,
it entered into a course of jugglery, not altogether unknown in more modern times.   Again the capital was
enlarged, by successive stages, until it amounted to the
enormous sum of £600,000, nearly all of which was
ultimately dissipated by gambling speculations on the
stock exchange.   It also "made advances," upon the
shares of several large building schemes, for lack of
better pledges.   The concern struggled on to the year
1731, having during that period 294 houses engaged in
Pawnbroking.   At one time, the £100 shares were at a
premium of £10 3s., but through the reckless speculations, mis-management, and embezzlements it sank
gradually, deeper and deeper still, to the final collapse.
Then it was discovered what a policy of fraud and deceit
had been pursued; for in addition to wholesale robberies, fictitious pledges were created to account for
the disappearance of the money.   Then a panic ensued,
the confiding and investing public had the glaring fact
staring them in the face that they had been gulled by
daring, unscrupulous, and designing rogues.   The
cashier, George Robinson, M.P. for Marlow, and John
Thompson, the warehouse keeper, both decamped in one
day.   The proprietary shareholders sent a petition to
the House of Commons, representing that by the most
notorious breach of trust they had been despoiled of
their money by persons to whom the care and management of their affairs were committed; the corporation
had been defrauded of the greatest part of its capital,
and that many of the petitioners were reduced to the

utmost degree of misery and distress.* On investigation of the accounts it was found that the £600,000 had dwindled down to £34,150 which amount represented the entire available assets. The legislature granted a lottery, as a means of relieving the distress of the many sufferers caused by the defalcations. Although the lottery was ostensibly for £500,000, yet after expenses, it only yielded about 9s. 9d. in the pound, which was distributed.

The affair was the greatest scandal of the time. The managers recklessly sold bonds, and there was a deficiency of £420,000, besides £110,000 in Bank of England notes, and £40,000 in notes and bonds of their own coining. On the managers being remonstrated with and reminded of the "necessitous poor," they are said to have replied "D——n the poor; let's go into the City and get money for ourselves."† It was reported that many Members of Parliament were expelled the House of Commons, amongst whom were Sir Robert Sutton, Sir A. Grant, Dennis Bond, and others who were all managers of the Corporation, and were called upon to give security before the Barons of the Exchequer for their not leaving the kingdom. What other punishment, if any, was inflicted upon them, is not disclosed.

All disastrous experiences which a previous generation endures, speedily dies away, and the successors know not, or care, of the dire consequences which may befall themselves, by entering into visionary schemes. So in 1823, a new scheme was launched called a "Philanthropic Loan Bank," and the prospectus said, "At this time when capital is so abundant and *British philanthropy so active and benign*," it behoved capitalists to study whether there were not opportunities to

* Smollett's *History*.

† *Gentleman's Magazine*, May, 1732.

secure advantages "by the *beneficent* employment of
their wealth," and it was confidently believed an
abundant remuneration would result. This sanguine
anticipation was, however, never realized, nor was the
capital ever subscribed.

Again in 1824, another infallible panacea for the cure
of poverty was projected under the high sounding title
of " The Equitable Loan Company of England. Capital
£1,000,000, (with power to increase) in 20,000 shares of
£50 each." The deposit was £2 per share, and no less
than 17 Members of Parliament were on the provisional
committee. How far the projectors understood the
subject, may be gleaned by an argument put forward
on more than one occasion that the Pawnbroker's
capital was so limited that considerably smaller amounts
were advanced than the borrowers required. The
Bill fell dead in the House of Commons, and Pawnbroking was still left to private enterprize. "It is
singular," wrote Cobbett, "that the pilot bubble of the
multitude previously sent aloft, was succeeded by
another new scheme of an " English Mountain of
Piety." Some £400,000 is believed to have been
subscribed, but it speedily vanished, as did the
funds of the Charitable Corporation.

We have not space to enumerate all the attempts
made, even to our own time, for establishing Charitable .
or otherwise Joint-Stock Pawnbroking. A "British
Pledge Society," to lend money at half the rates charged
by Pawnbrokers, with capital to the amount of £300,000,
which we suspect was only on paper, came to grief like
its predecessors. In 1843 the Earl of Devon introduced
a Bill in the Lords called a " Charitable Pawns Bill,"
which was referred to a Select Committee, but it never
got beyond that stage. In 1844 a Bill was introduced
into the Commons by the Hon. W. F. Cowper, Member
for Hertford, "To provide for the establishment and
regulation of Charitable Pawn Societies." Strong

opposition from the public and the Trade was evinced against it, and the *Times* in its commercial article said, the project "is one much discussed in the City, and held to be of a very questionable character; for past experience has shown the great difficulty of management, and almost *irresistable temptation to fraud*, which attends such institutions."

In 1846 another attempt was made to raise the modest capital of £30,000, to establish a *Mont de Piété* in Norwich, and it was said that the idea was warmly supported by the Bishop of the diocese. It went, however, the way of all other previous good intentions.

Many other schemes, similar in their character, have been attempted, and we believe there is one in embryo somewhere about Westminster at the present time. As this brief chronicle has no pretence to be an exhaustive history, we cannot stay to comment upon it or others. So likewise the *Monts de Piété* of Belfast, Limerick and other Irish towns, must pass here without comment. They are well known to have been disastrous and dismal failures, and have a peculiar and interesting history of their own, not unfamiliar to many of our readers.

CHAPTER XIV

HARBINGERS OF REFORM

Few but veterans in the Trade, have any knowledge of the various attempts made to remedy the defects in the Act of 1800, the general opinion being that the movement which originated in 1868, was the only campaign through which a valiant struggle was made. We have already shown, however, how in 1838 the London Pawnbrokers were anxious for some alleviation of the tyranny and oppression under which they suffered, and prayed the Government to amend the Act in many directions, but without effect. There was no popular clamour for a "reform" of that character, therefore Ministers could afford to turn a deaf ear to the desires of iron-ruled tradesmen. These latter had not the courage to take the field themselves, but had turned their backs on any fighting, and thrown away their weapons. But the idea was germinating, and if London soil could not develope it, there was an opinion that a trial by the provinces was worth attempting. Accordingly, the subject was brought forward at the annual meeting of the Liverpool Association, held on December 6th, 1843. After the report had been adopted, and other business disposed of, the Chairman said he wished to draw the attention of those present to the important subject of making application to

Parliament for an amendment of the Pawnbrokers'
Act. There would, he opined, be little difference of
opinion as to the desirability of such an alteration,
while he regretted that the London Committee had
declined proceeding in the matter.* It remained
therefore for the Provincial Trade to undertake the
duty, and their Committee had been considering the
subject for the previous few months; they had consulted their legal adviser, who had informed them
that with suitable outlay and proper exertions, they
could not fail to secure their object. After ventilating
the subject in all directions, it was resolved "That the
Committee of the Association be empowered to take
means for obtaining an amendment of the Pawnbrokers'
Act." Thus was the standard of "Reform" raised
nearly half a century ago, but it only inaugurated the
first demonstration in force, of an intermittent
campaign extending over many years.

A circular dated January 25th, 1844, was the earliest
intimation that the Committee had got to work. · It
was signed by the Chairman, Mr. Edward Byford—a
name still extant in the ranks of the Liverpool Trade—
and *inter alia* it stated that : "The views of the Trade
generally are, to reduce excessive penalties—to found
the regulations of the Act on an equitable basis—and
for the purpose of protecting the honest portion of the
Trade from the attempts of the common informers—
to reduce the interest from a percentage calculation
to specific fixed rates for the various sums lent—to
expunge the trivial requirements of the statute—and
generally to simplify the mode of conducting their
business. The Liverpool Trade have been subject of
late to much local annoyance, independently of the
general vexation caused by the introduction of the
Charitable Pawns Bill; for these reasons they are

* *Ante* p. 61.

determined, provided they receive the approval of any
considerable portion of the Trade, to endeavour to free
themselves from the shackles imposed by their Act.
At the same time if London, or any considerable town
will take a leading part, they are quite willing to
render all the assistance in their power, and to heartily
join in the endeavour to attain the most desirable
amendment."

The circular was sent to every Pawnbroker whose
name and address could be discovered in the United
Kingdom.

The first promise of support came from Newcastle
and Gateshead. At the quarterly meeting held Feb.
13th, 1844, the following resolution was adopted:
"That this Association approves generally of the
alterations proposed in the present Pawnbrokers' Act
by the Liverpool Trade, and that they are willing to
support them as far as lies in their power, in any
expense which they may incur upon that subject."

The progress of reform, however, was not, even at
that period, to run smoothly into the haven of success.
A sudden deadlock was produced by the introduction
of the Charitable Pawn Societies Bill into the House
of Commons by the Hon. W. Cowper, member for
Hertford. It was presented to the House on the most
appropriate day of the year, the 1st of April, and on
that day, read a first time, and was put down for the
second reading on Wednesday, 17th April. This was
not a good augury for a Bill likely to be opposed, and
there could be no uncertainty about the intention of
the Pawnbrokers in that respect. They were not slow
in realizing the unpleasant fact that the enemy was
at their very gates, and it must now be defence and
not attack. Reform became an unread drama, and was
pigeon-holed, to abide the result of a more stirring
performance. The whole country was roused into
activity to avert the unexpected and pressing danger.

Meetings were held in every town; subscriptions were
freely handed in; petitions against were poured into
the House of Commons. Day after day, honourable
members brought up from their constituents petitions
praying for the discharge of this bill, which consisted
of 20 clauses and 2 schedules, and threatened to put an
end to Pawnbroking as a private enterprise. In a few
days the following constituencies sent up petitions to
their representatives for presentation :—London (3),
Manchester, Liverpool, Birmingham (2), Newcastle,
Nottingham, Edinburgh, Exeter, Paisley, Brighton,
Rochester, Bromsgrove, Newark, Southampton,
Wednesbury, West Bromwich, Dudley, Warwick,
Leamington, Worcester, Coventry, Walsall, Wolver-
hampton, Sunderland, Glasgow, Warrington. These
were followed by others from great centres, as Leeds,
Sheffield, and many of the surrounding districts.
Invaluable services were rendered by two brothers
named Yardley, who were Pawnbrokers residing at
Hertford, and consequently constituents of the Hon.
W. Cowper, who had introduced the Bill. They wrote
to him most spirited and determined letters, full of
unanswerable arguments, and being supported by the
Trade generally, with the unanimity we have indicated,
the Government officials saw there was no other course
open but to sacrifice the bill. On April 18th the hon.
gentleman wrote to Messrs. Yardley as follows :—

" House of Commons.

" Gent",
     " After the communications you have addressed to
me, I think it right to inform you that the President of the
Board of Trade, having requested me to withdraw my Bill for
the present, on the ground that the question of Pawnbroking is
of such importance that it demands, and *will receive*, the
attention of Government, I have thought it right to accede to
his request, for it is only the neglect of the subject on the part
of the Gov^t that could justify an individual Member in attempting to legislate upon it.
     " I have the honour to be,
       " Your ob^t. Servt.
           " W. COWPER."

So the victory was on the side of the Trade; but a rude
blow had been struck at the reformers. The agitation,
the labour and the money required for the Campaign,
staggered the boldest and exhausted any enthusiasm
which had previously been aroused.

About the end of July, however, the redoubtable
reformers once more emerged from their enforced
retirement. The Liverpool men issued another address
urging that a meeting of Delegates from all parts of
the country should be held and that London should
take the lead. On the 31st of the month a deputation
from Liverpool waited upon the Committee of the
Manchester Association and produced a copy of the
amended Act which was read and fully considered. It
was then resolved: "That the amended Act now
proposed by the Liverpool Committee is considered
by this Committee an improvement on the present Act
of Parliament and ought to be adopted." Thus
Manchester became an adherent, and the following day
Warrington also joined hands. The Liverpool
deputation then visited Nottingham, Derby, and
Leicester, and at each place were well received, while
funds were subscribed or promised. Glasgow passed
approving resolutions and appointed a corresponding
Committee; Birmingham, however, was coy and
hesitating, for they considered it inexpedient to
introduce the Bill as Government had intimated that the
subject was already under consideration. On the other
hand, Portsmouth, Portsea and Gosport, gave early
support. Sheffield cordially agreed to the proposed
revision. Later, a deputation composed of Members
from the Manchester and Liverpool Committees visited
Leeds, and found the Trade unanimous for reform.
Elated, doubtless, with their success, the deputation
boldly made for Birmingham, and strangely enough
the Lancashire eloquence was so effective and convincing that the resolution which had been passed was

rescinded, and the meeting cordially approved of the movement, and engaged to give it "steady support." Wigan, Preston, and other towns came in with resolutions and subscriptions, and thus the march of reform seemed to be without impediment and promised to terminate in a glorious success.

London, however, held aloof, ostensibly because it believed Government would not adopt the bill, but would be tempted to introduce one of their own drafting and of greater stringency than would be likely to emanate from the Pawnbrokers themselves. The rumour became so general that this was to be the case that the late Mr. Jackson, editor of the *Pawnbrokers' Gazette*, wrote to ask for some definite information. A reply was received, dictated by Mr. W. E. Gladstone, in which it was stated that no such intention existed, finishing in true diplomatic style by saying, "That no step in relation to so important a subject will be taken without due deliberation and ample notice."

Reform meanwhile lay quiet. The once vigorous Committee were quiescent till March 31st, 1845, when came the deluge. In a report then issued by the Liverpool Committee, it regretted the secession of their "Manchester friends," who, continues the report, "at the eleventh hour, and when the Liverpool Committee were all but pledged to proceed, suddenly and unexpectedly changed their opinion, and notwithstanding their having for a period of six months joined heart and hand with the Liverpool Committee, after collecting a respectable amount for this object from the Manchester and Salford Trade—after affording assistance by deputations to various towns," they suddenly discovered that it was necessary to pause and remain neutral as a Committee. The Liverpool Committee therefore *had decided to abandon the Bill.*"

The Manchester Committee at once responded, and said the charge was incorrect, for it was the Liverpool reformers who had diverged from the lines laid down and agreed upon. The plan proposed was first to organize the Trade throughout England and Scotland, and afterwards elect a Central Committee. This was announced at every meeting that had been held, and, it was urged, the "Liverpool gentlemen well know that they departed from this the original plan; that the failure in forming a Central Committee does not lie at our door; 'nay we would have gone with them even at the eleventh hour,' in their own diverged plan of obtaining a new Bill, had they been able to demonstrate the practicability of obtaining it."

To think of Reform in the face of this unfortunate breach between the two most powerful bodies, was out of the question; therefore the matter remained in *statu quo*, although not forgotten. A firm hold had been obtained in parts of the country, and not a few were anxious to proceed. In December, 1847, nearly three years after, an address appeared in the *Gazette* from an anonymous correspondent, "To the Pawn-brokers of Great Britain," and said, "The days of reform are upon us; we cannot work many years longer with our present unjust and partial law—a law which would be submitted to by no other body of traders, even not possessing a tithe of the influence enjoyed by the Pawnbrokers of London alone. And why is it thus with us? Whatever may be the political bias of this or that administration * * * it could not be said, even by the most factious enemies of the powers that be, that a British Parliament ever refused to sanction *better and more equitable* laws for any class of Britain's subjects."

Possibly, since 1847, opinions may have been formed which are scarcely in accord with the enthusiasm of the above quoted writer. Many other correspondents took up the subject till the matter assumed so much reality

and earnestness, that a meeting was held in London on
March 1st, 1848, a Mr. Vesper, the convener, being
elected to fill the chair ; and many metropolitan
notabilities, with a few provincial representatives, were
present.   The following resolution was proposed by
Mr. Ashford, and seconded by Mr. Folkard, "That this
meeting deems it desirable to go to Parliament to
obtain an alteration of the existing Pawnbrokers'
Act."   An amendment was then proposed by Mr.
W. A. H. Hows, and seconded by Mr. Harrison, "That
this meeting is of opinion that to go to Parliament in
order to obtain a larger amount of profit from the
very poorest classes of the community, is a step calculated
to increase the prejudices already existing against the
Trade; and that there are no reasonable grounds for
supposing that such a proceeding would meet with
success."   A long and lively discussion took place,
when the amendment was declared to be carried.   The
minority, we are told, appeared to constitute about
one-third of the meeting.

CHAPTER XV

Nothing daunted by their crushing defeat at the London meeting, the little band of ardent reformers met in March, 1848, at the Ship Tavern, Bishopsgate-street, still determined to make a fight to obtain freedom from the thraldom of the Old Act. The Mr. Vesper, mentioned as taking a leading part at the previous meeting, now occupied the Chair, and the position of leader. A resolution was agreed to without a dissentient, that the meeting should then resolve itself into a Committee for the purpose of forwarding the views of those Members of the Trade who were desirous for an alteration of the Act of Parliament; also that there be a corresponding Secretary for the furtherance thereof. This step appeared to be definite, and likely to lead to business. Perhaps more so was the next resolution, which declared, "That this meeting is of opinion it would be very beneficial to the interests of the movement if each individual Member of the Trade, in town or country, who wishes an application to be made to Parliament for an amendment of the Pawnbrokers' Act, will forward his assent to the Chairman, *with a promise of a subscription of* £1, so soon as a Parliamentary Committee shall be appointed; this plan, the meeting considers, would enable the

F 2

friends of *the cause* to ascertain their real strength, and
it therefore earnestly recommends that it be adopted
by all those who are favourable." Although the foregoing
resolution extended almost to the dimensions of a brief
address, it was cogent enough, and emphasised practical
politics. Had there been any latent desire for reform
extensively permeating the mind of the country, such
an appeal should have enabled the gallant band to cry
"Once more into the breach, my friends, once
more!" But it seems to have been only a forlorn
hope, receiving no support; and gradually dwindled
into the forgotten.

Liverpool, still anxious to be in the van of progress,
but now under leaders whose names will be remembered
by the present generation—Mr. Jas. Fairhurst, and Mr.
Batten—about this time reported at a meeting in their
own town the result of their experiences at the London
meeting. They deeply regretted the apathy of the
Provincial Trade, which was only represented by
Liverpool, Nottingham, and Paisley. This induced
the members of the deputation present to refrain from
voting. They were encouraged by the fact, however,
that but a few years previously the London Trade *to
a man*, were opposed to any interference with the Act,
while now a portion of their body sincerely desired
Parliamentary reform.

With what result we have seen. The years 1848-9
went by and not another "note of busy preparation"
was sounded. There were disastrous reasons for
inactivity, not the least of which was a visitation of
the dreadful scourge known as the cholera. In 1849
it raged throughout the land; trade became paralysed.
Special religious services were held, new prayers
composed, and the people's thoughts and griefs were
devoted to the dead and dying. Ideas of reform and
trade matters were obliterated in the nation's sorrows
and calamities.

Then came the all-absorbing Crimean War, creating unexampled and intense excitement from its outbreak, in 1854, to the signing of the Peace, in Paris, in 1856.

It was early in this year that attention was recalled to the subject of Pawnbroking reform by a series of articles which appeared in the *Gazette* under the title of "The Pawnbrokers' Act considered with a view to its amendment." For many months the articles were continued, and drew forth favourable and other comments from numerous correspondents. In the annual report of the Liverpool Association, issued in July of the same year, it was stated that a Special General Meeting had been convened several months previously for the purpose of considering the advisability of appealing to Parliament for amendments of the existing Act. A resolution was passed declaring the opinion that the time had arrived for action; it was also decided to form a guarantee fund to the amount of £400, which sum should be the Liverpool contribution to a general parliamentary fund of £1000. The subscriptions in Liverpool up to the then date, exceeded £250, and there was little doubt—as the report expressed it—that the £400 would soon be reached. The time was considered favourable as the Government had just taken part in the repeal of the Usury Laws, it was therefore conceived to be the duty of the Liverpool Trade to make an effort to take up the important question without delay. Still time passed, and no movement was made. And no wonder, for disasters had come quickly on the steps of each other. First the case of Michael Duffy, who had been sentenced to seven years' penal servitude in Ireland for taking in pledge at Tullamore, a pair of brogues and three petticoats, stamped with the workhouse mark of that parish. The whole Trade quivered with indignation, for it was felt that the punishment was grossly in excess of the offence committed; meetings were held, and subscriptions generously contributed; while Manchester and Liverpool vied with each other in their unceasing efforts to obtain Duffy's release. A deputation composed of the leading officials from both Associations, went to Dublin and interviewed the Lord Lieutenant, Earl Clarendon, and presented petitions praying for a commutation of the excessive sentence. Meetings were held in London and other places, and petitions were also presented to the Home Secretary, and a strong deputation waited upon him at the Home Office. The Journeymen's Benevolent Society got up a large petition. In the end, after the expenditure of infinite labour, and large sums in travelling expenses, preparing petitions, &c., Duffy was released when he had suffered some eighteen months' confinement. The largest proportion of the money left in hand—some £20—was handed to Duffy's wife, and they left the country for America, at least £100 being given by Mr. Mackay the employer. Not very long after this, came the Shrewsbury case, in which the two only Members of the Trade in the town were arrested for knowingly having received a coat and trousers, which were stolen property. An officer had made inquiries at the respective shops, but so meagre was the description given, that the goods could not be found. The officer, *who had the tickets in his possession* all the time, obtained a search warrant, and entering the warehouses, discovered the property, which he alleged the Pawnbrokers had denied possession of. Again the country was aroused, petitions and deputations to the Home Secretary, Members of Parliament, and others poured in. When the circumstances came to be thoroughly investigated, it was found that a carpenter's house had been entered during the absence of the family, and among the articles stolen were the coat and trousers. Two tramps were apprehended on suspicion, and brought before the Magistrates. Notices had been circulated containing the particulars of the stolen property. After the arrest of the thieves, information was obtained *from them*, that some of the property had been pledged in Shrewsbury, and inquiries were made at Mr. Kent's and Miss Robinson's the Pawnbrokers, but without success. It was subsequently ascertained that the men in custody had sold two pawntickets to a lodging house keeper, *from whom they were* obtained by the police. Inquiries were again made at the two shops, but again, as the police asserted, without the goods being produced. A search warrant was then procured and the premises searched, when the trousers were found pledged on the Wednesday, and the coat on Thursday, the police notice being given on the Friday.

The Pawnbrokers were both committed for trial, being allowed free on bail, themselves in £50 each, and two sureties of £25 each. At the sessions the jury brought in a verdict of "not guilty" against Miss Robinson, and the case against Mr. Kent was abandoned.

The same year had not expired when the Trade was thrown into an unutterable state of consternation by the arrest of Mr. Jackson, a Pawnbroker residing at Doncaster. As the facts were evolved, it appeared that a charwoman named Collis, after reported as Collins, had been at work at the house of Mr. Thorpe, solicitor, of Thorne, about twelve miles from Doncaster, and while there, stole from the dressing table a diamond ring valued at £10. She afterwards pledged it at Mr. Jackson's shop for 5s. 6d., Mrs. Jackson taking the ring and believing it to be paste. An enquiry was instituted a day or two after the robbery, and on application at Mr. Jackson's shop, *the ring was immediately produced* for inspection, and being identified, was given up. The woman Collis or Collins, was taken before a Magistrate, and committed for trial, and Mr. Jackson was severely censured for taking in the

pledge, while the fact remained that *Mr. Jackson had
never seen the ring* until it was identified as stolen property.   At the Sessions held at Sheffield about a week
subsequently the prisoner Collis was arraigned on the
charge of stealing the ring, and she pledged guilty.   A
Mr. Blanchard, barrister for the prosecution, called
upon the Court to reprimand Mr. Jackson for his
reprehensible conduct.   Mr. Jackson was in attendance,
not by summons as a witness, but had accompanied his
wife, who had taken the ring in pledge.   He was
immediately after the trial arrested, on the indictment
of feloniously receiving stolen property.   The grand
jury forthwith returned a "true bill."   Bail was
offered but refused.   The next day he was put upon
his trial, when his counsel (Mr. Campbell Foster),
applied to traverse the case until the following sessions,
on account of the extremely limited time the prisoner
had at disposal for the preparation of his defence.   Mr.
Wilson Overend, chairman of the Bench of Magistrates,
refused the application, and the trial proceeded.   The
woman Collis had not yet been sentenced, and was
admitted as the first witness, her testimony being to
the effect that when she pledged the ring both Mr. and
Mrs. Jackson were present; that Mrs. Jackson offered
the 5s. 6d., saying the stone was paste; that Collis
accepted the money.   That a friend of Mr. Thorpe, the
owner, instituted inquiry, and the ring was found at
Jackson's, and at once given up.   Evidence was also
given that Mr. Jackson was asked why he advanced so
small a sum, he replied *he had not seen the ring*, but
that if he had he would not have hesitated to lend £7
upon it, as he could tell it was a diamond.

Many witnesses were called to prove the respectability of the prisoner, the valuable assistance he had
frequently given to the police, and the readiness with
which in this case he had facilitated the ends of justice.
The Chairman *summed up strongly against the prisoner.*

The jury consulted some time, and they expressed a
wish to retire; when the Chairman replied they could
retire if they wished, but if they did not agree to their
verdict within an hour, *they would be locked up all night.*
The jury then returned a verdict of "guilty," and the
Chairman, *without consulting* his colleagues, at once
sentenced the prisoner to twelve calendar months' imprisonment with hard labour. The sentence was
received with murmurs of disapprobation in a crowded
court. The prisoner appeared paralysed, but recovering himself said; "I am perfectly innocent of the
charge, and I feel that such a sentence at my age,
65, is extremely hard, and I trust the Bench will
reconsider it."

The Chairman replied "Sir, the sentence is passed,
and cannot be altered." The thief Collis was sentenced
to *one month's* imprisonment, at which some of the
bystanders cried out "shame."

Mr. Jackson was sent to Wakefield with a batch of
other prisoners, and Mr. Wilson Overend no doubt
retired to his home with the feeling that " The path of
duty was the way to glory," or as another poet expresses it, with "The secret consciousness of duty well
performed." He little knew, however, how notorious
his name would be throughout the length and breadth
of the land, in a few days. The Trade rose like one
man; petitions were rained upon Members of Parliament, the Home Office, and every possible official
likely to be of service. Every town in the Kingdom
vied with each other in their efforts; a large meeting
was held in London, attended by the Mayor of Doncaster, and representatives from nearly every large
town. They worked incessantly; deputations waited
upon leading Members of Government and Parliament,
and in the end, after suffering seven weeks' incar-
ceration, Mr. Jackson was released. But alas! the
shock had been too much, and he gradually sank

and died, to be followed in a few months by his mourning wife.

When these internecine and all-absorbing matters had been disposed of, the Trade was startled by discovering on the notices of motion of the House of Commons for May 2nd, 1856, an innocent looking announcement to this effect :—" 5. Mr. Wilson.—Pawnbrokers—Bill to amend the Acts relating to Pawnbrokers." On inquiry it was discovered that Mr. James Wilson was the Member for Westbury, which is now a division in the County of Wilts, and was also one of the Secretaries of the Treasury, and intended to legislate for the regulation of "leaving shops." This allayed the alarm at first created, so that no attempt at opposition was made further than an effort by the Liverpool Committee to introduce two additional clauses. The second reading was taken on May 9th, and the Bill consisted of two clauses only—the first defining a Pawnbroker in much the same language as in the present Act, and the second inflicting penalties for carrying on business without a Pawnbrokers' licence. Reformers believed their opportunity had come at last, and the Liverpool Committee entrusted their amendment to Mr. Horsfall, one of their Members, to be moved when the Bill was in Committee, to stand part of the Bill. These were afterwards withdrawn in the hope of obtaining a Committee of Inquiry. Important deputations were organised to the Chancellor of the Exchequer, composed of three Manchester Members, three from Liverpool, and two from Sheffield. A small London deputation waited upon Mr. Wilson. Then followed a meeting of the London Trade, a report presented, and the following resolution adopted, "That this meeting approves of the efforts made by the Committee of the Pawnbrokers' Society of London, and by the Trades Committee of Liverpool and Manchester, to induce the Government to consent to a Committee of

Inquiry into the laws relating to Pawnbrokers, in the
next Session of Parliament." A London Committee of
fifteen Members was elected, and a substantial amount
in subscriptions promised. The week following a
meeting was held at Leeds, and resolutions passed expressive of satisfaction and concurrence with the steps
taken by the Liverpool deputations, two members of
which were then present, to give the fullest explanations. There followed, in another few days, a similar
meeting with a like result, held at Preston, and again
the ubiquitous two from Liverpool—Messrs. Batten
and Fairhurst—were present. Nothing, however, was
effected in the Bill before Parliament, and the "Dolly
Shop Act" received the Royal assent on Friday,
June 13th.

On the 17th of that month, an important meeting
was held at Manchester, which was attended by delegates from Leeds, Sheffield, Halifax, Wakefield,
Huddersfield, Nottingham, Birmingham, Preston,
Blackburn, Wigan, Bury, Ashton, Staleybridge, Stockport, and Rochdale. Mr. Batten attended from Liverpool,
but there was no delegation present. Mr. Slater,
President of the local Association, occupied the chair.
The meeting became, as it were, by general consent a
conference, and long and animated discussions ensued
as to the desirability of "Free-trade" in profits, or
the "fixity of profits by law." Both principles had
their adherents, and a protracted meeting terminated
without any resolution being passed in favour of
either side.

In the same week a meeting was held at Birmingham and resolutions of approval of amendment
were passed. Other meetings were held in quick
succession in various towns. Willing helpers seemed
to fly from place to place, and succeeded in rous-
ing something like enthusiasm in the cause. The
London Parliamentary Committee up to this time

continued to work, and in August announced that
they had received £1,100 in subscriptions. In
November a special meeting was held in Liverpool,
when it was decided, as no Committee of Inquiry
seemed likely to be instituted, to endeavour to obtain
an amendment of the Act, and a call of 20s. per member
was made towards a Parliamentary fund. But in all
these movements, and meetings and resolutions, we
look in vain for united action. There existed a vague
desire to amend the Act, but no standard had yet been
raised under which all reformers could rally; consequently the absence of a common cause, of adhesion, of
confidence, seemed to threaten, once more, the failure
to obtain any degree of success. In November, the
London Pawnbrokers suddenly changed front. Erratic
and vacillating as it had proved itself before, the Committee now announced by resolution that it appeared
to them, from personal communication with the members, that the opinions of a large majority of the
London Trade were *not* in favour of an application to
Parliament for a new Act; therefore the Committee
were not prepared to sanction any proceeding for such
purpose; neither did they think it their duty to press
for an Inquiry before a Select Committee. In the event
of any other persons promoting either or both of such
measures, they would reserve to themselves the right
to take such steps in relation thereto as circumstances
might render necessary. It was only in the month of
May previous, that resolutions were passed approving
of a Committee of Inquiry, and they possessed funds
in hand ostensibly subscribed for that purpose.

The Liverpool Committee replied in a somewhat
warlike spirit ; and in retaliation declared that it was
agreed to take immediate steps to arrange a meeting of
the Provincial Trade for the purpose of forwarding the
appointment of a Select Committee to inquire into the
whole system of Pawnbroking. Thus they threw down

the gauntlet, but London allowed it to lay unheeded.
Then Manchester passed a resolution that they deemed
it inadvisable at that time to take any further steps to
promote a Parliamentary Inquiry. Sheffield and Preston
speedily followed this secession, leaving only Leeds,
Liverpool and Nottingham staunch and true. Reformers staggered beneath the blow, and for the
remaining portion of the year 1857 they remained
utterly prostrated.

Thus was the lack of organisation and unity brought
strikingly before the Trade, by the utter collapse of a
movement which, but a few short months before, promised such satisfactory if not brilliant results. Every
Association appeared to be an independent army corps,
commanded by its own officers ; but there was no
mobilization, no headquarters, no General, and no staff.
There existed the compound parts of a complex body,
.but an entire absence of organization.

CHAPTER XVI

When peace and security once more prevailed, attention was again directed to the subject of Reform. The several former attempts, however futile, could not but leave impressions in the minds of the courageous, that amendment of the derided old Act was a possibility. So, in March, 1858, another effort was made, and this time Nottingham led the van. This heroic little band of Pawnbrokers issued an invitation to the whole United Kingdom to send delegates to a meeting to be held in that town, and the response was a remarkable one. That veteran Reformer, Nathaniel Dickinson—"true till death"—was called upon to preside, and he was supported by Brooking (Exeter), Eaton (Sheffield), Holly (Derby), Batten, Fairhurst, and Deverill (Liverpool), Pickard (Halifax), Walker (Macclesfield), Ferguson (Edinburgh), Wild (Oldham), Pawson (Grantham), Hayhurst and Kellt (Preston), Jackson (Hull), Carryer and J. Y. Carryer (Staffordshire), Richardson and Cairns (Manchester), Thompson (Leicester), Middleton and Barker (Leeds), Travel, Pidcock, Fletcher, Palethorpe, Freeston, Tansley, Woodhouse, and T. Wood (Secretary), all of Nottingham.

A bold and spirited manifesto, containing the major points calling for consideration, was read by the Secretary. It stated that the first subject to bo settled and agreed upon was the objection to the imperatively fixed charge for interest, no matter how bulky the articles, or what additional care might be required. This diverted, it was contended, a large portion of the business into the hands of illicit traders, who charge exorbitant rates. The next objection to the Act was that it contained penal clauses for any deviation from the provisions of the Act, while, in many cases, these deviations were no offences at all, and only merited a mild punishment. There were other sections utterly indefensible, only tending to embarrass the Pawn-broker. There were still other sections which, all admitted, required amendment; but, unfortunately, they, as a Trade, could not agree as to what the amendments should be. The course, then, which tho Nottingham Association recommended was to agitate for the appointment of a Committee of Inquiry, rather than to begin a campaign with a sketch of a New Act. It was thought—the document pro-ceeded to say—that if they succeeded in obtaining the appointment of a Parliamentary Committee, the Trade would be prepared with witnesses and other proofs to substantiate their statements. The address concluded by expressing a hope that the meeting would, by its decision, set at rest the important question which had been agitating the Trade, more or less, for nearly twenty years. After the administra-tion of this sensible and honest advice, the meeting indulged in a long discussion as to whether or not the document should be "received," or "adopted," and it was ultimately resolved that it be "received."

Then came a business-like resolution, which was carried *nem. con.*, "That it is desirable to take the

preliminary steps for an enquiry into the working
of the present Pawnbrokers' Acts." Another resolution was passed to the effect that the meeting
resolve itself into an Association for the promotion
of an amendment to the Act relative to Pawnbroking. This hardly seems consistent with a Committee of Inquiry, unless the intention was to await
the result, or that attempted amendment would
bring about the enquiry. However this may be, the
meeting agreed to pay a call of ten shillings each
person to furnish the sinews of war, and concluded
by electing the following Executive Committee:—
Mr. Pickard, Mr. Middleton, Mr. Eaton, Mr. Dickenson, and Mr. Hayhurst. Mr. Fairhurst was elected
President ; Mr. Cairns, Vice ; Mr. Richardson,
Treasurer, and Mr. Batten, Secretary. Thus, once
more, the banner of reform being unfurled, waived
on high, and the campaign commenced under the
brightest auspices.

Immediately after the opening meeting another
was held in Manchester, under the Presidency of
Mr. Clegg, when resolutions were passed :—1st.
That this meeting forms itself into a Society to be
called "The Manchester Pawnbrokers' Auxilliary
Reform Association." 2nd. That the object of the
Association be to obtain an amended Act of Parliament. 3rd. That a President, Vice-President,
Secretary, and Treasurer, and ten other gentlemen
be appointed a Committee, and that such Committee
be elected annually. 4. That the officers of the
National Reform Association, who reside in the
district, be Members of the Committee *ex-officio*.
5. That the Committee shall have power to make
bye-laws, such bye-laws to be subject to the supervision and approval of the next General Meeting.
6. That any Pawnbroker in any of the adjacent
towns may become a Member of the Association on

complying with its rules.   8. That each Member
shall pay a call of 10s., to form a fund for the
promotion of the objects of the Society.

These rules or resolutions were eminently practicable, indicating determination, and a sincerity in the
cause which was most admirable.   The march onward
was not, however, to be achieved without encountering
obstructions and hostility.   The London Committee,
observing the activity prevailing in the Reformer's
camp, emerged from its seclusion, and reviewed its
forces.   To show they were not unprepared, the Treasurer reported that they had £1,185 9s. 3d. in the 3
per cents. reduced.   It will be remembered that this
money was subscribed to promote Pawnbroking
reform, when it was ingeniously, if suddenly, discovered that nobody in the Metropolitan district
desired any change, so the money appears to have
been invested for purposes of attack or defence, as
circumstances might require.   A curious stroke of
policy was now adopted.   A meeting of the executive
Committee had been fixed to be held on the 13th
April, at Manchester.   The London Committee decided
to penetrate the outposts, and as it were under a flag
of truce, enter the camp itself.   So it was resolved
that Mr. Richard Attenborough (Chairman), Mr.
Neate (Treasurer), Mr. Kelday, of "Defender" fame,
(Hon. Sec.), together with Messrs. Ashford, Lawley,
and Warre, should be appointed as a deputation to
attend the meeting at Manchester.   Whether they
went under sealed orders, or what the object to be
attained might be, did not transpire.   The matter
was made clearer when the meeting assembled, as
the Chairman announced, the London deputation
had been invited "rather out of rule," in the hope
that it would secure the co-operation of the whole
Trade.   It was evident every effort was being made
to conciliate London, for the letter of invitation from

the Secretary, stated that the meeting would be glad
as far as possible, to meet the wish of the deputies,
and to consider any suggestions which might be
made upon the general question of Parliamentary
reform.   The Chairman of the Executive informed
the meeting that it was most desirable that the whole
Trade should work harmoniously together; indeed,
he said they were prepared *to go any length* to secure
unanimity, short of sacrificing the principles upon
which the Association was based.   But there was no
response to this humiliation on the part of London.
The proceedings betrayed an unreality and lack of
reciprocity of sentiment, but indicated distrust rather
than sincerity.   Each party stood, as it were, posed
like the " masters of fence," toying with the foils.
The candour of the Chairman of the Executive, was
met by the London leader, who coldly announced that
he understood they had been invited to hear the
principles adopted by the new Association, and it
would be out of place for them to take part in the
details.   The deputation had come to hear the opinions
of the Executive, not to express any.   In the end a
resolution was huddled through pledging the meeting
to go to Parliament for "non-fixity of rate," which
we assume meant free trade in profits.

On their return to London, the deputation reported
that it was plainly and clearly stated at Manchester,
that the London Trade would not willingly be parties
to any parliamentary proceedings, preferring not to
interfere at all with the present arrangements; but
should they be compelled to take part in any such proceedings, it would only be in consequence of the proceedings of other parties.   So conciliation was a
failure, and for another period reform had all the
appearance of being scotched.

Fitfully, only, during the succeeding four months, the
existence of the Executive was made apparent to those

outside its own body.   Then in September a General
meeting was convened at Birmingham.   Here, several
Members of the London deputation attended, still
unswervingly adhering to their obstructive tactics.
That familiar, and by this time well worn, resolution
was submitted "That it is desirable to proceed in the
endeavour to obtain an amendment of the Pawnbrokers' Act, by means of a Committee of Inquiry
before the House of Commons."   A protracted and
tedious discussion ensued on a matter of novel policy
which appeared to have been sprung unexpectedly
upon the meeting, for the reception of votes by proxy.
Many were strongly against this course, but it was
finally decided by 31 votes to 7, that such votes should
be received.   London abstained from voting altogether.
Then came a long wrangling disputation on the
resolution itself, which was ultimately carried by a
curious and eminently unsatisfactory means.   Those
present at the meeting being in favour of the resolution numbered 24, and the proxies 272; total in favour
296.   The votes against were, members present 27;
proxies, 218; total 245; and the resolution was then
declared carried.

From this period, September, 1858, to May, 1859, no
evidences of the existence of any Association were
visible.   It was about the latter date that it was announced a meeting would be held, and was designated
as the First Annual Meeting of "The Trade Association
for the Promotion of Pawnbroking Reform."   It was
held at the Moseley Arms Hotel, Manchester, and Mr.
Fairhurst presided.   A report was brought up, stating
that the Association consisted of 386 members, and
although no votes had been taken at the previous
meeting at Birmingham on the questions of Free-trade,
or Fixed-rate, a scrutiny of the proxies disclosed the
fact that 143 were in favour of a fixed rate, and 99
against it.   The report further disclosed the important

G 2

announcement that the *influential towns* opposed to any *movement whatever*, now consisted of London, Birmingham, Bristol, Preston, Hull, Sheffield, and Leeds. No reason was publicly announced for these wholesale secessions, but it is not unreasonable to conclude that it was mainly owing to the fact that no matter how often the resolution was passed to proceed for a Committee of Inquiry, the Executive never appeared to act thereon. The waning fortunes of the Association were also indicated by the significant financial statement that the balance of funds in hand only amounted to £38 17s. 5d.

By no means encouraging were the facts that neither the Chairman or Secretary desired to be re-elected to their respective positions. Mr. Edward Heys, of Manchester, here came to the front and, in impressive language, put it before the meeting, that it would be more to the purpose if they discussed the general question first, and if the result proved that they were prepared to go on with the work of Reform vigorously, it might produce such a change that both gentlemen who desired to resign would once more accept office. This veteran Reformer, who in after years it was the writer's privilege to know, and pleasure to work with as a colleague, was truly a " man of unadorned eloquence." With a somewhat brusque and country manner, he possessed a faculty of logical argument and thoroughly Saxon diction, to which was wedded a calm, cool style of delivery which no interruption could disturb, so that his utterances were most convincing. At this meeting he urged the Association to persevere, and if £1,000 were necessary, let 100 Members of the Trade contribute £10 each, which might easily be done. He confessed he was not a rich man, but he was prepared to give his £10. It was their own apathy and neglect which had caused them to miss so many opportunities of improving their position.

After being put into straight line by these vigorous utterances, the evergreen resolution was adopted: "That it is the opinion of this meeting that an immediate application for a Select Committee of Inquiry, is necessary." Then the retiring Chairman and Secretary—as Mr. Heys predicted—were re-elected, with Messrs. Clegg, Cairns, Heys, Whitehead, Dromgoole, Middleton, and Pickard, as an Executive Committee. Some £230 was subscribed in the room, many of those present acting on Mr. Heys' suggestion and subscribing £10 each.

So, it might be supposed, commenced once more under the most favourable auspices a new era of reform. But in less than a month's time trouble was once more abroad. A gang of informers had descended upon Staffordshire towns, and were laying informations in all directions, for illegal charges for wrappers, hanging up, and other matters. So the Pawnbrokers, led by Messrs. Hannay and Kendrick, moved for the application of the Four Clauses to all the country. Those in ignorance of what was taking place were startled by the following unexpected announcement in the Parliamentary papers, "*Notice of Motion* for Tuesday, 21 June.—12. Mr. Henry B. Sheridan,—Pawnbrokers,—Committee on Act passed in the thirty-ninth and fortieth years of the reign of King George the Third, intituled 'An Act for better regulating the business of Pawnbrokers.'"

Great excitement, alarm and suspense was created by this announcement. Throughout the whole Trade it was regarded as a certainty that the motion meant nothing less than a hostile attack. Promptly the Chairman and Secretary of the Executive, accompanied by two members of the Dudley Trade, who were well-known constituents of the hon. gentleman, waited upon Mr. Sheridan, at his residence at Fulham. They were soon relieved in their anxieties by ascertaining that Mr.

Sheridan's intentions were found to be nothing more threatening than a desire to extend the "Four Clauses" from the Metropolitan Police Act to the Provinces.* The Bill was intituled, "The Mitigation of Penalties Act." After suggested modifications, the Bill was made applicable to the public at large.

Deputations were organised to Members of Parliament innumerable. Members of the Executive were ubiquitous, some of them always accompanying country constituents to see their own members. Even the London Parliamentary Committee was once more exhumed, and actually came to the conclusion to appoint a Parliamentary Agent as the most effectual mode of promoting the passing of the Bill.

The Bill was read a second time on Monday, July 18th, passed through Committee; was reported by Friday, and read the third time, Monday, July 25th. The progress through the House of Lords was equally rapid, being brought from the Commons, Tuesday 26th, passed through all its stages, and received the Royal Assent by commission on August 8th.

So although a good deal had been attempted, in another direction, there was attained some good for the Country Trade—but Pawnbroking reform remained much in its old position.

* *Ante*, chap. XI.

CHAPTER XVII

A MODICUM OF REFORM—AT LAST

The experience gained during the campaign in support of the Mitigation of Penalties Act, was of incalculable value to the leaders of the Reform movement. It was in its kind a "trial trip" by which their power, progress, and general going qualities were tested. They obtained introductions to a large number of Members of the House of Commons, and made acquaintances—if not indeed friends—which was of the utmost advantage in their future operations. The Members of the Executive instituted active canvassing throughout the country. In one report it was stated that Messrs. Batten and Brooking had visited the West of England, calling at nearly twenty towns, expounding the objects of the movement, and ·returned with additions to the funds of upwards of £120. They also made some curious discoveries, which future defenders of the Trade will do well to note. They found that many Members of the Trade took active and prominent part in every Parliamentary Election, and, in many cases, were personally known to their representatives. These valuable and important Pawnbrokers, it was endeavoured—not unsuccessfully—to win over to the ranks of Reform; a step which immeasurably increased the Parliamentary influence of the Committee, which influence could be used when the time should come, in promoting the interests of the Trade and the power of the Association. The deputation also discovered, during their travels, that many of the persons visited had never heard of any Reform movement previously, nor of the Mitigation of Penalties Act; indeed, that many of the Trade in those towns were not readers of the *Pawnbrokers' Gazette*.

Hearing of this benighted but haply contented condition of this "Darkest Pawnbroking," the Executive immediately made arrangements to send mission-like deputations to some fifty towns or more, which were remote from each other, and none of which corresponded on Trade matters or sought communication with other communities than their own, and few had any Association established. So the canvassing went on vigourously, with good effect, to the close of the year 1859.

In January, of 1860, the Executive met at Manchester. Favourable reports were given in by the various deputations. Encouraged by their success it was resolved to commence active operations preparatory to the opening of the Parliamentary Session. It was decided to wait upon Sir Richard Bethel, whom they had seen several times during the previous Session, the Home Secretary, and other influential Members of the House of Commons, and ascertain their opinions as to the best course to adopt.

On the 15th of February a deputation of the Parliamentary Committee, which consisted of Messrs. Fairhurst, Batten, Dickinson, and Heys, had an interview with the Secretary at the Home Office, and were accompanied by Mr. S. B. Horsfall, and Mr. J. C. Ewart, Liverpool Members; Mr. Thos. Basley,

and Mr. T. A. Turner, Manchester Members; the
Hon. Jas. Lindsay, and Mr. H. Woods, Wigan
Members; Mr. C. Paget, and Mr. J. Mellor, Nottingham Members; Mr. H. B. Sheridan, M.P. for Dudley;
and Mr. Hadfield, M.P. for Sheffield.

The deputation was introduced by Mr. Horsfall,
and a long and interesting conference took place,
which would be much too voluminous to re-produce
here. At the conclusion, the Home Secretary, Sir
Geo. Cornewall Lewis, replied as follows: "I must
say, gentlemen, that I think you have shown a *primâ
facie* case for relief, and, although I cannot promise
to make it a Government measure, owing to our
time being filled up; still, if Mr. Horsfall or any
other Member now present will undertake to introduce a short Bill, so far as I know at present, it
shall receive no opposition from within if it does
not from without, and, if opposed, it shall be referred to a Select Committee." Sir George then
asked Mr. Horsfall if he had not better take charge
of the bill; to which that gentleman promptly
replied that he had no objection. Then, speaking to
Mr. Turner, Sir George suggested that he too
should become a sponsor; to which the Member
replied that he did not object, as he thought it
would appear well that Manchester and Liverpool
should be side by side.

From the foregoing interview, it would be supposed that Pawnbroking Reform had at last commenced under most auspicious auguries. Every
encouragement was here given for the introduction
of a short bill to abolish the worst blemishes the
old Act possessed, and substitute substantial advantages in behalf of the Pawnbrokers. There was
little to fear, it might be supposed, in preparing
their bill and pressing the matter to a speedy issue,
for at the worst, if opposition arose, there was the

alternative of a Committee of Inquiry, *which was the legitimate object of the Association,* and which all sincere and unswerving Reformers most desired. But for some inexplicable reason, valuable time was consumed in a futile endeavour to induce the London Committee to join hands and cease to remain in the threatening attitude it had so long maintained. For some of the leaders there appeared to be a fatal fascination in the support of London, while actually the opposition of that body would have precipated the policy which had at so many previous gatherings received the support of the majorities. However, other councils prevailed, and a meeting of the London Parliamentary Committee was held, and the Chairman, Secretary, and Messrs. Dickinson, Heys, and Middleton attended. The Secretary laid bare to every detail what the Executive had done, and what they proposed yet to do, but they desired most of all the co-operation of the London Trade. It was proposed, as had been suggested, to proceed by a short bill which should be based upon—1st. The principle of extending ticket money to sums under 5s., which were then given gratis; 2nd. That the fractional rates of interest for intermediate sums should be abolished, and that $\frac{1}{2}$d. should be paid for every half-crown, or any part thereof, per month; 3rd. That half monthly charges should be abolished, and that seven days of grace be extended to ten. The deputation, the Secretary proceeded to say, had come to London to ascertain their views upon these questions, and they from the Country would be willing to concede many points of their original programme if by so doing they could secure the co-operation of the London Trade. After some queries put from the chair and replied to in a colloquial manner, the deputation were requested to retire until the points raised were discussed.

Then the flood-gates of the London eloquence were opened wide, and the proposals of the supplicating Executive were exhaustively discussed, the predominating opinion against co-operation strongly manifesting itself.

As might be expected, a resolution was agreed to, which declared shortly, that the London Committee were decidedly of opinion that the proceedings proposed would be prejudicial, and therefore they could not consent to co-operate in the application; but they should feel it incumbent upon themselves to watch the proceedings, and take such steps as circumstances might render necessary. The deputation was then re-admitted, and the judgment, as it were, of the meeting was delivered by the Chairman, in a long and elaborate summing up. They accepted the position with good grace, and deeply regretted that London had not seen it to their interest to assist in the movement. After this decisive repulse the Executive retired to their tents and spent some time in commune together. It was then decided to call the guarantors and subscribers together to hold conference at Derby. The notices for this meeting were accompanied by a proxy voting paper, which was to be filled up, and used by the Secretary, giving answers to the following questions: 1. Whether the member voting was in favour of going to Parliament by Bill, or Committee of Inquiry? 2. If in favour of a Bill, whether by a simple application for an extension of the ¼d. ticket fee to pledges under 5s.; or by one which should in a great measure re-model the scale of interest. Nearly one half the time of this meeting was absorbed by a discussion as to whether or not guarantors who had not paid should be entitled to vote, either personally or by proxy. In the end it was decided to receive such votes, and the meeting proceeded to discuss the points raised in the voting

papers. It was found to be of little use however,
save as a protest, to enlarge upon the various aspects
of these subjects, for it became known to the meeting
that the proxy votes were in favour of proceeding by
Bill, and that for *the halfpenny only.* Nevertheless
several veteran reformers expressed their opinion on
the proceedings. Mr. Dickinson said it was merely like
talking to the winds if the question was already decided by the voting papers then in hand. Still he, would
propose that they should keep to their original
intention and move for a Committee of Inquiry.
They underrated their own strength. He felt that
the Association had been lowered by its Committee
going humiliatingly to London to seek their assistance..
Such a measure as now proposed of asking only for
the halfpenny was a discredit to the Trade. The
speaker moved that they proceed by Committee of
Inquiry. All the Manchester Members present supported the resolution. Mr. Heys in that terse, incisive,.
logical manner which was always his great characteristic, said that the whole question had turned
from one of principle to one of expediency. In
political life he instanced that it might be wise to
compromise a great principle for the purpose of
allaying a powerful opposition, but they had no such
reason. No one had expressed a valid objection to a
Committee of Inquiry. No argument had been produced to show that such a course would terminate disas-
trously, therefore it was the best action to take, to go
for a Committee, and settle the question thoroughly.

No arguments could then however influence the
meeting, which at last proceeded to vote. Of those
present 26 were in favour of a Committee of Inquiry,
and 22 in favour of a Bill, but when the proxies were
produced the voting was :—

> For proceeding by Bill   319.
> „   „   Committee   115.

There were also 311 votes in favour of the Bill being limited to the one item of the ½d. for duplicates below 5s., and 105 in favour of other proposals.

No time was lost now in getting the Bill introduced into the House of Commons. Leave was given and it was read a first time on the 22nd of March. On Thursday, the 29th, the second reading took place, Mr. Edwin James moving that it be read a second time that day six months. The division was decisive, there being for the second reading 178; against 32; showing a majority in favour of the Pawnbrokers of 146.

Such a triumphant division practically settled the question, but the London Committee was determined not to die yet. They still, impotent as they were, hurled their fiery resolutions forth expressive of disapproval, believing that the proceedings would "bring opprobrium and injury upon the whole Trade," and resolved to reserve the right to take such measures—as they had been threatening to take for several years. There were, however, other and more reasonable Members of the London Trade who did not allow their prejudices to blind their better judgments. They recognised the Parliamentary power and influence possessed by the Country Trade, and they saw that further resistance was impossible. Therefore no less than 160 London Pawnbroking firms signed a requisition to the London Committee, urging them to withdraw from any further opposition to the measure.

The remaining stages through which the Bill had to pass, were easily accomplished, and it received the Royal Assent by commission on Tuesday, May 15th.

The London Committee tenaciously clung to life for yet another year, and in May 1861, a general meeting was held, and it was dissolved by a vote of the majority. Such balance of funds as remained in hand was to be returned to the subscribers; and yet another year expired before this was done, and many were the bitter letters of disappointment at the delay, which appeared for months in the *Gazette*.

A final meeting of the Reform Association was held in Manchester, on August 1st., 1860, when it was by unanimous vote dissolved. It was also resolved to return the funds in hand, amounting to £395 4s. 9d., to the subscribers and guarantors of upwards of £2. The report stated that the total cost of the movement had been £1,064.

And so at last some reform had been effected, and although producing great disappointment to many who longed ardently for more thorough reform, it resulted in the general benefit of the smaller capitalists. But what was the most valuable of all, it showed the lines on which future reformers could travel, who were not afraid to penetrate further than these pioneers had done.

CHAPTER XVIII

It was not to be supposed that consistent and progressive reformers would remain contented with the "Halfpenny Act," as a final settlement of their aspirations. It was thought by many that the result was not commensurate with the labour, time, and money which had been expended. They were not satisfied with a measure which, as Hood says: "May give a mite to him who wants a cheese," and which settled none of the points raised in the original programme. Opinion in the direction of complete, thorough and extensive reform was rapidly ripening; it was in the air; it formed the theme of many speeches at festivals and meetings, and confidence in its possible realization grew. The conference at Liverpool for the purpose of federation did much to advance the cause. London, in the person of Mr. George Attenborough, was now to the front. Most of the representatives from other towns were in favour of a new movement being commenced. That it was contemplated, was proved by one of the rules, which was proposed and accepted, to form one of those governing the Union of Associations. It provided that if any delegate at a meeting should propose any motion, which if carried would effect or cause any change whatever in any Acts of

Parliament governing the Trade, the President should
have power to adjourn the meeting for not less than
one month. A copy of the motion so submitted was
to be sent to each Association, and each delegate was
to attend the adjourned meeting, empowered to vote
as decided by the meeting of his own Association.
Had the Union been established there can be little
doubt that a motion of the kind provided for, would
soon have engrossed the attention of the delegates,
and with such an organization would have led to
practical results.   To many it will seem incredulous
that this rule with slight modification was actually
adopted by a meeting of the London Trade, but so
it was.

After the attempt to found this National Union had
failed, advanced reformers were provided with unexpected opportunities of preparing preliminaries. Early
in the year 1867 a section of the London Trade commenced an agitation for the promotion and support
of an appeal to Parliament for a further reduction
of the hours of business for Assistants in the
Pawnbroking Trade.   A strong and widely spread
conviction prevailed, that such a question as short
hours should not be settled by legislative enact-
ment.   Both London and the provinces became
divided into rival factions; but the Country majority
was largely against such a proceeding, for in many
large towns the hours observed were much shorter than
those it was proposed to apply for. Meetings in favour
and condemnation were held in all directions; while
contradictory manifestoes were issued, and the battle
was waged with fierceness and determination.   The
opponents, however, were anxious that it should be
understood, that they were in no manner unsympa-
thetic with the objects of the promoters, but they
believed that the whole question was one for mutual
agreement and settlement, rather than legislative

interference or regulation. It was felt that the
parties interested—employers and employés—should
adopt measures for satisfactory adjustment of the
difficulty, and not seek to forcibly impose fetters
upon the whole Trade.

The London opposition was led by Mr. J. A. Russell,
George Attenborough (Old Kent-road); and Mr. A.
G. Gush, and they appealed to the Trade to "stand
firm—shoulder to shoulder—London or Country—
that a stop may be put to this mischievous and
dangerous movement." The promoters issued
"counterblasts," and were admirably headed by
Mr. R. B. Starling and Mr. Cocks, and they championed
their cause with vigour and ability. But for the most
part the country was arrayed against them, for the
Bill was unnecessary and arbitrary.

Mr. Ayrton, M.P., then representing the Tower
Hamlets, and not long afterwards destined to take a
leading part in much more extensive Pawnbroking
legislation—took charge of the Short Hours Bill, and
in June he moved "for leave to be given to bring in a
Bill for regulating the hours for receiving and
delivering goods and chattels as pawns in Pawnbrokers' shops." This decisive step roused the whole
country to action. The first expression of opinion
was uttered at a small village to which the Manchester
and Liverpool Committees and friends had repaired
for a friendly contest at bowls, but the weather
proving unfavourable, an impromptu meeting was
held in the hotel. Resolutions were passed with enthusiasm that the Bill should be vigorously opposed.
This determination was confirmed by formal meetings
of the Committee held afterwards, and the Chairman,
Secretary, and one other member, were appointed by
each Association to proceed to London as deputations
to their respective Members, and induce them, if
possible, to obstruct the passing of the Bill into law.

Other constituencies adopted a like policy; so that in
June, 1867, there was quite a strong body of the
Country Trade assembled in London, all actively engaged in pioneer Parliamentary labours. A meeting
of the London Committee was called, and the Country
deputies were invited to attend, but little more
resulted than a colloquial discussion on the various
schemes of reform as compared to the advantages of a
Committee of Inquiry. The second reading of the Bill
was put down for June 17, but was postponed, while
interviews with Members were carried on with increasing vigour, and petitions from all parts were
presented daily.

On the 18th of the month a General Meeting of the
London Trade was held at Radley's Hotel, New Bridge-
street, and the Country Pawnbrokers were again
invited to attend. The late Mr. John Dicker—afterwards one of the most resolute Reformers and indomitable workers in the cause—in order to test the
opinion of London, proposed a resolution: "That in
the opinion of this Meeting, it is desirable for the
London Trade to join in the effort now being made to
obtain a Parliamentary Inquiry into the working of
the Act 39 and 40 Geo. III., cap. 99." Mr. Geo. Attenborough seconded the resolution, and in his speech
informed the meeting that he understood that Liverpool and Nottingham had both obtained promises from
their Members of assistance to obtain a Committee.
An amendment to the resolution was proposed : "That
a Committee (from those present) be appointed to
confer with the members of the Country Trade, in
order to ascertain their wishes in regard to an
alteration of the present Act, previous to London
deciding upon supporting the application for a Committee of Inquiry."

While the motion and the amendment were being
exhaustively discussed, several adroit attempts were

made to elicit from the Country deputies what schemes
of Reform they had prepared. The reply was, none.
Liverpool stated that a telegram had been received
from a meeting in their own town the previous evening,
with the result that it was unanimous for a Committee
of Inquiry. Nottingham supported this view, and expressed an opinion that the meeting then being held
was essentially one of the London Trade only, and that
those attending from the Country had no right to
express an opinion. Manchester declared that, so far as
their instructions went, they had but one single object in
view, that of opposing the Bill then before Parliament;
the question of an Inquiry had not been discussed by
them, but it was believed if the Bill could not be
defeated otherwise, the Manchester Trade as a body
would be in favour of such a course. Sheffield also
declared that their only object, so far, was to oppose
the Short Hour Bill. They had no instructions as to
an Inquiry, but they had informed their Members in
the House that they had no fear of an Inquiry, and
rather than that Bill should pass, they would prefer
to meet such a Committee. After several hours' sitting,
the meeting adopted the amendment by 51 votes to 3.
The Committee of Conference was then nominated, and
consisted of Messrs. G. Attenborough, Dicker, Harding, Russell, Starling, and J. A. Telfer.

Later in the day the conference was held with the
Country deputies, but no definite result ensued, as
only Nottingham and Liverpool had received positive
instructions either on Parliamentary Reform or a
Committee of Inquiry.

The Short Hour Committee now realized the dilemma into which they had plunged the London Trade,
and inadvertently dragged in the Country; they
therefore tried what effect conciliation would have, as
some of them at the meeting had been twitted with
having, like Frankenstein, created a monster which

they could not lay. However, they thought it worth
the effort, and Mr. Cocks wrote to the *Gazette*, "That
the Committee of the Short Hour Bill, whatever the
result may be, have resolved *not* to include the Country
Trade." The concession, however, came too late, as
the Bill was doomed, the Secretary of the Liverpool
Association having received a letter from T. B. Horsfall, Esq., M.P., in which the Honourable Gentleman
stated, that, "After several communications with Mr.
Ayrton, he told me last evening (July 2nd), he should
not proceed with the Bill." It was kept on the orders
of the House until August 7th, when Mr. Ayrton
formally moved that the order for the second reading
be discharged, and it was accordingly withdrawn.

The Short Hour Committee did not accept defeat
too readily, and there were those among them who
were hopeful enough to suppose that they would
resume active operations in the succeeding Session.
In October a General Meeting of the Subscribers was
called in London, and a Report was presented which
concluded as follows :—

"There are now three courses open to you, viz.:—
1st. To try conciliatory action. 2nd. Parliamentary
action. 3rd. Or let the matter rest in abeyance. And
it is for you, at this Meeting, to decide upon which of
the courses you will adopt."

After a long and devious debate it was resolved to
re-elect the Committee, and the management of all the
affairs of the Society to be left in their hands. It was
also decided that the balance of money in hand should
be retained for any future Parliamentary action.
This, however, was only a final heroic flicker, as the
Society dwindled away from sheer inanition; and we
find that in the following year the balance of money
subscribed was quietly returned—much to the indignation of a few, as being contrary to the resolution
passed at the Meeting—and notice given that all

surplus remaining unclaimed after May 1st, 1868,
would be handed to the Charitable Institution and
Assistants' Benevolent Society.

Thus, by the action of the London Assistants and
their Friends (their Leaders), those progressive Reformers, who had been disappointed in the previous
movement terminating only with the Halfpenny Act,
were provided with the opportunity of executing
valuable pioneer work, which was invaluable for the
proceedings which were speedily to follow. As we have
previously shown, the Bill was not required for, or by,
the Country, and had the promoters perceived the
logic of the situation earlier it would have kept the
Country quiet and at home, instead of unconsciously
affording them the golden opportunity of conferring
with the London Reformers and their own Members
of Parliament, and so preparing the way for the
victory soon after to be achieved.

CHAPTER XIX

The many conferences which had taken place between various Members of the Trade assembled in London during the Session of 1867, produced great confidence and hope that the time to strike a decisive blow to ensure Reform was not very remote. A better and more friendly understanding between all shades of thought and opinion, than had ever prevailed before, now existed. A number of new men had come to the front, amongst whom mutual friendships had developed, and coincident ideas prevailed. " Concord is strength," and the ancient motto was believed in.

Action, however, was not considered imminent. But the year 1868 was not yet a month old, when the call to arms was issued with startling suddenness by the Trade of Nottingham. A stirring and earnest appeal was promulgated calling attention to the various declarations which had been previously published by numerous Associations throughout the Country, of their readiness to support a demand for a Committee of Inquiry or to seek redress by means of a Bill. The address referred to the hopeful work which had been done in the previous Session, and then proceeded ;—

"Nothing has since occurred to suggest doubt that such application would not be successful; or to prove that it was less desirable or necessary than it was then; and the combined action of the whole Trade is now asked:

"To form a guarantee fund to meet the necessary expenses.

"To form a Committee to decide upon;—

"The course to be taken,

"The evidence to be offered; and

"To collect and arrange all necessary statistical information.

"The opportunity," continued the address, "is undeniable; the course is cleared and opened by the action of last Session; the temper of the House is pre-eminently in favour of removing all trade restrictions which are proved to be hurtful or unnecessary; labour has been for some time rising in value; expenses of all kinds bear no comparison with what they were 50 years ago; a remuneration which was then thought excessive now scarcely attracts attention; the Usury Laws have been repealed; the rate of discount little more than twelve months ago was for a period of three months as high as 10 to 12 per cent. on the best paper at the Bank of England; while we are tied down by an Act which was made at a time since when commercial dealings have very materially changed. * * * * The Trade are well able to show:—

"The unsuitable nature of our Act to meet the requirements of the present time;

"The severity and hardship of its penal clauses;

"The hindrance which compliance with it would inflict on the speedy transaction of business; and

"The inadequate remuneration it allows for the amount of labour each transaction involves."

The limited space at disposal prevents our giving this now historical document *verbatim et literatum*, but the concluding passages illustrate the sincerity and earnestness of the promulgators, who concluded by saying:—

"If only 50 earnest reformers will combine at starting, the thing may be done. Send in your names to us, and let a place be appointed to meet and make the preliminary arrangements; *but lose no time; too much has been lost already;* success is as certain as an application is made, and the result of the labours of the Committee will be a report on which an Act may be compiled in accordance with the spirit of the age and the usages of society. * * * Let us endeavour by a prudent and a fearless course to remove the difficulty—if not impossibility—of complying with the requirements of our Act, by applying for one which everyone can understand and conscientiously follow, and we shall confer an inestimable benefit on our Trade, and raise it in the estimation of every right-minded person."

This important, hopeful, and inspiring manifesto was signed by Mr. N. Dickinson as Chairman; Mr. Thos. Wood as vice, and Mr. Alfred Fletcher as the Hon. Sec.

From the numerous manifestations previously made by those Members of the Trade who were impatient for reform, it would have been supposed that this invitation to combine for a common cause would have been received with enthusiasm and approval. Unanimous response was doubtless expected from those who had confessed themselves so sanguine the previous year, but the general expression of opinion now was that the address was inopportune; that action was then premature, and altogether out of tune with the nature of the times. This idea manifested itself strongly, although a difference of opinion existed, but the majority considered it would be inexpedient to move, for many and various reasons. The commercial

distress, it was urged, was severe and widespread; the
poor were suffering horrible privations, and money
was lower than it had ever been in the memory of
living man. Thus, we had the antithises of the rosy
expectations, just expressed, placed before us.

But the strongest and most tenable reason for delay
which was advanced, was the fact that an announcement had been made, by some one in authority, that
a Report on Irish Pawnbroking was on the eve of
being presented to Government by Dr. Neilson
Hancock. This inquiry had been some time in progress, and the Report was looked forward to with
lively anticipation, not unmixed with anxiety, as it
was believed to be probable that it would map out, to
a fair extent, the way that Pawnbroking Reform
should or would be obtained. Even hitherto
clamourous Reformers shared this view, and
thought the Report would encourage progress,
or condemn interference with the existing law
other than in the direction of state Pawnbroking.
This was the uncertain condition of things when a
counter manifesto to the one issued from Nottingham,
emanating from the London Protection Society, was
published. Like its predecessor, it was addressed to
the Pawnbrokers of Great Britain, but recommended
delay. After dwelling on the depression of trade
and the wretched poverty to which the poor were
reduced, the address continued:—

"With regard, however, to the third reason, we
think it will be most imprudent to apply to Parliament before the Irish Commissioners' report is
published. Will that report be of so favourable a
character that an equitable and beneficial Bill is likely
to be founded upon it? Will its character be so unfavourable as to threaten results disastrous to the Trade?

"Are the present exigencies of the Trade so great,
or so sudden, that it is all at once necessary to bid

farewell to prudence, and petition for a Parliamentary investigation regardless of consequences?

"We think not. * * * When the proper time comes it is to be hoped that the Trade will then be prompt, energetic, and united as one man; but we do not believe that now is the proper time; and, therefore, our advice to you is, do nothing rashly, and remember that one false step, or unwise move, may cause years of anxiety, annoyance, and loss to every Member of the Trade and their successors."

The signatories to this address were Mr. J. A. Russell (Chairman), Mr. John Dicker (Treasurer), and Mr. George Attenborough, Hon. Sec. of the Metropolitan Protection Society.

The bias of opinion throughout the country also favoured delay, despite the courageous defences of their opinions made by Mr. Wood and Mr. Fletcher, that the time was then, and a blow should at once be struck. They availed little as against the set opinion of the Country Associations, who were constantly passing resolutions in favour of delay. On February 11th the Nottingham friends wisely accepted the general veto, and decided to postpone the meeting. The Association passed a resolution regretting that several important and influential Associations did not see the necessity "of now making any preliminary preparations for an application to Parliament," and so wisely announced that they did, in deference to the expressed wish of a large majority, agree to postpone further action on their part until the reception of Dr. Hancock's Irish report. In doing so they trusted that they might confidently rely upon the fulfillment of the promises previously made that the Associations would then proceed to the adoption of some measure most likely to procure a substantial improvement of the Act of 1800. By this cordial and ready acquiescence with the wishes of the majority, the amity of the Trade was preserved; but patience was on its trial through an anxious but not protracted interregnum.

At length, on March 16th, relief came with the eagerly anticipated report. It was a somewhat lengthy document, directly pointing to the road on which reformers desired to march. The Summary of "Recommendations" will be of the greatest interest as they relate to English Pawnbroking, and deserve a place in this brief history ; but as none of those relating to Irish Pawnbroking have yet worked any reform in that country, we therefore, for economy of space, omit them.

The principle recommendations were as follows :—

"1. That the abolition of the Usury Laws be made complete by being extended to contracts under the laws relating to Pawnbrokers, and that the exception of such contracts contained in the 4th section of the Statute 17 and 18 Victoria, c. 90, be repealed.*

"2. That the provisions of the existing law as to charges allowed on pawns be considered as regulating only the implied contract between the parties, in all cases in which there is no express contract.

"4. If the statutory restrictions as to the hours of carrying on the business of Pawnbroking *be not entirely abolished*, the Trade in Ireland should be subject to no further restriction than it is in Great Britain, and I recommend that the provisions of Statute 9 and 10 Vict., c. 98, should be extended to Ireland.

"16. That the periods for which the Pawnbrokers are required to keep pledges previous to sale are, for a large class of pawns, too long; and that they are fixed on a wrong principle, and should be repealed as compulsory regulations.

"17. That a period of three months for loans under 40s., and six months for all loans above 40s., should

* See Chap. IX., " Usury."

be fixed as the implied period for which pledges are to
be kept in all cases where no other term was fixed
by express contract. I recommend, however, that in
cases of loans on plate, jewellery, and watches, the
implied period should be extended to nine months.
"19. That the provisions of the English statute
(39 and 40 Geo. III., c. 99, s. 17), as to advertisements,
be extended to Ireland, the absolute forfeiture being
limited to pawns on which a sum of 4s. only has
been lent.

"WM. NEILSON HANCOCK."

Besides these encouraging recommendations, there
were opinions expressed in the body of the Report
which formed the bases of arguments to be used by the
Trade in the future, as proving the pressing necessity
for amendment of the Pawnbroking laws. He said,
"I recommend that the attempt to restrict charges on
the poor be abandoned." This was, of course, ultra
Free Trade. Again he said, "The English scale of
interest is too low." Such observations naturally
concentrated into one focus the straggling and somewhat incongruous ideas which had previously existed
on the subject of reform.

Nottingham, now in the greatest confidence, convened
the National Assembly for April 23rd. In preparation
for this important gathering, many large and influential towns held meetings and passed resolutions
with which the delegates were to be armed. About
a fortnight prior to the date then fixed, London held
a General Meeting of the whole Metropolitan Trade, and
a vast change in the attitude of that body towards their
Provincial brethren, was plainly visible. Reform ideas
had gained ground, and men of settled principles and
indomitable energy were now leaders. Expediency
had given place to sincerity and determination. No
less a person than the late Mr. Wm. Nathan proposed,
"That this meeting agree to co-operate with the Pro-

vincial Trade in their intended application to Parliament for a New Act," and what would have been a strange phenomenon, only a few years before, the resolution was passed in a large meeting, by three or four dissentients only. Free Trade, however, was less fortunate. Mr. John Dicker boldly proposed that the proceedings for a New Act should be on a free-trade basis, and this was ably supported by the late Mr. Geo. Attenborough. The dose was too strong for the patient, and it was rejected by a large majority. A Committee of 12 Members was then elected to confer with the Provinces.

Manchester decided to send representatives to the Nottingham meeting, but, after considering and discussing the Irish Commissioners' Report, resolved that the mode of procedure to obtain an amended Act should be by Bill in preference to a Committee of Inquiry. They were still, however, staunch to the principle of Free Trade as to profits, and that the term of forfeiture be not less than six months for all pledges not being plate, watches, and jewellery. Liverpool adopted a similar programme, with the exception that they were in favour of a fixed rate to regulate the implied contract, on all pledges under 40s., such rate not to be less than one halfpenny for every 2s., or any part of 2s., per month, for money lent. All sums above 40s., and not exceeding £10, to be entirely free both as to period of forfeiture and rates of profit.

Thus prepared, old reformers were "eager for the fray." After struggling for the unattainable for so many years, until "hope deferred" had brought despair to many, they seemed to stand on the Threshold at last, and longed impatiently for the portals to be thrown open.

CHAPTER XX

The morning of April 23rd, 1868, dawned bright and fair, and despite the fact that animated discussions had been heard far into the previous night, the Pawnbrokers were early astir in the streets of Nottingham, and might be seen in groups, in the vast Market-place and other notable localities, enjoying change of scene, while they emphasised their arguments by forcibly bringing down some printed document with a convincing thud on the palm of the left hand, or some equally demonstrative action. The Meeting was called for eleven o'clock in the forenoon, in the large billiard room of the Lion Hotel, Clumber-street, and shortly before that time the attendants began to troop in. At eleven prompt a record was taken, and the following gentlemen were found to be present. London: Messrs. Geo. Attenborough, J. A. Telfer, John Dicker, E. Bullworthy, W. A. H. Hows, Gush, Cook, and J. Walter. Manchester: Messrs. Grantham, Heys, Porter, Newton, and Fletcher. Liverpool: Messrs. Pickup, Beesley, H. E. Kidson, J. Jones, and Hardaker. Sheffield: Messrs. Eaton, Simmons, Jeffrey, Wright, and Gratton. Nottingham: Messrs. Dickinson, Robinson, Wagstaff, Wood, Samuels, Palethorpe, Tansley,

Priestman, Gell. Fletcher, and Clarke. Bolton: Messrs. Roscow and J. Vickers. Walsall: Messrs. W. H. Mold and T. Mold. Coventry: Mr. W. H. Marston. Derby: Messrs. Holly and Butters. Wakefield: Mr. Armstrong. Birmingham: Messrs. Buckler and Dukes. Glasgow: Mr. A. McKay. Edinburgh: Mr. Ormond Garland. Bradford: Mr. J. L. Morley. Ilkeston: Mr. Moss. Exeter and Bristol: Mr. J. R. Brooking. Hanley: Mr. Cooke. Greenock: Messrs. McGuckin and Mr. McKelly. Wolverhampton: Mr. Duncan Smith. Wednesbury: Messrs. Kilvert and Jones. Salford: Mr. Whitehead. Macclesfield: Mr. Walker.

The preliminary business consisted of the unanimous election of Mr. N. Dickinson as the president of the meeting, and Messrs. Alfred Fletcher and Alfred Hardaker as joint hon. secretaries. After the advertisement convening the meeting had been read, the Chairman briefly announced that the first question they had to decide was whether the Trade should take Parliamentary action or not. He had no resolution prepared on the subject, as it had been thought best that it should emanate spontaneously from the meeting.

Mr. Fletcher (Nottingham), then without many words of preface, proposed the following resolution: "That this meeting recognising the necessity for a comprehensive amendment of the Act 39 and 40, Geo. III., c. 99, relating to Pawnbrokers, pledges itself now to consider and adopt the best means for commencing and carrying on, an application to Parliament · to effect the same." This resolution was seconded by Mr. W. H. Robinson, who assumed, he said, that no one would have accepted an invitation to be present that day who was not favourable to a movement for a new Act. His assumption seemed to be rapidly endorsed as truth, for the resolution was at once adopted without further discussion, or a dissentient vote being recorded. A point was then raised as to the method of voting; it being contended by some persons present, that towns and localities were unequally represented, in many cases there was heavy voting power, while in others gentlemen had attended as individual Pawnbrokers, but in no sense as delegates from Associations, and having no instructions whatever. It was ultimately decided that no satisfactory system could, under the circumstances, be established, therefore the fairest and most equitable method would be for the personal votes of those present only to be taken. This course was eventually agreed to.

Mr. Geo. Attenborough then, in a brief speech, proposed, "That it is desirable that such application shall be made by Bill." This was seconded without comment, by Mr. Edward Heys, supported by two other speakers in as few words as possible, and immediately adopted.

Up to this point it appeared as if such perfect unanimity prevailed throughout the meeting that the entire proceedings would be concluded by the time the first hour had elapsed. But this apparent peaceful calm was as delusive as a placid smooth stream glides on before it dashes wildly over the rocks and becomes a cataract. Mr. Heys, in his composed, self-contained manner, rose and proposed, "That application be made to Parliament for Free Trade in profits." This, to many persons, seemed an unfair proposal, as they had been sent to the meeting as delegates, tied down to limited and defined propositions, and yet they could only give personal votes; while others who were present "unattached," were free to express their opinions and, as in some cases it occurred, acknowledge their conversion to the tenets advocated by the apostles

of Free Trade. However, nothing dismayed by any
considerations, other than testing the opinion of the
meeting on the subject, Mr. Heys proceeded with his
arguments in favour of the proposition. One chief
reason he urged in favour of Free Trade was that it
would place Pawnbroking upon the same basis as
every other trade. There existed no other the profits
of which were fixed by Act of Parliament, and if all
other trades were free to follow the natural laws of
Commerce, why should the Pawnbrokers be prevented from doing so too? As for protecting the
working classes, he contended that they were well
qualified to protect themselves. Nothing could be
more simple than a Pawnbroker's dealings. He
dealt in sovereigns, and every one who went to him
knew perfectly well the value of what he was
receiving, and precisely the measure of profit which
was to be paid, which was not the case in any
other retail trade whatever. If they went in for
Free Trade they would place the matter fairly
before the House of Commons, which was fully alive
to its value and advantages, and would, no doubt, be
prepared to carry it into Pawnbroking, just as it
had already done into every other trade.

Mr. John Dicker, of London, was the next speaker,
and warmly supported the proposition; not, he was
careful to explain "exactly" as a delegate from the
Metropolitan Pawnbrokers, for they had rejected
Free Trade. He was, however, in favour of a change
and believed Free Trade was the proper basis from
which to operate. He instanced the unsatisfactory
manner in which the (then) present Act worked.
They all knew that ½d. per month for 2s. 6d. lent
was at the rate of 20 per cent. per annum, but they
were not limited to that, for if an article were redeemed the day it was pledged it would really pay
about 600 per cent.; while if the loan were only 6d.

I

the protective statute really allowed about 3,000 per
cent. He argued that he ought to have the same
right to use his capital as others had, and he found
that many of those who had voted against him at
the late meeting in London were coming round to
the same doctrine. But it was urged that if they
made the business too profitable they would be
swamped by competition. His reply was that if his
present £100 share in his business was only worth
10 per cent. why should he object to others coming
in to share in a system which would raise the value
of his £100 to 20 per cent? Mr. Dicker concluded
by saying that the Trade was never in a better
position for going to Parliament than at that time.
Dr. Hancock's report was before the public. He was
a gentleman who had been appointed by the Government to inquire into the question of Pawnbroking—
not in the interests of the Trade—but in those of
the people, and the result had been that he had
recommended the abrogation of that remnant of the
Usury Laws which forbade Free Trade in Pawnbroking.

The Free Trade skein at this point became somewhat entangled by Mr. Hows moving, as an amendment, "That application be made for a fixed rate up
to £—, and provisions for enabling licensed Pawnbrokers to make special contracts for any sum under
£10." The author of this short history, who had
been sent to the Meeting, charged—with his colleagues—to support such a principle, had no alternative but to second it. Then the battle became a
very animated one, as the advocates for both questions were nearly balanced.

Mr. Wright, of Sheffield, said that while theoreti-
cally they were in favour of Free Trade, they could
not see any plan by which it could be made
applicable to Pawnbroking. Mr. Cook (London),

vigorously opposed the resolution as being contrary
to the opinion of the London majority. Mr. Robinson, Mr. McKay, Mr. McGuckin, Mr. Morley, Mr.
Kidson, Mr. Marston, Mr. Eaton, Mr. Gush, all
opposed Free Trade *pur et simple*, as being inapplic-
able to Pawnbroking.

After this diversion Mr. Grantham strongly supported his colleague, Mr. Heys, who had proposed
the resolution. He urged that fixed rates could
never enable them to meet all circumstances, which
Free Trade would. He believed that by adopting it
they would not lower the status of the Trade, and
he maintained that they had a right, equal with other
trades, to fix their own terms according to the market
value of that which they dealt in. He denied that the
status of the Trade had been lowered by the passing of
the "Halfpenny Act," in 1860, and said at the period
named they had 264 licensed Pawnbrokers in Manchester, while then (1868) there were 291, which did
not represent an abnormal number, considering the
ever-increasing population. He advocated that each
Pawnbroker should put up a scale of rates in his shop,
at which he was prepared to do business, and endorse
such rates on the duplicate. They had no reason to
fear Free Trade, as it was sound in principle; it was
adopted in large sums, then why should it not work
in small sums?

Mr. Telfer, who followed on the same side, admitted
that his opinions were not Metropolitan opinions, and
must not be taken as such. He thought that the
Trade was in danger of drifting into two things,
both of which were wrong. One party was advocating
Free Trade, above a certain limit, with a fixed rate
below that limit, for the protection of the poor; and
it was urged, against general Free Trade, that it
would admit a large amount of new capital into the
business. This was not unlikely; indeed, he regarded

it as their chief danger. But the most dangerous
proposition that could be put forward for enticing
promoters of companies into the Trade was that of
the 40s. restriction, with Free Trade above that sum.
It was just in this margin that these new-comers were
most to be feared, and not at all below 40s. A new
fixed rate would only repeat the failure that had
resulted from the "Halfpenny Act." Some small
capitalists had then come into the Trade, who could
not, even with its assistance, get a living without
trespassing beyond legal bounds. Under improved
fixed rates these would increase ; but with entire Free
Trade a number of honest traders would come in, who
would not be required to live upon a profit of 25 per
cent. upon a capital of £500 or £1,000. There was only
one other trade, besides their own, in which profits
were restricted by law. Cabs were limited to 6d. a
mile, and what was the consequence ? No one ever
got into a cab without having to pay more than was
lawful, or have a row with the cabman. But in
omnibuses—where trade was free—the public could
travel seven or eight miles for sixpence. So matters
under Free Trade would find their level. Any kind of
limitation would not make matters any better than
they were. The public prints complained of them
only because they were able to see their profits. If
a person laid out his money with a linen-draper
he did not know or see the profit; but he would
certainly think something if he knew what the profit
really was.

Now arose the "Hyperion" of the day—or, as one
enthusiastic speaker described him to the meeting,
"The Champion of Free Trade"—Mr. George Attenborough. This most revered and affectionate friend,
possessed a peculiar insinuating, persuasive, yet a
sort of "sledge hammer" kind of eloquence, which was
most effective for the time; and there can be little

doubt but that he carried the majority of the meeting
with him by his sincerity in his advocacy of the Free
Trade theory.   He answered one of the London
speakers, who had said that Free Trade had been
defeated by a large majority, by saying that he had
sent out 430 circulars in the metropolis, and in answer
thereto 91 attended the meeting, out of which 53 had
voted against and 22 for Free Trade, and he did not
take that as a fair expression of the opinion of the
whole of London. Competition, he contended, was the
life of all trade, and Free Trade especially. If there
were any man who would serve the public better or
more liberally than himself, let him come and set up
alongside.   He did not object to competition, yet he .
did not desire to lower the respectability of the Trade.
They already got the credit of what the dolly-shops
were doing, and could anything be worse than that?
Attention had been drawn to some severe remarks
indulged in by the public press, the purity of which
was doubtful, and also an article in *Good Words*, which
was falsehood all through. But was it that gave the
opportunity for abuse?   No, it was the law. It had
been said that law was not made for honest men, but
thieves; and in making a law for them (the Pawnbrokers) they had been classed with thieves.   The
moment legal profit was overstepped everyone could
see it, and immediately a lot of sensational articles
appeared, setting forth the villainy of Pawnbrokers.   The speaker then gave the familiar
illustration of leaving articles at the railway
station, and paying 2d. for each package, with no
money advanced. Yet the public regarded this as a
great accommodation and nothing was heard of Railway extortions. It was the law that made the
dishonest Pawnbroker. Take away that law and
they would take away the power of the Press to
write them down. If Free Trade were given upon

special contract, then all his business should be Free
Trade, as he would take in everything upon special
contract. But Free Trade could not exist without
an Act of Parliament to provide for the large
number of contingencies that must occur. Why
should they not have an Act to be binding upon
both parties in Pawnbroking ? The law was binding
upon the contracts between railways and the public,
and particularly upon the system of insurance of
travellers. Here was an elaborate contract, but it
was implied in a little bit of pasteboard, smaller in
size than one of their own tickets. Why then
should not the Pawnbrokers' ticket be equally
binding and comprehensive? If the Trade went to
Parliament for a limited scale, they would be bound
to abide by it, and yet this could not be done. He
must come back to Free Trade down to the smallest
article. All the principles of commercial experience
were in favour of it. Free Trade was good in every
other trade, why not in theirs? All the difficulties
raised against it were merely myths of their own
creating. If other trades could be trusted, why
should not they? There was one point to which he
must allude before he concluded. *If the result of*
that day's discussion was to split them into two sec-
tions it would be a most unfortunate calamity. They
must stick together. The first question members of
Parliament would ask would be, "Are you united
among yourselves? If not, we cannot touch the
subject." They ought then first to agree among
themselves.

Several other speakers followed Mr. Attenborough,
including Mr. Brooking, Mr. Bullworthy, Mr. Vickers,
&c. The meeting was by this time becoming impatient for the division, so Mr. Heys very briefly
replied. The division was then taken, when it was
found there were

For Free Trade in profits   31
Against 25
                                     ——
Majority in favour of Free Trade   6
                                     ——

The remaining business was speedily disposed of.
A resolution was passed without dissent, "That in
the opinion of this meeting the term of forfeiture
should not be less than six months, but beyond that
time there should be freedom of contract for any
term they pleased." The Meeting, after very dis-
cursive conversation, elected the following Executive
Committee: Messrs. Geo. Attenborough, John Dicker·
and J. A. Telfer (London); Messrs. Grantham and
Heys (Manchester), Hardaker and Kidson (Liverpool), Buckler (Birmingham), Brooking (Exeter),
Cooke (Hanley), Vickers (Bolton), and Wright
(Sheffield).

A very hearty vote of thanks was given by
acclamation to the Chairman for the impartial
manner in which he had presided. The Meeting
then dissolved after its deliberations had extended
over six hours.

Thus the good ship "Reform," was safely launched
at last.

CHAPTER XXI

The newly-elected Executive Committee met for
the first time the morning immediately succeeding
the general gathering. Their first and most important duty consisted of the appointment of
officers, which was speedily effected, as there appeared no difficulty in the selection, nor much difference in opinion. Mr. George Attenborough was of
course elected Chairman, he being the hero of the
previous day's meeting. Mr. N. Dickenson was
appointed Treasurer; Mr. Ed. Heys, Vice-chairman,
and Mr. Alfred Hardaker, Honorary Secretary.
Some time after, when the work had become very
extensive and onerous, Mr. H. E. Kidson was appointed Financial Secretary, and the labour connected with the guarantees and subscriptions justified
the Executive in creating such a new department.

As a proof of the earnestness and determination of
the new Committee, it is only necessary to state
that after completing the appointments we have just
named, the consideration of the old Act was taken
in hand and the desirable amendments freely discussed. Before the members departed for their
various homes on that day, they had come to

a decision to repeal entirely 13 sections of the Act
of 1800; 13 other sections were to be redrawn with
extensive modifications, and the remaining sections
were to stand without alteration. Not content with
this rate of progress, the Meeting closed with a
resolution "That the Hon. Sec. should to the best
of his ability, draw up an experimental Bill,
embodying the projected changes, and place it
before the Executive at their next Meeting."

But this was not to be. The ardour of the new
reformers had shut out from their ken the existence of the Trade at large. They had adopted the
philosophy of the ostrich, and anticipated no danger.
It soon became manifest, however, that the good
ship "Reform" was to encounter squalls and contrary currents from the very commencement of its
voyage. The snap division with its majority of six
in favour of Free Trade down to the indispensable
flat iron, did not receive general support and
approval from outside. Liverpool was the first to
rebel, and at a Meeting held seven days after
the Nottingham gathering, passed a resolution of
protest. This protest was to be sent to the
Executive Committee asking them to reconsider
that portion of their programme relating to Free
Trade in profits, and to solicit proxy votes from
the whole of Great Britain upon the subject.
It was also further resolved that the Liverpool
Association take no further proceedings for or
against the movement. The non-Free Traders from
London, published an address to the whole Trade,
asking if the majority of six, was to be the means
of bringing disaster upon upwards of 3,000 Pawnbrokers in Great Britain? At a meeting of the
Committee of the Metropolitan Protection Society,
held early in May, Mr. J. M. Walter brought up an
elaborate resolution which was little less than an

indictment of treason for having violated their allegiance to the body who sent them, against those members who had voted for Free Trade at Nottingham. They regretted, said the resolution, that the members of the Parliamentary Committee who attended at Nottingham had voted for an alteration of the Act, had done so on principles opposed to the opinion of the Meeting at which they were appointed. Mr. Telfer moved an amendment that the debate be adjourned, so that they might fight the battle, as it ought to be fought, elsewhere. The present meeting had practically nothing to do with the matter. The amendment was defeated by the casting vote of the Chairman. The discussion then continued in a most accrimonious tone, and when the question was about to be put all the Free Trade members left the room, therefore the incriminatory resolution was declared to be carried unanimously.

A few days later a crisis was precipitated by the resignation of the Secretary of the Reform Association. He felt he was in an anomalous position, as there could be no hope of carrying out a Free Trade programme in the face of the attitude assumed by the Liverpool Association. Nor was that all. Mr. Gratton, the Hon. Secretary of the Sheffield Association, wrote to say that a fixed rate would have their unanimous support, whereas, if the resolution for entire Free Trade was persisted in by the Executive, he was inclined to think that Sheffield and an extensive neighbourhood around would put in an appearance in opposition. Here an impediment to progress was presented, but having a strong desire to disarm such opposition it was considered that the Executive should be called together at once and discuss the position.

The Meeting was held at Birmingham on the 13th May. It was admitted by the most ardent Free

Traders that the situation was a critical one, and that the Nottingham programme would not satisfy a large portion of the Trade throughout the country unless *a revised fixed rate* should constitute an integral portion of the draft Bill. After earnest discussion it was decided that a simplified fixed rate should become a portion of the programme in connection with the movement. After this decision the Secretary's resignation was withdrawn, and amity and unity were established.

The following evening a General Meeting was held in Liverpool, when it was decided that the Trade there would now co-operate with the Executive and was prepared to give individual guarantees to meet the expenses of an application to Parliament for an amendment of the Pawnbrokers' Act. This action was speedily followed by other towns, and the anticipated crisis was averted.

On the 23rd May, exactly one month after the inaugural Meeting, the manifesto of the Reform Association was issued. It was a somewhat formidable document and was signed by the Chairman, Treasurer, and Hon. Secretary. We have space too limited at our disposal for its reproduction, but we may briefly summarize its contents.

As a matter of course, it was addressed " To the Pawnbrokers of Great Britain," and referred briefly to the many unsuccessful attempts previously made to obtain an amendment of the Pawnbrokers' Act. The movement which originated in 1858, and resulted in what was known as the " Halfpenny Act," was the only one which had resulted in any gain, but that was described as only a modicum of amelioration, and totally inadequate to remove the disabilities under which they laboured. It was felt that the time had at last arrived (this had frequently been said and believed before) when a more extensive and satis-

factory measure should be applied for. The Usury
Laws had been repealed to the benefit of every
person in the Kingdom, save the Pawnbrokers. After
referring to the Royal Commission which had been
issued to Dr. Hancock, and his satisfactory report
after two years' investigation of the subject, the
programme and policy of the new Reform Association was boldly announced as follows :—

"The great and undeviating leading principle which
actuates the promoters of the present movement, is
to obtain the repeal of this clause,* which would
emancipate the Pawnbrokers from the operation of
the anomalous portion of our Act, which allows only
15 per cent. per annum profit on pledges over 42s.,
and empower him to regulate his own scale of charges
on all transactions according to the nature and value
of the security offered; in other words, it would
establish perfect Free Trade between the Pawnbrokers
and the customers, as to the rate of profit to be paid
for accommodation. Dr. Hancock says, 'I think it
impolitic that the legislature should deal with the
system of lending money to the poor on a principle
different to that adopted in dealing with loans to the
rich.' 'I recommend that the attempt to restrict
charges on the poor be abandoned.'

"It will require no further justification of the objects
the Committee have in view, when the importance
of the language quoted above, and the sources from
which it emanates are considered; at the same time,
as they are not in a position to say how far the present
system of express contract can be modified to meet
the requirements of the Pawnbroking Trade, the
Committee, after earnest and careful deliberation,
have resolved to apply for a special rate which shall
regulate the implied contract where it may be found

* 4th clause of the Usury Laws Repeal Act.

impolitic or inconvenient to transact business under
the express contract.

"This will tend to simplify the operations of large,
low, businesses, where it might bo thought inconvenient to have a special contract with every pledge
received.

"This portion of the subject will receive the utmost
consideration, so that a rate may be adopted by the
Committee and submitted to the Trade and Parliament, which will be free from the embarrassing sub-
divisions, fractional charges and portions of a month,
which characterizes the present rate.

"The hope that this concession will be obtained, is
strengthened by the words of the report, already
quoted, that 'The English scale of interest is too low.'"

The address then dilates on the desirability of
shortening the term of forfeiture, and gives the
reasons, now well known, why, with the rapid changes
of fashion, the transient and delicate fabrics which
were manufactured, the period of twelve months was
much too long for which pledges should be kept.

"It is hoped," continues the sanguine document,
" that a clause may be inserted and acceded to, whereby
the Pawnbroker may be indemnified if property comes
into his possession through the gross carelessness or
immoral conduct of the owner. An effort will also be
made to amend an Act, recently passed, by which the
Pawnbroker is precluded from participating in money
found upon a felon, while the purchaser is permitted,
at the discretion of the judge, to receive such award.
The Auction Clauses will be modified and modernized,
and no opportunity will be lost to make the present
Parliamentary movement a large and comprehensive
one, calculated to materially improve the present
position of the Pawnbroker."

This tolerably bountiful programme was sent where-
ever a Pawnbroker could be found. If one man in a

district was known, he was solicited and implored to furnish a list of all in the Trade in his locality. Secretaries to the Associations were, in like manner, appealed to, and so generous was the response that in a short period the address was in the hands of nearly 3,000 Pawnbrokers, and a form of guarantee was, in no case, omitted to be enclosed.

CHAPTER XXII

PARLIAMENTARY BILL MAKING

Little time was allowed to elapse, when harmony had become established, before the Executive Committee plunged into hard and practical labour. Such preliminary work, as issuing the address, and preparing documents required for the next meeting, was completed by the end of June, and the Executive body met at Manchester, the conference extending over the 2nd and 3rd July. The Secretary had, as desired, prepared draft copies of the intended amendments of the Act, in consonance with the opinions expressed at the first Meeting held at Nottingham. These were now discussed with greater deliberation and care, and the result indicated wonderful unanimity as to the direction in which the efforts to achieve reform should be devoted. It was agreed that sections 1 to 5 were to be repealed; sections 8 to 14 were to be retained; while sections from 15 to 19 with 21 added were all condemned to annihilation. Sections 22 to 36 were to be allowed to remain undisturbed. After these alterations had been decided upon, the Secretary was instructed to draft an experimental Bill, and that being completed, a Sub-Committee consisting of the Chairman and Secretary, with power to add to their number, if necessary, was elected, and advised to seek, at as early an opportunity as possible, an interview with Dr. Hancock, and solicit his advice and assistance upon the subject of the intended legislation.

It was at this Meeting also that the prospects of the Reform Association appeared to be of the brightest; as within about six weeks after the circulation of the inaugural address, the guarantee fund amounted to little less than *two thousand pounds*, and this announcement supplied cheering and convincing evidence that the battle for reform was, after many attempts, at last going to be fought in earnest. An important regulation as to future voting was also adopted. It was declared that all guarantors up to July 1st, 1868, should be entitled to vote at General Meetings; but that in future all guarantees for any less sum than £2 should be treated as subscriptions only, and should not entitle such donors to a vote. This course was found necessary as guarantee papers had been sent in for sums as low as five shillings, which would entail trouble and labour to collect by calls of 5, 10 or 20 per cent. It was also very definitely resolved that under no conditions should proxy votes be received.

For a time after this meeting, circumstances did not contribute to rapid progress. Dr. Hancock was on the continent, and could not of course be approached. The Sub-Committee awaited his return anxiously and impatiently. At length on the last day of July a letter was received by the Secretary, informing him that Dr. Hancock had returned to London, and was at liberty to consult with the gentlemen appointed to wait upon him. No time was lost, as the Secretary joined the Chairman in London the next day, and they proceeded together to the office in Victoria-street, Westminster, and

were received with great civility and courtesy. They
entered at once into a free and friendly conversation on the subject of an alteration of the laws of
Pawnbroking. The deputation had previously expressed between themselves the hope that possibly Dr.
Hancock might be retained in the interests of the
Trade, and his assistance secured in drafting a Bill.
Their hope, however, was speedily dispelled when
he informed them that he was not at the time free
to accept any private engagements, as he had been
appointed Commissioner by the Government to conduct an inquiry into Irish Railways. But while he
could not accept any responsibility in connection
with an application to Parliament, he was quite at
liberty to consult and advise on a subject he had
studied and inquired into. The wishes of the Trade
were then fully explained, with the course the
Executive thought it wisdom to pursue, and all the
points were discussed with considerable freedom.
The draft Bill was then handed to him, when he
deprecated unhesitatingly and somewhat strongly
the number and length of the clauses it contained.
The author confessed it was the work of an
amateur draftsman, and that he had had no previous experience. The Doctor then good humouredly
expressed his belief that a Bill to succeed in
modern times, should consist of as few clauses as
possible; in fact that it should present as small a
surface of resistance compatible with the desires
and necessities of the Trade. He further strongly
advised that a Parliamentary Agent should be consulted and the Bill properly drawn before submit-
ting it for adoption by the Trade. He grounded
his reasons for this course, on the fact that the
Bill contained certain proposals which would affect
the stamp duties, the law of contracts and other
points, so that the Bill should not be drawn as

K

antagonistic to the common law. He recommended
non-interference with any clause in the old Act
which might appear to the mind of a Member of
Parliament to give any protection to the poor;
especially would it be dangerous to interfere with
the auction clauses. In parting the learned gentleman reiterated the advice that a first class Parliamentary Agent should be consulted and instructed
to draw the Bill in a most brief and concise manner.

All this information, so kindly given, was of inestimable value to the Sub-Committee. They were
moving along an untrodden path and in a strange
land, therefore these directions were most acceptable. Neither of the Members to whom this task
of Bill making was allotted, were experienced in
Párliamentary tactics, and therefore accepted any
information most willingly.

On leaving Dr. Hancock's office it occurred to
them that they were in the locality where Parliamentary Agents "most do congregate," and that
no time should be lost in putting the practical
lesson they had just received to account. They saw
the spacious offices of Messrs. Baxter, Rose and
Norton, and their inexperience emboldened them to
seek an interview with that eminent firm, in the
steadfast belief that Pawnbroking affairs were as
important as any other business, and as worthy of
attention. They were introduced to Mr. Spofforth, then a junior member of the firm, and
unfolded their hopes and aspirations. After hearing
the nature of the business Mr. Spofforth undertook
to have a Bill drawn, providing "there was nothing
radical in it," and promised a draft in a few weeks.
He advised, however, not to attempt to repeal the 4th
clause of the Usury Laws Repeal Act, as he did not
think it necessary ; besides it would complicate the
question too much to be understood by Members of

Parliament.   So the high sounding sentiment expressed in the address that "Tho great and undeviating leading principle" should be such repeal,
went by the board.

The matter was then, with a feeling of confidence,
left in the hands of Mr. Spofforth, and the Sub-Committee had a feeling of self gratulation that they
had completed rather an important day's work. Their
elation was not of permanent duration, for after
waiting patiently for nearly a month in the daily
expectation of receiving a copy of the draft Bill, Mr.
Spofforth wrote to say, that after some consideration
of the subject, he and other members of the firm had
come to the conclusion, that an amendment of the
laws affecting Pawnbrokers, was not a measure
suitable for them to undertake, and they must decline
further connection directly with the promoters.
This rebuff, which it was undoubtedly felt to be, was
partially neutralized by the suggestion of a suitable
gentleman in Mr. Coates, of the firm of Messrs. Dyson
and Co., Parliament-street.   Heavy hearted enough,
thither the Chairman and Secretary wended their
weary way and related their instructions and explanations to Mr. Coates *de novo*.   It was now discovered that the period of the year when it was
desired to commence operations was inauspicious, for
Parliament had been prorogued, and professional men
were generally in vacation, and dispersed all over the
world. Mr. Coates, however, promised to give the
subject his best consideration, but feared that he
could promise to make no progress till about October.
After the lapse of considerable time Mr. Coates wrote
and suggested that the Bill with full instructions
should be placed in the hands of F. S. Reilly, Esq.,
Parliamentary Barrister, Draughtsman and Commissioner.   This was agreed to, and on the 28th
October the "first revise," or uncorrected proof of

the Bill, was received, but on examination it was
found to be very defective and insufficient on many
important points, so that an application was made for
a personal interview with Mr. Reilly. This was with
some difficulty acceded to, as it was contrary to professional usage to receive instructions except through
Solicitors or Agents. The Chairman, Secretary,
and Mr. Dicker attended and went exhaustively
into the subject, pointing out the omissions of
many of the requirements, stated by the Executive
as necessary. Mr. Reilly expressed his sense of
the great difficulty of dealing with such a subject,
and pointed out that he had yet to be supplied
with the rate of profit to be inserted in the First
Schedule, and the conditions which it was intended
should regulate the Special Contract. His opinion
was very decided that it would be dangerous to
interfere with the Usury Laws Repeal Act, as it
would be very much better not to encumber the Bill
with it.

After this interview it was decided that the Secretary should call the Executive together at Leeds, for
a thorough discussion of the Draft Bill. The meeting
was convened for the 11th November, but extended
over two days. The draft, and Mr. Reilly's opinions
thereon, were laid before the Committee and the
clauses discussed seriatim. · The Bill was considered
too massive and voluminous, consequently several
clauses were deleted. It was then returned to the
draftsman with instructions to re-draw it as amended.
It was also decided that so soon as the Secretary
received the new draft he should call a general
meeting of the Guarantors, to give them the opportunity of expressing their opinions and approval, if
not in that, in some still further amended form.

A very gratifying and enjoyable event took place
in connection with the labours of the Executive,

during their stay in Leeds. The Pawnbrokers of
that town most generously invited the whole of the
Committee to a banquet, which was attended by over
fifty guests. Mr. Councillor Linsley presided, and the
vice-chairs were filled by Major Middleton and Mr.
Councillor Scotson. The festival, which was on a
grand scale, was given in the Queen's Hotel, and
was a brilliant and successful event, and a splendid
specimen of true Yorkshire hospitality. The toasts
were brief and effective, including success to "The
Parliamentary Reform Association," coupled with
the names of the Chairman and Secretary. The
genuineness and sincerity of the toast could not be
put to better proof than the fact that guarantee notes
were handed to the Secretary for no less a sum than
£107, £20 of that sum being contributed by two
gentlemen from Bradford.

The year 1868 expired before the Draft Bill could
be completed, the draughtsman having found the
subject so intricate, that he was compelled to break
down the barrier of professional etiquette and seek
inspiration from those who had more practical
knowledge of the matter, and this led to repeated
interviews with the officials of the Association.

After all the wasted months the draft was received
still in an incomplete condition. It was at once put
in the hands of the printers, and circulated without
delay to the Guarantors, who were, at the same time,
summoned to attend a general meeting at the Midland
Hotel, Derby, on February 12th, 1869, to consider,
amend, and approve of a Draft Bill.

CHAPTER XXIII

Prior to the Meeting of Guarantors at Derby, London was again seized with paroxysms of exasperation at the conduct of the gentlemen who represented them at the Nottingham Meeting, and felt little less at the action of the country in forging ahead with the agitation for the achievement of Pawnbroking Reform. In the van of the discontents was that "Mother Carey's chicken," whose presence generally presaged a storm—Mr. John M. Walter, who revelled in the delight of inciting his fellow tradesmen against the Reform Association, and all who supported it. He said at one Meeting that they had attempted to carry Free Trade by "sleight-of-hand," and he believed the whole Trade would be disgusted with it. He had explained the measure (according to his own biassed vision) to a Member of Parliament, whose opinion was that they need not distress themselves as such a Bill had no chance of passing. As the American humorist said, it is much safer to prophecy after the event, and probably Mr. Walter may now share this view, for although that Bill did not actually pass, a better one did, and Mr. Walter knows, and regrets it, that the Act is not, through his own efforts in opposition, better still.

At the same Meeting, which was one of the Protection Society, Mr. Lawley moved, "That in the opinion of this Meeting, the Draft Bill prepared by the Parliamentary Committee appeared to be highly detrimental to the best interests of the Trade; and that it was absolutely necessary that the strongest opposition should be given to it." Mr. Geo. Attenborough (Fleet-street), seconded the motion. An amendment for adjournment was defeated by a large majority, and the resolution, on a division, was carried by 48 votes in its favour against 21 dissentients.

On the Friday in the same week a General Meeting of the London Trade was held at the Terminus Hotel, Cannon-street. Mr. J. Dicker presented a short report detailing the labours of the Executive, and explaining the principal proposals contained in the Draft Bill. Again Mr. Lawley represented the obstructionists, and moved a terrible amendment to the motion that the Report be received, in these words, "That this Meeting, having considered the Draft of the Bill* (submitted by the Executive of the Parliamentary Pawnbroking Association) for the amendment of the law relating to Pawnbrokers, is of opinion that if such became law it would be entirely subversive of the best interests of the Trade, and that it is framed directly contrary to the instructions given to the London Parliamentary Committee, this Meeting is strongly of opinion that if it is pressed into Parliament the London Trade should offer to it the strongest opposition in their power." This was carried by 84 votes against 52.

* Up to the time of the speaker making this observation the Meeting had mainly complained of the action of the gentlemen who had been sent to Nottingham. The only consideration of the Bill was by Mr. Dicker.

The repeated fulmination of these impotent but adverse resolutions did not deter the Executive from pressing onward. They met in Derby the evening before the General Meeting and again the following morning, completing details of the business on the agenda. The great gathering took place on Thursday, February 11th, 1869, and Mr. George Attenborough, the President of the Reform Association, occupied the chair. The sight was an impressive one, and the assembly would have done credit to any organized representative body in the world. There were no less than 161 Pawnbrokers present, hailing from 43 different cities and towns.

After a brief introduction to the business before the Meeting the Secretary was called upon to read some important and voluminous correspondence, which included some letters which had passed between the Parliamentary draftsman and himself. Most of it is too technical and uninteresting to reproduce, unless the clauses of the Draft Bill were also laid before our readers, and as the Bill itself has these past 20 years been consigned to the limbo of good intentions, we have no desire to resuscitate it. Mr. Reilly's opinion as to the difficulty of defining a Special Contract may be given as an illustration of the knotty points the Executive were called upon to face. He wrote :—" It would be useful if persons interested would suggest amendments, rather than content themselves with criticizing what is proposed. The note is intended to be, and made by Act of Parliament to be, evidence of a Special Contract for a higher rate of profit. Whether it can properly be called a contract or not is a verbal question, which I am not disposed to discuss. It would be well if attention were given to the inherent difficulty of the plan, namely, that there is nothing to fairly fix the pawner with the knowledge that he is to be charged the higher rate, whence it must be apprehended that in some cases pawners when they come to redeem will profess to be surprised at being asked to pay the higher rate, and will dispute their liability. It appears to me that those who concern themselves about the Bill should endeavour to devise some plan of getting out of the difficulty. The signature of the pawner on the counterpart would probably go a long way towards getting over it, but I understand that was considered impracticable. Something might be done by coloured paper for the note, or other devices of a material kind which might be prescribed in the schedule."

The correspondence disposed of, the Meeting addressed itself to the consideration of the Draft Bill, taking it clause by clause. The preamble and first clauses numbering 1 to 5 inclusive, were agreed to without comment. With clause 5 the real business of the day began, as its purport was to define the fixed rate for sums lent of 42s. and under. Two scales were submitted marked A. and B., one of which was to be determined upon and inserted in the first schedule. Scale A. provided that the profit on any sum lent *under* 3s. should be at the rate of one halfpenny per month, or any part of a month. Then for the full 3s. and *under* 4s., there should be taken ¾d.; for 4s. and under 5s., 1d.; for 6s. and under 7s., 1¼d.; for 7s. and under 8s., 1¾d.; for 9s. and under 10s., 2¼d.; for 10s. and under 11s., 2½d.; and so on up to 20s. and under 21s., when the monthly charge should be 5d.

This scheme found little favour with the meeting, for although it demolished the per centage rate, it was complex and involved the dealing with farthings, which it was the hope of reformers would disappear in any new scale of charges which might be adopted.

Scale B will require no explanation, for it was the
one eagerly adopted by the meeting; was recommended in the report of the Select Committee; it
passed through the scathing ordeal of the Houses of
Commons and the Lords, became law, and forms
to-day a portion of third schedule of the Pawnbrokers'
Act of 1872.

The Executive, in their experimental draft bill, had
not proposed to carry the fixed rate higher than the
42s., as arranged in the old Act, but Mr. Nathan
expressed the opinion that such a stipulation did not
seem reasonable, as the increasing the profits below
42s., and not above. If they increased the former
from 20 to 25 per cent., they ought in fairness to raise
the old 15 per cent. rate, to 20, which would be a
charge of one-halfpenny per month for every 2s. 6d.
lent. Mr. Cooke, of Hanley, seconded the proposal, and
after some discussion it was unanimously adopted.

As will have been seen, the rate to be charged was
per month, or any part of a month, thus excluding
days of grace. The clause was drawn to the effect
that a Pawnbroker should take the aforesaid profit
for "anything pawned with him for any time during
which the same remains in pawn, not exceeding one
month, and so for every month afterwards, including
the current month in which the pawn is redeemed,
although that month is not expired."

Mr. R. B. Starling objected to the omission, and
thought the Bill was too much of a one-sided
character, he therefore proposed that a third paragraph
be added to the clause, enacting " that the first seven
days after the expiration of any calendar month,
should not be chargeable with any additional interest
beyond that due for such month, but that after the
expiration of those seven days then another whole
month's interest should be chargeable." Mr. Grantham
was the seconder. An amendment was proposed by

Mr. May, seconded by Mr. Webb (Worcester), that fourteen days' grace be allowed; the original motion for seven days was adopted by a large majority.

The Special Contract clause was next for consideration, and led to a long discussion, which was not surprising when the difficulties raised by Mr. Reilly are borne in mind. The first paragraph read as follows; "Notwithstanding anything in the principal Act, or any Act amending the same, or this Act, a Pawnbroker may demand and take from any person applying or offering to redeem anything pawned with him a greater profit than that prescribed in the principal Act or any Act amending the same or this Act, provided that at the time of pawning a Special Contract for such higher rate is entered into in the form, and according to the regulations set forth in the second Schedule to this Act."

Mr. Vickers moved, and Mr. Brooking seconded, that the first paragraph be adopted.

Mr. Starling in a long and earnest speech moved an amendment, in the hope, as he asserted, of creating harmony between all sections of the Trade, but he was afraid the clause as it then stood would meet with the most stubborn resistance. He moved that after the work "*take*" in the third line, the words, "not being an article of wearing apparel, silver plate, watches, or jewellery," be added. Mr. Hows seconded the amendment, which, strangely enough in the face of the Free Trade phalanx, met with general support. Free Traders, who had at Derby declared that nothing less than free and fetterless profits down to the humble flat-iron (so dear to sensational writers), would satisfy them, now declared that if unity of action could be secured, and factious opposition cease, they would support the amendment. Even the Chairman, Mr. Heys, Mr. Grantham, and others said that if these objects could be secured, they would sink

their individual opinions and go with the feeling of
the meeting. The motion was then withdrawn, and
Mr. Starling's amendment carried by acclamation.
Thus, Free Trade "pure and simple," as was Mr.
Walter's favourite phrase, became an incorporeal and
visionary principle.

The difficulties surrounding the Special Contract,
as mentioned by Mr. Reilly, were next discussed.
There existed little difference of opinion on the subject
of requiring the signature of the pledger, as it was
felt the scheme would never work satisfactorily
without it. The proposal to adopt that course was
quickly agreed to.

The six months' forfeiture next claimed attention,
but this was a matter on which the opinion of the
meeting appeared to be so unanimous that it was
adopted with little discussion. Several details as to
declarations, numbering pledges in rotation for each
month, and a few typographical errors, were settled
and corrected, when the discussion on the Draft Bill
was brought to a close.

It was then decided that a call of 25 per cent. should
be made upon the guarantors, as the Association had
then been in existence ten months, and considerable
expense had been incurred.

A cordial vote of thanks to the Chairman brought
this most important Trade Meeting to a close.

A third Meeting of the Executive, while at Derby,
was held on the day following. Messrs. Nathan and
Starling were added to the Executive, as their
assistance at the General Meeting was invaluable.
The amended clauses of the Bill were revised
and drawn in accordance with the resolutions
passed on the previous day, and the Chairman,
Mr. Dicker, Mr. Starling, and the Secretary, were
deputed to arrange for the final draft of the Bill to
be prepared.

A Parliamentary Committee was also appointed, consisting of the Chairman, Mr. Dicker, Mr. Linsley, Mr. Heys, and the Secretary, to conduct the Parliamentary business so as to prevent the calling together too frequently the whole of the Executive.

And so, hopeful, cheerful, and contented with their efforts to promote unity and unanimity in the Trade, the Executive separated and returned to their respective localities. They were animated with the full confidence that great progress had been made, and that Parliamentary Reform was almost a near certainty. They were utterly unconscious, however, that at the moment of their exultation a serious danger threatened the Trade, and, like the sword of Damocles, might descend at any moment and destroy them. Little, indeed, did they anticipate, that, in a less period than a month, Reform would be, for a time, cast aside, and that they would be engaged in a severe hand to hand struggle with an unsuspected but powerful enemy.

CHAPTER XXIV

DENOUNCED AS HABITUAL CRIMINALS

Quite a month elapsed before the amended Draft Bill, as completed at Derby, was received from the Parliamentary Draughtsman. It was circulated to the guarantors without delay; and with the brightest hope the Parliamentary Committee were convened to meet in London, with a view of getting the measure introduced into the House at once. The Meeting took place at Ridler's Hotel, Holborn, then, and for many years previously, a famous hostelry for Country Pawnbrokers, and it was a rare chance when one or more could not be met with, "up in Town" for either business or pleasure.

The Meeting was fixed for March 10th, with the intention of deciding on a line of action; but "the native hue of resolution" had its current turned "awry" by a circumstance which had occurred almost simultaneously with their own determination to proceed. A Bill had been, but a few days previously, introduced into the House of Lords by Lord Kimberley, with the alarming title of the "Habitual Criminals' Bill," and it contained three stringent police clauses directly applying to Pawnbrokers. The measure emanated from the Home Office, when Mr. Bruce—now Lord Aberdare—was

Secretary, and it had the active support of the
Earl of Shaftesbury and others equally as eager
for the suppression of crime, but having no
practical knowledge of the subject.

Fortunately an early copy of the Bill was obtained
by the Editor of the *Pawnbrokers' Gazette*, and, its
character as affecting the Trade being ascertained,
that gentleman at once printed copies, and with
admirable promptitude, circulated them to every
Pawnbroker whose address could be ascertained.

Thus there dropped a thunderbolt, which effectually obliterated all thoughts of Reform. An article
in the *Gazette* commenced with the words :—
"Whilst the Pawnbrokers have been organizing
themselves for approaching the portals of the Legislature, the latter has astonished them by anticipating
the movement, and sounding an alarm upon the
doors of the Trade, which has been in no small
measure a startling one." And so undoubtedly it
was; but the surprise might have been more
alarming and perhaps disastrous, had there not been
already a strong organization for Reform. Here
there was strength which was at once diverted
into the channel for defeating the obnoxious clauses.
The first burst of indignation permeated the whole
country, which could not but be bitterly incensed
at the degradation sought to be imposed upon them,
by including them with the criminal classes. But
there was no time to indulge in execrations against
the Bill as immediate action was imperative. The
situation was grasped by the "leaders" of the
Trade, and a Meeting was hastily convened in London for March 10th, only a few days after the
alarm had sounded. The Parliamentary Committee
stayed in London and rendered all the assistance
in their power, while delegates from all parts of
the country attended the Meeting, which was held on

the day when it was hoped the struggle for Reform
would have commenced within the Parliamentary
arena. But as we have said all these hopes and
aspirations were hushed for the time. The "Habitual
Criminals" clauses were strong enough to divert
men's minds, and thoughts of defence for self-
preservation predominated. At this there could be
little surprise; the astonishment arose when it was
calmly proposed to legislate for Pawnbrokers in such
disreputable company.

The clauses which the Meeting had to consider,
and against which every Pawnbroker in the land
was up in arms, read as follows :—"15. This part of
this Act shall be construed as one with the Act of
the session of the thirty-ninth and fortieth years of
the reign of George the Third, chapter ninety-nine, 'for
the better regulating the business of Pawnbrokers,'
in this Act referred to as the Pawnbrokers' Act.

"Any Pawnbroker who acts in contravention of the
provisions contained in this part of the Act shall be
deemed guilty of an offence against the said Act, and
on summary conviction thereof *may be punished
accordingly.*

"Pawnbrokers to produce books on demand.

"A Pawnbroker in any place shall at all times
during his hours of business, produce, on demand, to
the Chief Officer of Police of that place, *or to some
police-officer appointed by such chief-officer,* all books in
which any particulars respecting the articles received
by him by way of pawn or pledge are entered, and
shall allow such officer to examine such books. He
shall also exhibit to such officer all goods which the
officer, on the information given to him, *reasonably
suspects to have been stolen, embezzled or fraudulently
obtained,* and, if required, *shall deposit the same with
such chief-officer,* for the purposes of public justice, on
receiving a receipt for same.

" Report by Pawnbrokers of stolen goods.

"16. If in any place any officer of the police force of such place gives information, in writing or print, or partly in writing and partly print, to any Pawnbroker, that any goods described in such information, have been stolen, embezzled, or fraudulently obtained, and if any of those goods are in or thereafter come into the possession of any such Pawnbroker, or are offered to him for pawn or pledge, such Pawnbroker shall forthwith give information thereof to the chief-officer of police of such place, and shall state the name and address given by the person from or by whom the same were received or offered.

"Where the goods are wearing apparel, or articles which it is difficult to identify, the Pawnbroker shall not be liable to any penalty for acting in contravention of this section, unless it appear to the justices or magistrates that the goods, or the offer of them, were knowingly concealed by the Pawnbroker.

"If stolen articles be altered or defaced by the Pawnbroker, "he shall be held to be a receiver of stolen goods.

"17. If any Pawnbroker, after receiving information of the theft, embezzlement, or fraudulent disposal of any goods of whatsoever description, melts, alters, defaces, or puts away the same, or causes the same to be melted, altered, defaced, or put away, without having previously received the permission of some justice or magistrate, and if it is found that such metals, goods, or articles, were stolen, embezzled, or fraudulently disposed of, *then such Pawnbroker shall be deemed to have known* that such goods were stolen, embezzled, or fraudulently disposed of and may be proceeded against, and punished accordingly *as a receiver of stolen goods*, or as being a party to the fraud, and no other evidence of his guilt shall be necessary' than evidence of such melting, altering, defacing, or putting away, after receiving information as aforesaid."

L

After these tyrannical clauses had been circulated to
the Trade, meetings were held everywhere and strong
condemnatory resolutions were carried, accompanied
by declarations to use every possible effort to ensure
Pawnbrokers being exempted from such degrading
legislation.

The meeting in London, as we have said, was
strengthened by the support of country delegates.
Mr. John Dicker was called upon to preside, and Mr.
Geo. Attenborough, the Chairman of the Reform
Association, stated that Mr. Dicker, Mr. Starling, and
himself, had realized the imminence of the danger,
and saw it would not do to stand still, but that
immediate steps must be taken both energetically and
promptly. They had, therefore, on their own responsibility had a form of petition drawn up, copies of which
had been circulated throughout the country, so that
the Trade might at once proceed to address itself to
the House of Lords. They had also obtained interviews with several Peers—amongst others Lord
Shaftesbury—and they had an appointment to see him
next day, and they were sanguine enough to hope that
he would accompany them to an audience with Lord
Kimberley and Mr. Bruce, the Home Secretary.

Mr. W. Nathan, in a long and eloquent speech,
moved, "That, in the opinion of this meeting, the
principle of legislating for Pawnbrokers in any Bill
intended to deal with habitual criminals is most
objectional, and calls for the combined opposition of
the Trade." The motion was seconded by Mr. Middleton (Leeds), and supported by representatives from
Sheffield, Hull, Bradford, Liverpool, Bolton, Manchester, Gosport, and Leeds, all being accredited
delegates.

Mr. Heys, next, in an earnest and powerful speech,
moved, "That the clauses included in part 4 of the
Habitual Criminals' Bill, will, if passed into law, be-

unjust and degrading both to Pawnbrokers and
customers, harassing in the conduct of their business,
and will also expose them to risks which no honest
tradesman ought to be liable to; and this meeting
pledges itself to oppose them to the utmost of their
power." It is needless to say that both resolutions
were carried with great enthusiasm.

It was also agreed that a Committee should be
appointed empowered to collect subscriptions and
conduct the defence of the Trade. The following
gentlemen were appointed:—Messrs. G. Attenborough
(Fleet-street), Geo. Attenborough (Old Kent-road),
F. Cotton, John Dicker, Harding, Hows, Lawley,
Nathan, Starling, and Telfer (all of London), Messrs.
Dickinson, Heys, Hardaker, Jeffreys (Sheffield), and
Linsley. A vote of thanks (Grantham—Hardaker)
was enthusiastically passed to the Editor of the *Pawnbrokers' Gazette*, for his kindness and promptitude in
making the Trade acquainted with their threatened
danger. The meeting closed with the usual thanks to
the Chair, and the cheering announcement that a sum
of between £700 and £800 had been subscribed in
the room. There has never yet been lack of funds
when the Trade was attacked from without.

The day following the Meeting, a deputation
waited upon Mr. Bruce at the Home Office. The
Members in attendance were Messrs J. Dicker,
Attenborough, Starling (now made Hon. Sec.), Heys,
Hardaker, and Linsley. Mr. Coates, the Parlia-
mentary agent, introduced the deputation to the
Home Secretary, with whom was Lord Kimberley.

Mr. Coates said that the Pawnbrokers objected
most strongly to be legislated for in a Bill which
was specially intended to deal with Habitual
Criminals, and they repudiated the charge that anything could be brought against the Trade to justify
such legislation.

L 2

To this Mr. Bruce demurred, saying that when he
was a Magistrate he became quite familiar with the
faces of Pawnbrokers' Assistants, from their frequent
attendance before him as witnesses. To this remark
several members of the deputation replied, and pointed
out that much as they regretted the frequent
appearance of their assistants at the Criminal Courts,
it was impossible it could be otherwise, when the
large number of Pawnbrokers was taken into account,
and also the enormous number of pledges annually
received by each. In further explanation of this
point, a member stated that in his own town, if each
Member of the Trade had but one police case annually,
there would be 25 Pawnbrokers to appear at each
Session or Assize. A London Member exhibited
the police notices of articles lost or stolen for four
consecutive weeks, and there were no less than 2,927
articles enumerated and described. To this Mr.
Bruce replied emphatically, that those were not the
kind of notices intended by the Bill. The deputation
then dwelt on the small per centage of forfeited
pledges, and the fact of a large portion being exposed
in public sale rooms. Great emphasis was laid upon
the mischief that must arise to pledgers if police
constables were allowed to make themselves acquainted with the names and addresses of persons
driven by misfortune to the Pawnbroker, and
the unfair use which might be made of such
information. It was still further urged that
the law was strong enough as it existed. Magistrates could order a search warrant to be issued,
and the Trade did not object, but they did object
and that strongly to such power being relegated to
an irresponsible police officer. It was also shown
that any article of gold or silver ware might be
purchased twelve months or more after any notice
had been given, and broken up and melted, an act

which under the Bill would become a crime, while
jewellers and refiners could buy and break up or
melt immediately.

Lord Kimberley remarked that the clauses already
existed in Scotch law. In reply it was stated that
they were not wanted in England nor were they
required. The Trade were willing to submit to any
investigation or inquiry as to the mode in which
their businesses were conducted, and urged strongly
that such stringent enactments should not be passed
without careful collection of reliable information
proving the necessity for them. In conclusion the
Home Secretary said: "Well, gentlemen, you have
made out a very good case for yourselves, and the
matter shall have the careful consideration of the
Government."

This might be considered as an opinion expressed
in a fair and conciliatory spirit, but what can be
thought of a noble Earl who took great interest in
the subject, when he exhibited his ignorance in a
speech he made in the House of Lords? It only
requires a portion of his Lordship's utterances to
be quoted, to show how little he or his hearers
understood what dire result would follow on their
blind and ignorant attempts at such special legislation. The Earl of Shaftesbury, in the debate on
the second reading of the Bill, did, according to the
report in the *Times*, make the following remarkable statements:—"Of the many valuable provisions
of the Bill," said his Lordship, "I think none will
be more effective in the repression of crime than
that which refers to the receivers of stolen goods. . . .
As for spoons, forks and jewellery, they were not
taken so readily to the smelting pot; but to well-
known places where is a pipe which your Lordships
may have seen—I hope none may have seen it of
necessity"—(perhaps a few of the West End Pawn-

brokers would know more on that subject than the speaker)—in a Pawnbroker's shop. I have had a description of the process from practitioners (?). *The thief taps, the pipe is lifted up, and in the course of a minute a hand comes down covered with a glove, takes up the jewellery, and gives out the money for it.*"

Believing such romancing drivel as this, our hereditary legislators were prepared to inflict indignities upon a body of respectable tradesmen who to a man resented it (except Mr. J. M. Walter) without there being searching and exhaustive inquiry made into the whole subject. It was soon apparent, however, that the Pawnbrokers were not so abject and spiritless as to accept such proposals. Every possible effort was now made; petitions, signed in every district by every Pawnbroker were showered into the House of Lords. Interviews with Peers were taking place all day long; introductions were obtained from all parts of the country, and in many cases men who were known personally to some noble Lord were sent for to London, and accompanied by members of the Committee obtained interviews. The influence and combined action of the Trade made itself felt. Many friends were made, and foremost in the rank was Lord Lyveden, who undertook to move the rejection of the clauses.

The decisive battle was fought in the House of Lords on Monday, March 15th, when the Bill was down for the Committee stage. The outlook was not bright at the commencement, for Earl Grey moved an amendment to clause 14 to the effect that if any person should be found to be in possession of goods proved to be the proceeds of three or more separate robberies, he should be liable to be separately punished for as many offences as there had been robberies. This was speedily negatived. On clause 15 Lord Lyveden moved the omission of that and the two following clauses which related to Pawnbrokers. He made a very excellent speech full of statistics and arguments, but as his Lordship's remarks travelled over ground more than well known to most of our readers, it would be useless to produce them here. The Duke of Cleveland urged that any measure proposed affecting Pawnbrokers should be done in a separate Bill. It might be true that a certain amount of stolen goods finds its way to respectable Pawnbrokers, but it is utterly impossible to prevent that even by the strictest investigation. Provisions relating to men who, for the most part, were respectable should not be placed side by side with habitual criminals.

The Earl of Kimberley said that the Pawnbrokers had shown themselves perfectly capable of defending themselves. He had had some communication with them, and he thought, that in some respects they had made out a case. He offered no opposition to the withdrawal of the clauses. The Earl of Shaftesbury also did not object to the withdrawal, but thought some provisions of a similar character should be enacted for the Pawnbrokers.

CLAUSES 15, 16 AND 17 WERE THEN STRUCK OUT !

CHAPTER XXV

The battle—crowned with victory—against the noble Lords and the Home Office, had been short, sharp and severe; but it had a most encouraging effect on the spirits of the Parliamentary Committee. They had not only "fleshed their maiden sword," but routed the enemy, so they returned to the work of Reform with renewed courage and confidence. The completed Draft Bill was in their hands, and it was plainly their duty to lose no time in enlisting the kindly services of a friendly Member of the House of Commons to ask for leave to introduce the Bill. Mr. Sheridan, member for Dudley, was the first gentleman thought of, and it was decided to apply to him at once, and ask him to take charge of the Bill. The Secretary wrote to the hon. gentleman, and at the same time to Mr. Hannay, Pawnbroker of Dudley, who was a prominent constituent, and personally known to his Member, to go to London and accompany some Members of the Committee to an interview with Mr. Sheridan. Unfortunately Mr. Hannay was unable to leave home, but wrote to his representative explaining the wishes of the Committee. Mr. Sheridan was away from town, and no reply was received as the letters did not reach him until he returned. Being surprised at the silence, it was

decided to go down to the House and endeavour to
obtain an interview. It was then discovered that
he had not been in attendance for some days. An
introduction was obtained to Mr. Mundella, who appeared to be very friendly disposed towards the
Trade, and a copy of the Bill was handed to him, the
leading features and principles being freely discussed. He was also informed of the Committee's
desire that Mr. Sheridan should introduce it into
the House. At the conclusion of the interview Mr.
Mundella promised to convey the wishes of the
Committee, and to hand the Draft Bill to Mr.
Sheridan on his return to town.

A few days later letters were received from that
hon. gentleman by Mr. Hannay and the Secretary,
the tenour of which was that he would be happy to
see the Members of the Committee at the House of
Commons the next evening at six o'clock.

Hopeful that this apparent friendly attitude was
indicative of the willingness of Mr. Sheridan to
comply with the Committee's request, they went to
the House at the time fixed, inspired with every
feeling of confidence. They were doomed, however, to
early disappointment, for they were informed that
the hon. gentleman had already his hands too full;
but he advised that application should be made to
the Home Office to ascertain if Mr. Bruce would
consent to take the Bill in hand. Mr. Wheelhouse,
then Member for Leeds, recommended the same
course, and both gentlemen avowed their readiness
to accompany a deputation, but neither gentlemen
would accept the responsibility of taking charge of
the measure, which had taken so much time and
labour to prepare. The difficulty of the position
was now fully realized, and it was felt that private
Members would decline to be sponsors to a Bill on
such a subject as Pawnbroking.

The Committee therefore welcomed the suggestion,
as they had long entertained the wish, that the
Government would adopt the measure, which would
assure its success. Accordingly the same evening
the Secretary addressed a letter to the Home Office
asking for an interview. The next day a reply was
received dated " Home Office, Whitehall, March 19th,
1869," and saying, "I am directed by Mr. Secretary
Bruce to acknowledge the receipt of your letter, and
to inform you, that before he can entertain the
question of receiving a deputation from the Pawnbroking Parliamentary Association, he requests that
the Committee will forward a copy of their Bill
with their observations thereon. Signed A. F. O.
Liddell." In compliance with this reasonable request
the Secretary prepared a series of "Observations
and Reasons on behalf of the Pawnbrokers' Bill,"
which were afterwards published and circulated to
many Members of the House.

The copies of the Bill and the Observations were
forwarded, as soon as completed, to the Home Secretary, and the result was awaited with considerable
curiosity mingled with some anxiety. On the 8th April
Mr. Liddell wrote :—" Mr. Bruce desires me to say that
he cannot at present fix a day for receiving a deputation from the Pawnbrokers' Association, but Mr. Bruce
will consider the Bill drawn by the Association, *and
he will fix a day for receiving a deputation from them*,
if they should continue to desire it before introducing any measure into Parliament on the subject
of their Trade." A reply was sent to this that the
Committee did still desire an interview, as they had
no intention of introducing a Bill into Parliament
which Her Majesty's Government might consider it
their duty to oppose. Five days later another letter
—the last—was received from the Home Office. It
said :—" Mr. Bruce desires me to express his regret

that he cannot give an interview to the Pawnbrokers' Association at present; when a Bill is
before Parliament affecting the interests of Pawnbrokers, Mr. Bruce will give his consideration to
what may be said with respect to it on behalf of
the Pawnbrokers."

This was not only a disappointment but a breach
of faith. The letter of the 8th said *and he will fix
a day*, on certain conditions which were at once
complied with, and the second letter was a direct
contradiction. However the mandate of the 8th was
carefully preserved, and did good service in after
time, in enlisting the sympathy of Members,
who believed the Committee had not been fairly
treated.

But the little band of Reformers were not yet dis-
couraged, so at once determined, notwithstanding the
official rebuff, to attend at the House and procure
friendly assistance, and, if possible, make another
endeavour to penetrate the portals of the Home
Office. Messrs. Heys, Dickinson and the Secretary
proceeded to Westminster. Mr. Sheridan was soon
found, and the new trouble fully explained to him.
He suggested a letter to Mr. Bruce to be signed by
Members, asking for the desired interview, and he
promised to sign first. Shortly after Mr. Mundella
was seen and informed of the unexpected dilemma.
He at once made the more practical suggestion that
"Bruce" should be personally seen that evening,
and his final answer obtained. A little later Mr.
Wheelhouse was seen, and put in possession of the
latest intelligence. He at once adopted Mr. Mundella's suggestion, promised to find him—no easy
matter on busy evenings—and act with him, and
they would go to the Home Secretary together.

Hours passed, and the deputation paraded the lobbies,
weary but expectant. Mr. Bruce must be at leisure be-

fore he could be approached, and that favourable event
did not occur until a late hour. At length the desired
interview took place, and the two gentlemen who
had taken such a kindly interest in the subject
returned to the deputation and reported Mr. Bruce's
ultimatum, which was as follows :—" That the amount
of business at the Home Office would not allow time
to see the Pawnbrokers; that if Mr. Hugessen—
(the Under-Secretary and now Lord Brabourne)—
received them he might make a vague promise,
which it would be impossible for Mr. Bruce to keep;
that if Mr. Mundella had any influence with the
Pawnbrokers, to advise them under any circumstances to keep quiet for the present. He (Mr.
Bruce) had taken them from the *Habitual Criminals
Bill*, and he would promise nothing should be introduced *into that or any other measure* during the
present Session, which should affect Pawnbrokers,
nor at any time without giving them a full opportunity of being heard. Mr. Mundella had mentioned
a Committee of Inquiry to Mr. Bruce, but the reply
was that he could not entertain such a proposition
at present, as they had already more Committees on
hand than could possibly be got through."

The effect of this message was depressing almost to
the point of despair. There was a sudden barrier raised
against any onward movement. Certainly there was
as it were a verbal compact binding both sides
not to trouble each other; a truce, or an established neutrality was for the time to be observed.
The Pawnbrokers were constrained to keep it, and to
have full belief that it would be as honourably
observed on the other side. But however satisfactory it might be to know they were safe from
attack, there was a feeling of blank despair that all
hopes of immediate progress were so utterly for the
rest of the year dispelled.

It was decided to call the Executive together, report and take counsel. The town chosen for the Meeting, on this occasion, was Sheffield, and a very pleasant and memorable reception was accorded to the dejected band of reformers.

The report merely dealt with the proceedings taken since the Meeting at Derby, and the steps adopted to introduce the Bill. After the report had been discussed and received, it was decided that in deference to the wish of the Home Secretary, no further Parliamentary action be taken that Session. It was reported by the Financial Secretary that up to that date (June 8th), the amount guaranteed was £2,300, and £93 in subscriptions. It was afterwards decided, that although held in check at present, the policy of the Committee was one of progress. There was no symptom of wavering, hesitation, or failure, to be perceived; nor was there felt to be any cause for despondency, for there was the possibility that in the autumnal months, when the Session and its work had died away, the Committee might obtain the long desired interview with the Home Secretary, and if they were successful early preparations could be made for prompt and decisive action on the opening of the Session of 1870.

It is a pleasure to turn for a moment from these dry and dull incidents in history-making, with all their ever recurring disappointments and wasted labour, to the enjoyments and relaxation provided by the Members of the Trade in each town in which the Executive met. "Some relaxation is necessary to people of every degree," said a deep thinker; "the head that thinks and the hand that labours must have some little time to recruit their diminished powers." So these friends appeared to believe, for they provided right royal welcomes for the Members of the Committee. At Nottingham, Manchester, Leeds,

and lastly, Sheffield, they were profuse in their
hospitality; but the season of the year, beautiful
weather, and the proximity to the magnificent
ducal palace at Chatsworth, with its inexpressibly
lovely surroundings, made the Sheffield visit
ever memorable. Carriages were provided in which
to drive from the town; lunch and dinner at
Edensor; saunter through the magnificent halls
adorned with priceless works of art; a visit to
Haddon Hall, and the drive back to town, are all
vividly impressed upon the writer's mind, there to
remain an indelible picture "while memory holds
her seat." *Floreat* the "Field on the Sheaf."

CHAPTER XXVI

As the peremptory dictum of Mr. Bruce enforced inactivity, no attempt was made for progression until towards the close of the year, when it was thought the Home Secretary might again be approached. The Secretary made application for a deputation to be received from the Pawnbrokers in relation to their Bill. A reply was soon to hand,. stating that Mr. Bruce would either receive a deputation or state to the Pawnbrokers' Association the course he was prepared to take with regard to the Bill. This appeared to be candid and satisfactory,. and the long looked for missive was anticipated with considerable anxiety. But a long and unaccountable silence ensued. Despondency, even with some Members of the Committee, was fast taking the place of confidence. In fact the impression extensively prevailed that Reform was doomed, and would be heard of no more. The *Pawnbrokers' Gazette*, in the summary for 1869, said: "The Trade generally are now looking upon this subject with a very different feeling to what they did in times past; they are beginning to appreciate the immensity of the task, while the rude lesson they received has taught them to regard Parliamentary action as a two edged weapon, and to look

with much less confidence towards a future success.
Indeed we have been much surprised at the change
which has come over the popular feeling among the
Country Trade—in London, Reform has never been a
favourite—but we believe that it is not too much to
say that if the provincials could now be polled upon
the subject, fully three-fourths of them would be
against any further action for some time to come."

This expression of opinion, no doubt, found a ready
echo in the minds of many Members of the London
Trade, while it could not but have a discouraging and
depressing effect, even upon sanguine and ardent
Reformers. Nor was it of an encouraging character
to the little band forming the Parliamentary Committee, and who were waiting impatiently for Mr.
Bruce to break the intolerable silence. But, "Was
there a man dismayed" amongst those who were
labouring to achieve success? Not one had yet
yielded to despair. But the thought was rapidly
being developed that Mr. Bruce was deliberately
breaking faith with them, as on a former occasion,
and the position was one of great perplexity, as
several months had now elapsed since the letter had
been received from the Home Office promising to
receive the deputation. February had now arrived
and the House was in Session, and yet no indication
as to the course Government might adopt. It was
therefore decided to remind Mr. Bruce of his promise,
which was done, when lo! the knotty enigma was
at once solved and the mystery dissolved, by the
following letter, under date of February 18th, 1870:

"SIR,—I am very sorry that, *through my neglect*, no day
was named in December for receiving a deputation from the
Pawnbrokers' Society, nor any steps taken for otherwise
giving the Society the information it desired. The questions
raised by your Bill were, however, carefully considered in
December last, and Mr. Bruce will cause the opinion at which
he then arrived to be communicated to you with as little
delay as possible. I hope that by to-morrow or the following

day you will hear from Mr. Bruce on this subject, and that there may be no delay in putting you in a position to act as you think best in regard to the Bill, with full knowledge of Mr. Bruce's opinion in regard to it.

I am, yours faithfully,

A. O. RUTSON."

So after all, the dreaded and ominous silence was nothing more than the neglect of a Government clerk, though it had been provocative of much anxiety to those who so longingly desired to proceed; but they had not long to wait now before the explanatory letter came from Mr. Bruce. It was dated February 18th, two days only after the preceding one and was from the same writer. It stated:—

" Mr. Bruce directs me to say in regard to the Bill of the Pawnbrokers' Association recently submitted to him, *that some changes in the law in the direction of the Bill seem to him to be desirable.* Mr. Bruce cannot, however, promise the assistance of the Government to the passage of the Bill in its present shape, until he has before him more evidence on the subject. This evidence—and Mr. Bruce refers particularly to the experience of those who avail themselves of *loans on pawn*—would probably be best obtained if the subject were referred to a Select Committee of the House of Commons. Under these circumstances Mr. Bruce will not oppose the introduction of the Bill ; and will consent to its being read a second time on the understanding that it be referred to a Select Committee, and that the action of the Government, in regard to the further progress of the Bill *will depend on the result of the inquiry* to be made by the Select Committee."

On the receipt of this important communication the Secretary at once summoned the Executive to a meeting to be held in London. Copies of the letter were extensively circulated to all the Associations, and the whole aspect of the situation was changed into hopeful animation and activity. Meetings were held all over the provinces, and resolutions, approving of the line proposed by the Home Office, were readily passed. Within a week, Manchester, Leeds, Liverpool, Sheffield, Nottingham, Exeter, Edinburgh, Hanley, Glasgow, and Bolton, had all spoken, with no uncertain meaning. They accepted the terms suggested with alacrity, and urged the Executive to proceed.

M

There were no signs now of despondency, or of the
probability that "three fourths of the Trade" would
vote against reform.   Courage and hope had rapidly
revived, and the determination to go on with the
work was stronger than ever.   The Executive were
unanimous to a man, and speedily passed resolutions
empowering the Parliamentary Committee to resume
active operations without delay.   This they did, and
commenced a system of daily visits to the House,
and were hours at a time in the lobbies interviewing
members, as the sponsor for the Bill was yet to be
found before the Committee could act on Mr. Bruce's
advice.   No Member seemed bold enough to accept
the position.   At length one gentleman made the
valuable suggestion that a conference should be held
at the Westminster Palace Hotel, and as many members asked to attend as could be secured.   This course
was without hesitation adopted; all the members who
had been previously seen were written to, and invited
to attend.   The plan was eminently successful, as no
less than fifteen representatives, for the most part
of large constituencies, were present.   The Chairman of
the Association first read and expounded the Bill
clause by clause, thus making each member familiar
with the subject.   The Hon. Sec. next briefly related
the origin and progress of the movement, and its
then present position in regard to the Government,
Mr. Bruce's second letter not being forgotten.   A very
friendly conversation then took place as to the best
means of getting the Bill introduced, but no one had
yet volunteered to perform the friendly act.   It was
at last decided that a deputation should at once wait
upon Mr. Hugessen at the Home Office, and ten
members agreed to accompany the Pawnbrokers.
They proceeded without a moment's delay, and were
admitted to an audience.   After hearing the deputation, Mr. Hugessen promised to confer with Mr.

Bruce, and if that gentleman saw any reason to alter his opinion already expressed upon the subject, or could advise the appointment of a Select Committee, without introducing the Bill, the fact should be immediately communicated to Sir Thos. Bazley (Manchester), and Lord Sandon (Liverpool), now the Earl of Harrowby, both gentlemen being with the deputation.

No time was lost, for the next day Lord Sandon wrote to the Secretary; "Mr. Bruce is of opinion that it will be the best course to introduce the Bill at once, and have it referred to a Select Committee." On the same day the members of the Parliamentary Committee attended a meeting of the London guarantors, at which the Secretary read Lord Sandon's letter, and it was unanimously resolved that the Committee be requested to proceed in the recommendation contained therein.

But the difficulty still existed as to how the introduction of the Bill *at once*, was to be effected, for no one appeared anxious to take charge of it. The Parliamentary Committee again went down to the House, and obtained several introductions, but with no success. Later in the evening. Mr. Wheelhouse, who had evinced great interest in the Committee's proceedings, introduced those present to Mr. S. Plimsoll, then M.P. for Derby. That gentleman's kindly offices were solicited, and he was so far favourably disposed, that he accepted a copy of the Bill, promised to study it, and would give a reply the next day. In some trepidation his answer was awaited. Fortunately he was prompt and relieved all suspense by accepting the responsibility of introducing the Bill, and obtained the support of Mr. Sidebotham, Member for Stalybridge, as a seconder.

The Bill was brought in and read a first time on March 17th, and the second reading was fixed for the 22nd of that month, but unfortunately Mr. Plimsoll

was taken ill and the matter was postponed from day
to day. On the 25th the first masked battery of the
enemy opened fire, by Mr. Hambro, Member for Weymouth, giving notice of his intention to move that the
Bill be read a second time that day six months. This
gentleman had been approached by a hostile Member of the Trade, who openly confessed to violations of the law, and took his interest "long;"
made Special Agreements for any sum over £2, and
yet objected to legal redress being obtained for his
fellow Tradesmen. He had the audacity to villify the
promoters of the Bill, grossly distorting its effects
upon the poor, and using every possible means, other
than scrupulous ones, to bring about the wreckage of
the measure.

Seeing danger ahead, the Secretary sought the
assistance of Lord Sandon, who kindly obtained a
postponement of the second reading until April 4th.

During the respite many Members were seen, and
a large number of petitions in favour of the Bill were
prepared and forwarded to various constituents to be
signed and sent to their representatives for presentation. Meanwhile every effort was made to mitigate
the rancour of Mr. Hambro's opposition, but he was
inflexibly obdurate in his resolve to obstruct the
passage of the Bill, and expressed himself determined
to press the matter to a division. Renewed and
vigorous exertions were put forth to enlist the support
of Members; Pawnbrokers were summoned from all
parts of the country to attend in London and assist in
the work of waiting upon their own representatives,
and, when personal attendance was impossible, they
were requested to send letters of introduction to the
Parliamentary Committee.

This state of excitement continued until March 30th,
when Mr. Hadfield, then Member for Sheffield, wrote
to Messrs. Wright and Eaton, who were in London

working heartily, to the effect that Mr. Bruce would not permit a division, and, if one should be pressed, the Government would vote against the Bill, which must be withdrawn, and a Select Committee appointed.

A conference was held next day between Mr. Plimsoll, Sir Thos. Bazley, Lord Sandon, and Members of the Parliamentary Committee. The Home Office letters were read, and it was considered that the Pawnbrokers had a claim upon the Government. Mr. Hugessen was seen, but insisted that no other course was practicable than the one proposed. Mr. Baines, then Member for Leeds, Mr. Chadwick, M.P. for Macclesfield, with Mr. Plimsoll, saw Mr. Bruce, but it was impossible to shake his determination. The three gentlemen named then brought out of the House a resolution, which had been written by the Under Secretary, and ran thus: "That a Select Committee be appointed to consider the state of the law with regard to the Pawnbroking Trade, with a view to its consolidation and amendment."

The Parliamentary Committee were, of course, compelled to accept the inevitable, and so, on behalf of the Reform Association, consented to the appointment. The same evening Mr. Plimsoll moved that the order for the second reading should be discharged and the Bill withdrawn.

And thus the labour, thought and time, extending to close upon two years, involving great expenditure, terminated in the death of the much debated Bill, and the curtain fell on the first act—consisting of many and varied scenes—of the drama of Pawnbroking Reform.

CHAPTER XXVII

On the 4th of April, 1870, Mr. Plimsoll, in the House of Commons, moved for the appointment of a Select Committee on Pawnbroking, which was agreed to, after the Home Secretary stating that, "I have no objection to offer; I think it impossible to examine the Law without seeing it is defective in many respects, and I think the proceeding a very useful one."

The day following the Parliamentary Committee met for the last time for many months to come. The situation was exhaustively discussed, and the probable difficulties of conducting an Inquiry were speculated upon, and suggestions made as to the best course to adopt. From experience it had been found that a Parliamentary Agent was so hopelessly ignorant upon the subject, as to be able to render no practical assistance. Besides, being an Inquiry into the working of Acts of Parliament of a public, and not a private character, the Trade could not be represented by Counsel. After long and serious deliberations it was finally resolved, "That the Hon. Sec. be requested to undertake the management of the Inquiry before the Select Committee, and with a view to this purpose he be requested to take up his residence in London during

·the progress of the work." This proposal was adopted
in the belief that the heavy expenses which would be
incurred by engaging an Agent would be avoided.

Time then passed away until the 9th of May was
reached, without any sign being given of a forward
movement. On that day, however, the Select Committee was nominated; and, as in future generations
it may be a matter of interest to know who were the
Members that composed this important body, we append their names. The first Member, who was elected
Chairman, and represented the Government was—

The Right Hon. Acton Smee Ayrton, member for
the Tower Hamlets, and Chief Commissioner of
Works.   Born, 1816.

Richard Arkwright, member for Leominster. Was
.called to the bar, 1859, but had ceased to practice.
Born, 1835.

Robert Meek Carter, member for Leeds, and an
Alderman of that town.   A coal merchant and cloth
finisher.   Born, 1814.

Charles Joseph Theophilus Hambro, member for
Weymouth and Melcombe Regis.   Called to the bar,
1860.   Born at Copenhagen, 1835.

Thomas Hughes, member for Frome, and author of
"Tom Brown's Schooldays."   Called to the bar, 1848.
Born, 1823.

Charles Henry Mills, member for West Kent.   A
member of the firm of Glyn, Mills & Co., bankers.
Born, 1830.

John Whitwell, member for Kendal, a manufacturer.
He was the warmest and the most sincere friend the
Trade ever possessed, and it was through his firm-
ness and energy, the Act of 1872 was ever obtained.
He was born in 1812.

Mathew White-Ridley, member for North Northum-
berland.   Graduated B.A. 1st class in classics, 1865.
Fellow of All Souls, and M.A., 1867.   Born, 1842.

John Simon, member for Dewsbury, and known as Serjeant Simon on the Northern circuit. Called to the bar, 1842. Born in Jamaica, 1818.

Colonel Beresford, member for Southwark, and a wharfinger. Was Hon. Colonel to a volunteer regiment. A convert of the enemy's, and familiarly known to reformers as "the potato merchant."

Samuel Morley, member for Bristol, well known as a philanthropist. Was a member of the firm of J. and R. Morley, London. Born, 1809.

James Sidebotham, member for Stalybridge, and a cotton manufacturer. Born, 1824.

Montague John Guest, member for Youghal, Ireland, afterwards for Wareham. Magistrate and Deputy Lieutenant for Dorset. Born, 1839.

William Thomas Charley, member for Salford, now Common Serjeant of London. Called to the bar, 1865. Born, 1833.

Samuel Plimsoll, member for Derby, which seat he resigned in favour of Sir William Harcourt. Was a coal merchant and author of several pamphlets relative to that trade. Afterwards widely known as " the Seaman's Friend." Born, 1824.

This was the complete list of the original nominations, but on the 30th of the month, there were added, we believe at their own request—

Archibald Orr Ewing, member for Dumbartonshire, and a Glasgow merchant. This gentleman entertained an inveterate dislike to Pawnbrokers and all their works, but this was unknown at the time. We find, however, that in May, 1864, petitions were presented to the House of Commons, by Mr. Smollet, from Messrs. Orr Ewing and Co., praying for an inquiry into the cause of the great increase of Pawnbroking establishments in Scotland, *with a view to their suppression.* Other petitions were presented by Mr. Crum Ewing from Mr. Hector and others, containing a

similar prayer. On five days in one week, and four
in the following week, such petitions were presented.

From the 4th of April to the 30th May, nothing had
been done by Parliament. But the interregnum was
very welcome to the little band—which, for better
title was called the Parliamentary *Sub-Committee*—
which was busily employed in the preparation of
evidence to be given when the Select Committee
should sit. An office was taken at No. 11, Bridge-street,
Westminster, and a regular routine of business was
established. Here could be found every day Mr. G.
Attenborough (the Chairman), Mr. John Dicker, Mr.
J. A. Telfer, and the Hon. Secretary, who devoted
their time to the invention and compilation of the
evidence. A vast amount of trouble was involved in
the working out of figures connected with the businesses of the three gentlemen named, in calculating
per centages, and otherwise endeavouring to prove
the unprofitable condition of Pawnbroking. The
evidence, which was compiled in the form of question
and answer, and afterwards written in duplicate, on
brief paper by a law writer, presented a voluminous
result. All this was satisfactory as far as it went, but
there was an ever-present doubt as to whether or not
the work had been prepared in accordance with the
regular requirements of Parliamentary procedure,
and no information could be obtained.

The end of May having arrived, and no indication of
the Select Committee proceeding to business, the
Sub-Committee began to feel anxious for a start to
be made. Two Members went over to the House and
were fortunate in finding Mr. Ayrton. He was reminded of the appointment, and that the Pawnbrokers,
observing the rapid waning of the Session, were
despairing of being able to get through before the
prorogation. After the explanation, Mr. Ayrton confessed, that if anything was to be attempted, there

was no time to lose. He at once entered the Committee Office and instructed a clerk to enter the first sitting of the Select Committee for Thursday, June 9th.

Just about the commencement of June, the Sub-Committee was called upon by the late Francis Turner, Esq., Barrister-at-law, author of *The Contract of Pawn*, and other works, to confer as to the points it was desired he should give evidence. The opinions of the Sub-Committee were expressed, and he agreed to confine himself to a certain line. This settled, he was shown a mass of evidence which had been prepared, and his opinion requested as to whether or not it was in accordance with the rules of the House. Unfortunately the learned gentleman's experience was no greater than that of the amateur Parliamentary Agents who had prepared it. But he expressed himself strongly that the evidence should be submitted to a solicitor for examination. It so happened that the late Mr. Henry Bremner, then the Solicitor to the Liverpool Pawnbrokers' Association, was engaged on the Pilotage Committee, and was visiting London for two or three days in each week. He was written to, and urged to call and examine the evidence, and this, to the intense relief of the Sub-Committee, he promised to do. Mr. Bremner, however, was not able to be in London till June 9th, the day the Select Committee would sit for the first time. Meanwhile, every effort was made to perfect the evidence of those who it was intended should open the proceedings. Balance-sheets were copied, books were checked, and all that could be, was done to prove the plaintiff's case.

On the day that Mr. Bremner arrived, the Select Committee were to sit at three o'clock to select the Chairman and arrange the order of procedure. The first omission Mr. Bremner discovered, was the absence of a syllabus, which should be prepared for the Chairman to be made acquainted with the names of the witnesses,

the order in which they were to be taken, and to what
part of the subject they would address themselves.
No such document had been prepared, as it was
thought the case would be opened by Mr. Dicker, Mr.
Attenborough, and Mr. Telfer; but the quick eye of
the lawyer detected another weakness.   Strong
evidence he supposed had been prepared, but no case
had been stated, therefore, a witness must be put
forward to explain the whole laws then regulating the
Trade, the defects of them, and the grievances they
inflicted, and the remedies proposed by the promoters
of the Inquiry.   Thus, in an instant, the result of
months of labour appeared to be seriously jeopardised
by this almost fatal omission.   After a serious
conference, no opening presented itself, but the Hon.
Secretary undertaking the task.   It was the *dernier
ressort*, and, whatever the result, the risk must be run.
He had been busily assisting in preparing the evidence
for others, and attending to a torrent of correspondence,
but not a line had been prepared for him. The desperate
situation was, however, accepted, the syllabus was
prepared in the order arranged above for the opening,
supported by Mr. Richard Attenborough (Piccadilly),
Dr. Hancock, Mr. Turner, Mr. Stubbs (Magistrates'
Clerk of Liverpool), Mr. Keeson, and others.   From
the country, to prove the practices which prevailed
and the hardships experienced, it was proposed to
call Messrs. Heys, Grantham, Dickinson, Fletcher,
Brooking, Blackwood, May, Kidson, Tatton, Cooke,
Makin, McKay, Middleton, with one or two Auctioneers.

At a few minutes to three o'clock the Secretary, Mr.
Bremner, Mr. Attenborough, Mr. J. Dicker, and Mr.
Telfer, attended in the Committee-room.   Mr. Ayrton
had been elected Chairman before the door was opened
to the public, so the Secretary then presented the
hastily-prepared syllabus to him.   He then announced
that the Committee would meet at twelve o'clock on

the following Monday, and the first witness (the least prepared), Mr. Hardaker, would be taken. The Chairman also requested a list of the various Acts of Parliament regulating the Trade, to be furnished to the Clerk of the Committee.

On that evening Mr. Bremner took away several copies of the evidence for examination, and the next day returned them with the pleasing and encouraging information that the evidence was strong and well drawn, and a strongly opened case would come in with convincing effect. He considered the work reflected the highest credit on those concerned, and that it was decidedly the best attempt he had ever seen made by unprofessional men. This was very flattering to those who had simply blundered into the right track. The valuable services Mr. Bremner had rendered were highly appreciated by the Sub-Committee, who voted him their special thanks.

The Parliamentary Sub-Committee then separated for the week, to meet on the following Monday, leaving the Secretary a little time to prepare for the much-feared ordeal he had to undergo on that day.

CHAPTER XXVIII

It was under no slight apprehension, nor inconsiderable trepidation, that the members of the Parliamentary Sub-Committee—especially those set down for examination—entered Committee room, No. 17, in the House of Commons, at noon, on Monday, June 13th, 1870. Fourteen out of the seventeen members of the Select Committee, were present, a sufficiently imposing array to produce nervelessness and depression of spirits on the first witnesses, as though they were culprits of the deepest dye, and might expect condign punishment.

It is impossible, with the limited space at our disposal, to give more than a skeleton outline of the evidence adduced, the reader will therefore be required to fill in details from his imagination. He must also forgive what may appear to him to be frequent irrelevancy, as after the examination in chief was conducted, by the Chairman (Mr. A. S. Ayrton), up to the conclusion of one part of the subject, each of the other thirteen members, who had been busily engaged taking notes, cross-examined the witness in turn. The answers in many cases may be inconclusive, and erratic, not to say stupid, but it must be remembered, that probably the questions which evoked them, were in themselves so utterly wide of any practical object, as to prevent any other replies being given for the moment. As in the case of the first witness, who had handed in evidence to the extent of 38 questions and answers, which were made to expand to 425, it follows, that to many of the questions, he had not a satisfactory reply ready.

The reader—if never in a committee room—must also imagine the appearance from a brief description. The table around which the Members sit is something of the horse shoe shape, the Chairman sitting at what may be called the apex, and the other Members on the right and left of him to the ends of the table on each side. A square table is placed between these ends at which the witness sits facing the Chairman; at the same table to the right of the witness, the short-hand writer sits. A duplicate copy of the evidence as supplied to the Chairman, is before the witness, who may also have, for reference, any books or documents necessary for the purposes of the inquiry. Behind the witness are two rows of desks, as in a court of law, and these on a private Bill inquiry, are occupied by Barristers, Solicitors, and Parliamentary Agents ; but on this occasion by witnesses and friends of the promoters. Behind these again is an open space in which stand spectators and persons generally interested in the subject under inquiry.

As it states on the first page of the blue-book, " Mr. Alfred Hardaker called in and examined," as the first witness. In answer to questions put, first, by the Chairman, and, as already explained, by other members of the Committee, he said he was a Pawnbroker of some 24 years' experience, and was Hon. Sec. of the Liverpool Pawnbrokers' Association, as well as Hon. Sec. to the Parliamentary Reform Association. He had given much study to the various Acts of Parliament which regulated the Trade, and went

through them section by section, to explain them
for the information of the Committee.

In the principal Act (1800) the scale of interest was
illustrated by the witness, who showed the faulty and
inconvenient manner in which it worked, how it broke
off at £2 from 20 per cent. per annum to 15, so that if
he lent £2 he would be entitled to charge 8d.
per month, while if he advanced £2 3s. he
would only be entitled to charge 6¼d. and ¹⁶⁄₁₅
of a farthing for the same period. He then showed
that these rates could not be adhered to, as it was
impossible to take the correct sum. He admitted that
the difficulty could be overcome by abating the fractions, but the Trade could not afford to do that,
because their remuneration was already too low. The
uniform and inflexible rate of interest was objectionable, as for a watch which occupied a small space in
storage, the same rate per month was charged as for a
bed or other bulky article which involved labour in
porterage, and occupied a large space in the warehouse, for which no additional charge could be made.

Section 3 applied to "intermediate" sums, or
amounts which were not composed of complete half-
crowns, and these resulted in fractions, for which
there was no known coin to meet. He would suggest
that a simple rate of not less than one halfpenny for each
2s. or any part of 2s. lent should be substituted for the
(then) present scale up to £10. In Clause 4 was the
proviso that farthings should be given in change by
the Pawnbroker. This regulation was, the witness
believed, carried out by the majority of the London
Trade, but in the Country the Act was frequently
violated, and the whole halfpenny charged. In respect
to Clause 5, he thought the limitations on parts of a
month should be abolished,* and instead of seven days"

* For a full description of the Act, see Chap. X.

grace, let the Pawnbroker charge the whole month
after the expiration of 14 days. The object they had
in view was to attain simplicity, by having only one
step in the calculations. He desired to get relief from
all fractional calculations. With respect to articles of
large bulk, many Pawnbrokers refused to take them
under the existing scale. Asked what was the custom,
the witness replied that he could not speak with certainty, but it would be fully explained by subsequent
witnesses. He knew the Act to be extensively evaded
in Liverpool, and would consider that charging two
months for one month and seven days was a violation of
the Statute. In Ireland the rate was $\frac{1}{2}$d. for each 2s.
or any part of 2s. for each month, and this was the
rate the witness desired to see substituted for the
(then) present English one. The days of grace allowed
in Ireland were only three. To the general principle
of Section 6, relating to booking pledges, he raised
no objection, as it was absolutely necessary to keep
books in which to enter all transactions, but there
were points of detail in the section which were
objectionable and which it was impossible to carry
out. It was not in the power of a Pawnbroker to
be certain that the names and addresses given by
pledgers were correct, and he saw no utility or
value in writing in H. for housekeeper, or L. for
lodger. People very commonly concealed their real
names and addresses, and frequently gave fictitious
ones. That the time for entering a certain class of
pledges was limited to four hours, while others
must be entered at the time of pledging, was
anomalous and of no value, and the system
set down in this Section involved the keeping of three books, but he considered two were
sufficient, one for pledges of 10s. and under, and
another for those above 10s., which were to be sold
by auction. In regard to the tickets, witness would

suggest that the amount of interest per month should be placed on the face of that given to the pledger, which would prevent overcharges. He wished that the rate should be fair compensation, beyond the implied rate for warehousing bulky articles, and that the power to charge above the fixed rate should be conceded to the Trade. Evidence would be produced thereafter which would show that pledges for small sums and short dates did not pay. In addition to an improved rate he was in favour of retaining the charges for tickets as then existed; as for endorsing the interest taken on the ticket, it possessed no practical value to the pledger; the intention of the Act was doubtless to prevent overcharge, but it did not do so, for the pledger could not see what was written by the Pawnbroker. Subsequent witnesses would give the proportion of pledges above and below 10s. Those below, in an ordinary business, were much in excess of those above that amount. In Liverpool he estimated that between nine and ten millions of pledges were received during the year, of which about fifty thousand would be for sums over forty shillings. Those of two shillings and under would probably amount to about four millions and a half. They, as Pawnbrokers, could sell forfeited pledges of ten shillings and under in any manner they pleased; above ten shillings all must be sold by auction. It would be injurious to all parties if small pledges were required to be sold by auction, as the expenses of sale would be out of all proportion to the small value the goods would realise. It would be a question for a higher authority as to whether or not, a pawner ought to be subject to fine for giving a false name. He would not recommend that there should be an endorsement on a ticket, when the pledger sold it to another person; it would

N

be no protection as there would be no proof of the
genuineness of the endorsement. The witness then
went minutely through the 8th section, dealing with
declarations, but the particulars would not be of
interest now, further than that opinions were expressed in the direction of limiting the time for
which a declaration should be in force, and proving
ownership in the goods pledged, both ideas being
adopted in the present Act. A Pawnbroker was
not liable for loss by robbery committed on his
premises, neither was he for damage by fire, or any
other accident which he was powerless to prevent;
but he would be held liable for any loss arising from
his own wilful negligence or "misbehaviour," or
from the negligence of his servants. Clause 17 was
the next step of interest as it related to the period
of forfeiture, and the witness went into the subject
at considerable length. He considered the time was
too long, and advocated the adoption of six, instead
of twelve months. He maintained that the change
would be no hardship upon the pledger, but a great
advantage to the Pawnbroker. The former would
have only half the amount of interest to pay for
renewals, while the goods would bring more at auction
by being sold at the expiration of six, instead of
twelve months, and it was in the interest of the
pledger that goods should realise the highest price,
as he was entitled to the overplus. Dr. Hancock
recommended that in Ireland some pledges should be
kept for three months only, but witness thought a
uniform period would prevent misunderstanding and
confusion. If the short period of six months was
adopted, it would enable the Pawnbrokers to lend
more liberally than was possible under a twelve months'
forfeiture, as goods became forfeited at the wrong
season, and, practically, were on hand for 18 months.
Eighty per cent. of the pledges were redeemed in the

first three months. Saw no reason why, if gross
negligence was proved, a Pawnbroker should be ex-
cused from making compensation. Overplus was not
very often claimed, and thought the period too long
to keep a pledger's account open. Admitted, if the
limit was not fixed by law the claim would be good
for six years. Was agreeable that the age of young
persons pledging should be 16 as in Liverpool, but
that would be a great inconvenience in many large
towns and manufacturing localities. Hours of business should be regulated by local requirements. It
should be remembered that the rate of interest was
an annual one, and that goods redeemed in the first
month only paid one twelfth of 20 per cent., or less
than 2 per cent. on the turnover, which could not
possibly pay, considering the necessary working expenses. A business consisting of pledges paying $1\frac{1}{2}$d.
each all round would result in loss. If 1000 pledges
per day were to be received, a staff of at least seven
persons would be required. Saw no objection to bed
or body clothing being pledged ; people parted with
what they could best spare. Did not believe that the
money obtained from Pawnbrokers was spent in intemperance. Pawnbrokers' profits were considerably
enhanced by the sale trade, which in one house came
to about 27 per cent., while those on Pawnbroking
only came to about 6 per cent. Witness thought the
legislature should make the Trade more remunerative,
in order to enable Pawnbrokers to advance money on
goods which they were now compelled to refuse. If an
article should be redeemed weekly, and the apparent
profit was 1300 per cent., the transaction would still
be unprofitable. He was confident that the facilities
afforded by a properly conducted Pawnbroking business did not tend to foster intemperance. The few
concluding questions were " speered " by Mr. Orr
Ewing, who persistently endeavoured to wring

affirmatives from the persons under examination.
The witness then retired, after being under examination two hours and a half.

Mr. John Dicker, Pawnbroker, of Commercial-road,
Limehouse, was the next witness. He stated that he
had been in the Trade all his life, and was the son
of a Pawnbroker; he had been a master 29 years, was
Treasurer of the London Protection Society, and had
four establishments. He superintended them himself,
but they were managed by his sons and responsible
managers. They were working businesses fairly representing "low," "medium," and "auction" classes
of pledges. In the house from which he would lay the
statistics before the Committee, there was a capital
of £14,217. About £11,182 of this amount was invested
in pledges, and some £3000 in sale. He was anxious
to have an Act which could be easily understood.
When the old Act was passed, the expenses of the
Trade were much lower than at that period. His
father's business was chiefly worked by apprentices,
now they had to pay salaries to all assistants.
Rents and expenses of living had largely increased,
but the profits had remained fixed. He wished
for an Act which did not compel evasions, as the
tendency was bad, and it effects demoralising. He
considered the manner in which the contract
was regulated bad in principle, and thought freedom
of contract much better with a higher rate of
interest, as a large number of their transactions
were unremunerative. The witness was prepared
to submit his books to any scrutiny which might
be desired. (Mr. Dicker here read and explained
elaborate balance-sheets of the operations at different
houses; showing the general movement and disposition of capital, with the proportions of profit
received on the Pawnbroking and the sale branches
of each.) Then, proceeding, he said that a simple

rate, like the Irish one, would be generally understood. In special cases it was desirable that
contracts should be made in a regular way, and
bear the signatures of the parties. He was certain
that the then fixed rate worked hardly on the public.
The accounts kept by Pawnbrokers were systematic
and simple, and were balanced every day, again
made up every month, and checked every six or
twelve months by stock-takings. The process of
book-keeping was then explained at length. In
reply to a series of wide questions, Mr. Dicker
said that in addition to forfeited pledges
Pawnbrokers bought goods over the counter,
besides large quantities of new goods. In the
case of the business, the figures of which were
before them, the £3,000 sale stock would include
only some £800 or £900 forfeited "low" pledges.
To sell these at auction would be productive of
great loss. He then went into a detailed explanation
of the earnings for the year both by pledge and
sale stocks. Seven assistants were engaged in that
house, without himself. There was great advantage
of sale over pledge stock, as the former could be
kept conveniently in the front shop, while the
pledges occupied a large series of warehouses. The
net profit on the pledge stock, as he had proved,
showed 5½ per cent., while that upon the sale was
27 per cent. He did not believe there was any other
business but Pawnbroking, with £11,000 capital,
which would produce so small a profit as was shown
by the earnings of his pledge stock. The charges
made in his establishments were rigidly in accordance with the Act, and he never suffered an overcharge to be made.

At this point, Big Ben boomed out the hour of
four. At the same moment there was a knock at
the door of the Members' entrance, followed by a

voice, "The Speaker's at Prayers," and the Committee adjourned to the following Thursday.

The conclusion of this important day's business
was signalised by a comical incident, which has
doubtless been many times recited. It had been
the custom with the Sub-Committee all through
the preparation of the evidence to dine in the office
to economise time. There was an excellent cook
resident somewhere in the mysterious upper regions
of the building, and on this day dinner was ordered
to be ready for four o'clock. The Sub-Committee
returned from the House, mentally and physically
fatigued, hot and excited with the day's work.
Noticing the fagged condition of those who had
been under examination, the Chairman, with his
usual consideration, said the Committee had decidedly
made a "notch," and deserved, what he jocularly
called, a "cruet" of champagne. It was duly obtained,
the glasses charged, and "Success to our labours"
proposed, when the door of the room slowly
opened, and the well-known voice of a midland
counties' Pawnbroker exclaimed, "Oh! This is the
way the Committee's killed with work, is it? That's
the way the money goes." After the astonishment
of the Committee had subsided, the visitor was invited
to join in the toast, which was drunk in all sincerity.

CHAPTER XXIX

. Precisely at twelve o'clock Mr. John Dicker resumed his evidence at the point where he had discontinued on the previous Monday. In reply to some cross-questions, he said he had done a large sale trade at the house for which the returns put in related. It employed two persons, a salesman and a junior. He was not able to state what the retail profits were in other businesses, but he had heard a wholesale grocer say they were about 40 per cent. on the capital per annum. In Government contracts he had been informed that 15 per cent. was considered a fair profit. Mr. Dicker then explained at considerable length what was meant by "weekly pledgings." He then came to the figures of a second business which were handed in, and showed the average amount per pledge to be 4s. 3d., and the loss on all pledges delivered within the first month ⅜d. each. He arrived at these figures by taking the amount of the expenses and dividing by the number of pledges. By this means he found that each pledge cost 2¼d., while a pledge of 4s. 3d. only returned one penny interest and one halfpenny for the ticket, thus showing a loss of three-farthings. Mr. Dicker then put in a remarkable statement showing the redemptions on one

Saturday, at the house of a relative.* This was on
May 7th, 1870, and we believe the Saturday before
Whit Sunday. The total number of pledges redeemed
on that day was 1,899, and of these 1,553 had been
pledged within one month; the remaining 346 were
for longer periods. The capital lent on the larger
number was £304 17s. 4d., and on the latter £72 8s. 2d.
The interest on the 1,553 was £5 18s. 8½d., and on the
remaining 346 £8 6s. 2½d. The pledges averaged
3s. 11d. each, and the yield of profit per pledge 1¼ $\frac{7}{10}$ths d.
including ticket money. The cost of each pledge to
the Pawnbroker was 2½d., so that there was a loss of
¾d. each on the 1,553 pledges delivered. The witness
then produced a detailed statement of each of the
1,899 tickets, on a roll of paper of the enormous
length of 58 feet, showing the amount lent, the time
each parcel remained in pledge, the interest, ticket-
money, and the total profit. This "sea serpent," as
it was playfully designated, had been prepared in the
office by the Sub-Committee, and its production caused
considerable amusement amongst the members. One
hon. gentleman occupied most of the afternoon in
rolling up the document, much in the manner that a
draper rolls up ribbon. In addition to this statement
there was also produced a large carpet bag, containing
the whole of the 1,899 tickets, to prove the vast
amount of labour which had been performed in one
day, and for a profit on the turnover of £304, including
ticket money, of only 3.05 per cent.; and on £72 18s. 2d.
of 12.57 per cent. The witness further explained that
had the 1,553 pledges remained for two or three
months they would have become profitable. He could
not state what amount should be the minimum charge
on small pledges, but they cost 2½d. to 3d. to receive,

---

* Mr. Barnett's, Lambeth.

warehouse, and deliver. He was in favour of an
implied rate to stand in all transactions where a
special agreement was not entered into. On the
subject of forfeiture he considered it would be better
to have the term for six months. It would benefit
the public as much as the Pawnbroker, because it
would be easier to pay half-a-year's interest than for
twelve months. A long accumulating charge worked
badly for both parties. Many pledges were left at the
end of twelve months on account of that accumulation.
He objected to prolong the term beyond a year, as a
large portion of unredeems were prolonged in that
way. Many Pawnbrokers were glad to clear their
forfeited goods at a discount: the redemptions
amounted to about 90 per cent. of the pledgings,
and it was frequently the case that a Pawnbroker
speculated on the redemption. If the Pawnbroking
and sale trades were separated, he did not think
Pawnbrokers could exist. Any ordinary dealer with
a capital of £5,000, turning it over at a small profit,
would make a much larger profit than a Pawnbroker.
He could not understand why any man became a
Pawnbroker except by inheritance. The old privilege of the Trade had gone since the Usury
Laws were repealed, and he thought that the
Legislature should remove the last restrictions
which were imposed upon them. Mr. Dicker
here mentioned a case in which a Pawnbroker had
lent £6 upon a piano, which remained for 15 months,
the total charge being 22s. 6d., a sum much below
what would be charged for warehousing only. He
produced a bill and receipt from a City pianoforte
maker, for the sum of £3, which had been charged
for storing the same piano for the same period and
no money advanced. He had written to the proprietor
of the Baker-street Bazaar to ask the charge for
warehousing a lot of goods, similar to one he had

in pledge for £5, which were redeemed in 6½ months,
yielding a profit of 8s. 1½d., but the Bazaar people
required 50s. for the first six months, and 7s. 6d.
per month afterwards. Pawnbrokers should be entitled to the privilege of charging for storage or
warehouseroom. He could not define the class of
goods, as it was difficult to do so, but he thought
persons should have facilities for pledging what they
could best spare, bulky or otherwise, and that the
contract should be left open, as it would be regulated
by competition. The Pawnbrokers' scale of interest
was a hard and fast one, which forbad, under heavy
penalties, any extra charge to be made. He had heard
of such an event as the redemption of a pledge on a
Sunday, but the rule was to close. It might be
desirable to stamp a ticket with the words "extra
charge," but he preferred a distinct contract to which
the borrower should sign his name. He did not think
a pawner would be constrained to accept terms offered
by a Pawnbroker; competition would reduce all to
some uniform principle of charge throughout the
Trade. People took articles of small value to "leaving shops," because the Pawnbroker would not receive
them. If driven to borrow from persons in their
own position of life they would have to pay more
than to a Pawnbroker. He referred to the circumstance, that a few years previously, his place of
business had been visited by the late Charles Dickens,
who made the event the subject of an article in
Household Words,* which periodical he then conducted.
In the sketch the author had given the name of
"Mrs. Flathers" to one of the customers he had seen
on the Saturday night of his visit. Some time after
the woman described to witness the extortionate

---

* The article was published in No. 89 of "*Household Words*,"
on December 6th, 1851, and was entitled " My Uncle."

amount she had been charged for a small loan from
some person in private life, and the charges appeared
to him so oppressive that he wrote to Mr. Dickens
enclosing a statement of " Mrs. Flather's " sufferings,
which called forth a reply from the great novelist,
which the witness handed in. The letter, which was
as follows, excited great interest in the Members of
the Select Committee, several of whom were anxious
to read it. It was dated from

> " Tavistock House, Tavistock Square,
> " Twentieth December, 1857.
>
> " SIR,—I assure you I have received your letter with much
> pleasure, and it is a great satisfaction to me to have helped to
> render justice to a deserving body of men.
> " You owe me no thanks—on the contrary, I feel indebted to
> you for your valuable assistance and for the great intelligence
> and moderation with which it was rendered. The case you
> mention occurred to me as a suppositious one, when I was
> looking at your customers. I have no doubt whatever that
> Mrs. Flathers would be infinitely worse off with an obliging
> neighbour than with any Pawnbroker whatsoever.
> " I am, Sir, faithfully yours,
> "CHARLES DICKENS.
> " Mr. John Dicker."

The witness, resuming his evidence, gave a description of " Dolly Shop " operations, and was then drawn
on to the question of stolen property. He did not
believe, he said, that any Pawnbroker would knowingly receive stolen property; it was against his
own interest, and every precaution was taken to
prevent its coming into his hands. In seven
years he had received no less than 1,334,011
pledges, out of which only fifty-three had been
given up as stolen property. Many of the
pledges would be sold by public auction, and,
if stolen, could be identified when on view. Thieves
did not take their plunder to Pawnbrokers as a rule,
for they were more liable to detection. He thought
any interference of the police with their books or
stocks would drive respectable and conscientious men

out of the Trade, as they would feel they were placed
under public stigma.   As a rule the Pawnbrokers
lost more by the deficiency on sale of goods than they
gained by unclaimed overplus; they set off the gain
of one side against loss on the other.   Mr. Dicker
then retired, having been under examination about
two hours, in addition to the time occupied on the
previous Monday.

Mr. George Attenborough, of Old Kent-road,
London, was the next witness called in.   He said
he had been a Pawnbroker about forty years ; was
Hon. Sec. to the London Protection Society.   By
request he read the rules which defined the objects of
that Society, and said his connection therewith
brought him constantly into contact with the Trade.
He had heard the greater part of Mr. Dicker's
evidence, and generally agreed with it.   Knew short
date pledges were unremunerative, and approved of
the substitution of the Irish rate.   He considered it
most desirable that they should have the right to
make special contracts ; he dealt in loans above £10
when he could, as it was the best part of the business,
being complete free trade.   He believed pawners
generally were very well able to take care of themselves.   The witness then went into a long and
elaborate explanation of how Pawnbrokers were
defrauded by the professional " duffer," who earned
quite a good living by pledging "duffing" goods;
and he believed there were at least 10,000 persons
always employed in defrauding Pawnbrokers.   Their
Society punished them when they could establish a
fair and clear case against them ; but the great
difficulty was to detect them, as they were too wary
to make false representations.   The witness then
followed those who had previously given evidence,
as to the insufficiency of the profits and the desirability of freedom of contract.   He was also of

opinion that the time of forfeiture was too long, and approved of six months. He gave it as his opinion that it would be quite impossible for the Trade to combine to fix the prices to be lent; no union of the kind could be sustained in consequence of the keen competition which existed. As to the set off on the sale of a pledge, witness stated that the Protection Society had then a case pending, in which a person presented five tickets to a Pawnbroker for pledges which had been sold by auction. The man demanded to see the account of each sale, and finding there was a loss upon two of the pledges, and a profit on the other three, he demanded the profit, but repudiated any liability to pay the loss on the others. The insurance of the pawner's risk was then gone into, and a great deal of the ground already traversed by previous witnesses was again passed over. The examination of Mr. Attenborough was much curtailed, as the Chairman announced that he thought both he and the Committee quite understood the promoters' view of the subject.

Mr. John Ashbridge Telfer was the next witness called, but as with the preceding examination, the prepared evidence was much abbreviated. He proceeded to say, that he had two houses of business at the East of London, and had, like Mr. Dicker, succeeded his father in the possession. He produced a balance-sheet of one business, and the net profit on the Pawnbroking branch was 3 and ¼th per cent. But for the sale trade his business would be very unprofitable. He concurred generally with the evidence already given, but did not quite agree with the method of ascertaining the cost per pledge, as large amounts were reckoned in with the small ones. He found it cost him 3½ per cent. upon his loans to pay working expenses, therefore any transaction paying less than that resulted in a loss. The rate allowed by the Act,

nominally 20 per cent., was in reality only 1⅔rds per
cent. per month. A clause in a new law fixing a
minimum payment for the first two months would
pay; then the interest could run on as it did under
the old Act. If he could be sure of two months'
interest as a minimum, he would not desire any increase beyond that now allowed. The Trade, however,
preferred the Irish rate; therefore it might be better
to adhere to that. A pledge for £1 paid, in interest
and ticket money, 6d. for one month, which was 2½
per cent. on the turnover, which he contended was a
losing rate. If a pledge for 2s. were taken on a
Monday and redeemed on the Saturday, it would pay
4s. 4d. in the year, but it would cost 2½ and a fraction
per cent. each time, and if that were multiplied fifty-
two times, it would be found that the cost was much
greater than the receipt. Reckoned as interest on
money it would appear heavy, but still it would only
represent the working cost. The short date pledgers
were their worst customers—except those who left
their goods altogether, after having obtained a long
price upon them. The witness placed in the hands
of the Chairman a large amount of interesting and
carefully prepared evidence, calculated to strongly
confirm the testimony of those who had preceded him;
but the Committee considered that many portions of
the subject already treated, had been sufficiently and
explicitly explained, and therefore confined their
questions to the comparatively few points given in
the above brief abstract.

Mr. William Nathan, of Limehouse, Pawnbroker,
was the next witness, and his examination was exceedingly brief. He deposed that his business was a
large running one, which paid net about 9 per cent.,
but he was not deducting interest on capital, which
should be 5 per cent. ; then his net profit would only
be 4 per cent. He did a large sale business, which

paid about 26 per cent.; he would be quite satisfied with the Irish rate for interest, and concurred in shortening the period of forfeiture to six months. Also thought special contracts should be allowed, but was in favour of limiting them· to sums of 40s. and upwards, with the statutory rate below. He would not allow contracts to be made by persons under 21 years of age.

With this, the proceedings of the second day were brought to a close, lasting up to five o'clock, or one hour longer than the previous sitting. The Chairman asked the Secretary to arrange for evidence from the Country to be given on the following Monday. The case for the promoters may be said to end here, all the succeeding evidence being either in support of the opening, or mildly appreciative with suggested modifications; or, on the other hand, fierce, implacable and unreasoning hostility.

CHAPTER XXX

FRIENDS AND SUPPORTERS

It is not within the scope and purpose of this brief chronicle, to present further lengthy abstracts of the evidence given before the Select Committee. The first five witnesses may be said to have opened the case for the promoters, and it may be assumed, so far effectually as to satisfy, if not to convince, a majority of those present on the first and second days. The witnesses who followed may be described either as friends or enemies, with the exception of three—Sir Wm. Bodkin, Mr. Keeson, and Mr. Rayner Storr—who may be classed as neutral. Many of those who were both in support and opposition, did of necessity travel over the same ground many times, and to re-produce these endless repetitions would convert this modest recital into a wearisome mass of unreadable verbiage. Besides, in the space at our command, it would be impossible to render the evidence intelligibly, for the Blue-book consists of 316 pages, containing 5157 questions and answers.

We therefore propose to indicate, in a few words, on which side a witness ranged himself—whether as friend or enemy—and we will deal with our friends in the first instance, as they were called to *prove*, from their own experience, the statements put forward by the opening witnesses.   The first gentleman called in our friendly category was

Mr. John Frederick May, of Salford, Pawnbroker, and a member of the Manchester and Salford Pawnbrokers' Association.   This witness occupied the chair about two hours and a half, and he detailed in the most minute manner, the illegal practices which had grown, in the course of seventy years, so as to have become general throughout his locality.   These included excessive charges as to interest; dispensing with the Magisterial declarations; taking pledges from children under the legal age; not endorsing interest on tickets; not selling pledges by auction as required to do by the Act; not taking or giving farthings in change; splitting pledges; with many other infringements and evasions of the law.   This evidence, which required considerable courage to impart, was of the most valuable character, as it proved indisputably the pressing necessity for extensive amendments of the Act of Parliament.   As proposed remedies, Mr. May strongly supported the programme of the Reform Association.

The succeeding witness was Mr. Joseph Brooking, of Exeter, a well-known Pawnbroker, a keen and patient student of Pawnbroking law, and for many years a voluminous contributor to the *Pawnbrokers' Gazette*.   He was, too, what in these days would be irreverently termed a "faddist," for although a sound and earnest reformer in the main, he preferred his own panacea to any proposed by others. He approved of the six months' forfeiture, but not of the proposed rate of interest.   He had invented a system of what he called "brokerage," and would reduce the rate of interest from 20 per cent. to 12½.   He would charge one halfpenny per shilling for brokerage and the interest for all sums below 4s. ½d. per month, and then by 4s.

steps at the same rate, but he admitted to
the Committee that he had not found any general
acquiescence in his ideas.   He was in favour
of free contracts and unlimited hours of business.
Mr. Brooking was also an earnest advocate for some
system of insuring the pledgers' goods; he did not
unfold his scheme when giving evidence, but he forwarded to the Members of the Select Committee, we
believe, a pamphlet on the subject, which was a re-
print of his views as expressed in the columns of
the *Gazette*.   The next advocate for reform was Mr.
Benjamin Blackwood of Bradford, a Pawnbroker,
and Secretary to the Association of that town.   He
generally supported the Irish rate and freedom of
contract.   He believed the Act was fairly carried
out in Bradford, with the exception of charging and
giving farthings.   The majority of the Trade in the
town were in favour of twelve months' absolute forfeiture with no extension beyond.   The auction clauses
were properly carried out, and he did not consider
with Mr. Orr Ewing, that improvident and intemperate people only pledged goods.

The next witness called in was Mr. Archibald
McKay, a Pawnbroker of 26 years' standing in
Glasgow.   He told the Committee that he estimated
that 6,960,000 pledges were deposited annually in
that City, and that about £1,392,000 was lent upon
them.   (Expected asphixiation of Mr. Orr Ewing,
but his efforts to take copious notes averted any
serious consequences).   The witness considered that
the pledges throughout would average 4s. 6d. each;
but his own would not be more than 3s. 1d. each.
His gross earnings for the year amounted to
£613 13s. 6½d., and after paying working expenses
and deducting 5 per cent. for capital, he had a net profit
of 1·9 per cent. on the turnover.   He adhered to the
Act as to the sale of auction pledges.   Was in

favour of six months' forfeiture, and freedom of
contract with persons not under 21 years of age.
This witness was considerably "heckled" by Mr.
Orr Ewing, who insistently endeavoured by every
insidious means he could command to compel Mr.
McKay to confess that the majority of the immense
number of pledges were deposited for the purpose,
mainly, of obtaining drink. But with all his artful-
ness, the scheme signally failed.

William Neilson Hancock, Esq., LL.D., was the
next witness called. He described his vocation as
Barrister-at-Law and a Government official in Ireland.
He had directed his attention to the system of Pawnbroking in Ireland and England, as far back as the
year 1849, when he read a paper on the subject at the
meeting of the British Association for the Advance-
ment of Science. In 1866 he was appointed by the
Lord Lieutenant of Ireland to inquire into the Pawnbroking laws in that country; he made a report
thereon which had been presented to Parliament.
The Pawnbroking laws originally arose from being
an exception to the usury laws. All the usury laws
had been repealed, and Pawnbroking was the only
remnant remaining. He had formed a very strong
opinion that the repeal of the usury laws should be
made complete, as Pawnbroking was the only trade
subject to restriction as to the rate of interest on
money. He would not have a compulsory rate, but
an implied rate if there was no actual contract. He
thought freedom would be beneficial to both parties;
those who pledge and the Pawnbrokers, as if the goods
were being sold instead of being pawned. He saw no
reason to modify anything he had stated in his
report. He would have no compulsory time of forfeiture. As to searching by the police for stolen
property, it could not be made without a warrant
in Ireland, owing to portions of the English law

which prevailed, but in the City of Dublin, which
was under very efficient Government police, they do
not wait for a warrant, but they make a contract
with the Pawnbrokers that they shall carry on business beyond the hours allowed by law, if they will
give the police the right to search.

Mr. Richard Attenborough, then a Pawnbroker on
a large scale in Piccadilly, London, was next called.
He said he dealt chiefly in pledges of large value;
they were mostly above £10 and under Special
Contract. He found by investing his money at
fifteen per cent., after expenses it left him 7½
per cent. net profit. He did not consider the money
lent on pledges under 2s. 6d. was interest, but
a fee for the loan of the money. There should be no
odd days or parts of a month in the calculations. He
agreed with the proposal for six months' forfeiture.
He should prefer, he thought, a fixed rate up to £5, and
then open contract. He had been 20 years in business,
and in all that period had not more than thirty transactions in goods dishonestly come by—or about one
and a half per year. The police could be very
offensive, and he objected to their coming into his
house to search his stock; no honourable man would
submit to such degradation. Many other opinions
were expressed on the subject generally, but they are
already sufficiently familiar to our readers.

Mr. Francis Turner, Barrister-at-Law, was also
called, and he reviewed very exhaustively every clause
of the Act, and gave his opinion thereon, and pointed
out the defects which he considered existed. He
showed that the rate of interest could not be placed
on the ticket, as it was too intricate; he considered
the system of making declarations as then arranged,
little better than a farce. The evidence was given
at great length, but being for the most part legal
and technical, it produced no novelties.

On another day, Mr. Lucas Peter Stubbs, a Magistrates' Clerk, of Liverpool, was examined, and said he was the author of a work entitled "A Guide to Pawnbroking," which he intended as a manual to simplify the understanding of the law by the poorer classes. From inquiries he had made, he had come to the conclusion that the profits on Pawnbroking were low compared to other trades. By his position in the police courts he had come in contact much with Pawnbrokers; and his experience was that Pawnbrokers frequently lost money by having to restore stolen property. He never knew of a Pawnbroker being convicted for knowingly receiving stolen goods; he believed, as a body, they were a very efficient protection to the public and aid to the police. The clause relative to lost duplicates, did not work well; in his court the declarations were handed to the usher, who asked if the statement was true; he then stamped them and handed them in batches, to be signed, to the magistrate. Sec. 4 in respect to farthings should be repealed; he had not seen a farthing in Liverpool for six years. Agreed in a six months' forfeiture. Pawnbrokers, he considered, were fair dealing respectable people.

Mr. Wm. B. Raynor, the head superintendent of the Borough Police, of Nottingham, was called and deposed that he had been 41 years in the police. There were about twenty Pawnbrokers' shops in Nottingham. The police circulated notices relative to stolen property, but it did not frequently happen that the goods went to the Pawnbrokers. The number of robberies in the town for the previous twelve months was 302. Pawnbrokers always gave him the fullest information, and never knew of a Pawnbroker being convicted. Did not see any advantage in searching the warerooms for clothing, as they could not identify other peoples' clothes. The articles found at Pawnbrokers' shops for the twelve months were 44 out of 302 robberies.

Mr. Wm. Scoular, an old and well known Glasgow Pawnbroker, and at one time Secretary of the Association, tendered some evidence as to his experience of the Trade. He related the curious fact that there was only one Pawnbroker in Glasgow in the year 1811, and he carried on the business on the "wee pawn" system, for it was not known up to that year that the Act of 1800 applied to Scotland. The solitary Pawnbroker died, and the Sheriff of Lanarkshire issued a warrant that a public notice should be sent round *by the sound of the drum*, that all goods not redeemed in one month would be sold. No Pawnbrokers' licence was taken out in Glasgow before 1811. Up to 1856 there were probably from 200 to 300 "wee pawns" there. The witness sold all his forfeited goods by auction without reserve, as he had no sale shop. From June, 1867, to June, 1868, goods which cost £1,469 sold for £1,198, thus showing serious loss. He objected to the rate of interest as being too low, and for the fractional calculations it involved; he was in favour of the six months' forfeiture.

Mr. Arthur Davidson, auctioneer, of Glasgow, volunteered evidence as to the custom of the Trade. He stated that he sold largely for Pawnbrokers, and was in the habit of selling five days in the week, commencing at half-past 12 at noon, and half-past 7 in the evening. The value of a day's sale of unredeemed pledges would vary from £150 to £30. Pawnbrokers did not buy at the sales because they did not keep sale shops; the sales were properly advertised. Pawnbrokers did not bid at the sales for their own goods, but they sometimes reserved them. The witness exhibited books and explained the system of entries.

Mr. Geo. Scotson, of Leeds, a Pawnbroker, also

supported the case in favour of reform. The greater
part of the Trade in the town endeavoured to carry
out the Act, but some took the "long" interest.
Farthings were not much used, but where the legal
interest came to complete pennies or half-pennies
the legal amount was taken. The Pawnbrokers were
a respectable class, many of them had filled offices
of aldermen, councillors, poor law guardians and
other positions. The auction clauses were strictly
observed. He calculated that there would be from
£150,000 to £170,000 invested in the Trade at Leeds.
On one day he had delivered 860 pledges on which
£291 was lent, for a profit of £8 1s. 6½d. He was in
favour of the Irish rate, six months' forfeiture, and
freedom of contract above £2.

The last witness who could be classed as favourable was Mr. George Russell, Manager of the Equitable Loan Company of Scotland, carrying on the
business at Edinburgh, with a capital of £27,000. It
was raised by 3,000 shares of £9 each. They received 72,000 pledges per annum, and about 8,400
would be for smaller sums than 2s.; the average
amount lent per pledge was 11s. 3d., including pledges
above £10. Without those the average would be
about 9s. 8d. The forfeited goods would amount to
about 10 per cent. They sold all pledges above 10s.
by auction, and everything was sold without reserve.
The Company had paid dividends of 5, 5½, and 7
per cent. He objected to the rate of interest laid
down by the Act as being insufficient, and involving
fractional parts; he always gave and took farthings,
which cost them 1s. 8d. in the £ to obtain. There
were very few in Edinburgh who gave farthings;
for 3s. lent most of the Trade charged one penny
for the first month. He was in favour of six months'
forfeiture. From the Superintendent's report on
crime he found in 1869 there were 3,355 articles

stolen in the whole City, and the number found in
the possession of Pawnbrokers was 380. Of these
126 were illegally pledged by watchmakers, tailors,
dressmakers, bootmakers and others, leaving 254 lots
as petty thefts, and of those his Company had taken
six. He was in favour of freedom of contract over
40s.

Thus concluded the case for the promoters ; it only
remains for us to show what could be said against
it by our opponents.

CHAPTER XXXI

As we have already instanced, Sir William Bodkin
the Assistant Judge of the Middlesex Court of Sessions; the late Mr. Alfred Keeson, editor of the *Pawnbrokers' Gazette;* and Mr. Rayner Storr, auctioneer, may
be considered as strictly neutral and unbiassed witnesses. The first-named gentleman gave his evidence
with exceeding fairness, taking broad and liberal
views upon so difficult a social problem. He declined
to express an opinion on any portion of the subject
which he did not understand. He was not in favour of
giving power to the police to search the books and
stocks of Pawnbrokers; he thought small loans were
useful to the poor, and objected to give licensing
power to Magistrates.

The evidence of Mr. Keeson was mainly technical,
relating to Pawnbroking on the Continent, conducted
by the Monts-de-Piété, and the Kleine Pandjes Huis,
or Little Pawn House in Amsterdam. As regards
English Pawnbroking, Mr. Keeson's very first answer
to the Chairman was: "I cannot pretend to answer
any questions in reference to the practical details of
Pawnbroking, as I have never had experience of
the business." Mr. Rayner Storr's evidence related
entirely to his experience as a Pawnbroker's

Auctioneer, and he gave no opinion as to the practical
working of the Act.

The first hostile witness—summoned we have little
doubt at the instance of Mr. Orr Ewing—was Mr.
Alexander McCall, the Chief Constable of Glasgow,
who gave his evidence and his opinions highly
flavoured with most potent prejudice. He stated
that there were 109 Pawnbrokers in Glasgow, or 1
to every 4,220 of the population; he also gratuitously
and irrelevantly stated that there were not less than
1,500 publicans and spirit dealers. The Chairman
here adroitly interposed with the remark, that pro-
portionately there would be 15 times as many publicans as Pawnbrokers, which the witness ingenuously
admitted. He then went on to say that he believed
the pledgings in Glasgow would amount to about $5\frac{1}{2}$
millions annually, and of these about 5 millions
would be under 10s. He had heard complaints
about a few of the Pawnbrokers. There was one who
engaged people to sell tickets, and he had issued
one for a gold chain for £2 15s., which was from his
sale stock and not as valuable as represented, the
purchaser being imposed upon. Very few members
of the Trade indulged in these practices. There were
cases where people could not get their own articles
back when they had applied to redeem, as inferior
goods were substituted. There had been a case in
which a woman pledged a quantity of work, some in
an unfinished state. When arrested she confessed
where she had pledged the goods, but when applied
for the Pawnbroker said they had been redeemed.
Witness *thought* that the Pawnbroker finding himself likely to get into trouble, had obtained the
tickets from the thief *and so redeemed the goods
himself.* The witness could not say he was certain
of the fraud, *he only suspected there was something
wrong.* A number of people were handed over to

the police by Pawnbrokers, but *he thought*, they might make more enquiries than they did. He was not of opinion that they would knowingly receive stolen goods or that any kept a melting pot. He thought it desirable that Magistrates should grant licences or certificates; thought also that Pawnbrokers' premises should be better lighted. His notion was that all pledging should be put down under ten shillings. Asked if he did not consider that a high limit, the witness admitted that it might be, so he would say 5s. After further pressing questions put by the Chairman, witness replied that he was strongly of opinion there should be no pledges for such sums as 9d., or 1s., or 1s. 6d., or 2s., for he believed such amounts were spent with spirit dealers. Special Contracts would enable Pawnbrokers to take advantage; but people who pawned for more than 10s. might protect themselves. The time might be shortened for keeping some goods, but they should be scheduled. He had experienced difficulties in tracing stolen goods pledged for more than £10; had known a case where goods to the amount of £300 could not be recovered, because they were not entered in the books kept under the Act. He invariably found pawn-tickets on thieves and in their houses. He believed everything so pawned was turned into whiskey or strong drink: he could take a drop himself now and then, and did not consider it a sin at all events. He would do away with pawnshops altogether, and did not think it would be a national calamity. He thought as they did without them up to 1800 they could do so now. In answer to the Chairman, witness admitted that Scotchmen. thought proper to go without *breeks* at one period, and that it was no reason that they should go without them still.

Mr. Bailey Miller was a magistrate of Glasgow and justice of the peace for the county. He

considered that Pawnbroking contributed to the de-
moralization of the lower classes, by the facilities
it afforded for getting drink. If Pawnbroking were
abolished people would rely more upon themselves;
suppression might produce inconvenience for a time,
but had they never been established the habits of
the people would have been much better, as he
would not leave it open for people to reduce themselves to distress, misery, and disease. He would
prevent existence of the facilities for pawning, but
could not say how. Being pressed by the Chairman
to expound some plan, the witness sat silent for
some time, being utterly unable to express himself.
His examination was then resumed. He admitted
that if every transaction in the post office savings
bank cost the Government 6d., they would be justified
in charging 1s. Pawnbrokers, he said, should be
under magisterial control; he would have them on
the same footing as publicans, and all unclaimed
overplus should be paid over to the charities of the
city. Yes, he would make the Pawnbrokers bear
all the losses, and give the Charities all the profits.
He frequently visited the poor and observed the
evil influences of Pawnbroking; he had tried to estimate the amount of money paid in interest, and
thought it would come to £150,000 or £200,000 a
year, or more than was paid to local charities.

    Another Scotch witness, of a similar type, was Mr.
William Hector, who described himself as Procurator
Fiscal for the Eastern District of Renfrewshire, and
Sheriff Clerk Depute for the same District. His
examination in chief was conducted by Mr. Crum-
Ewing. The witness's public position, he considered,
had afforded him good opportunities to become acquainted with the affairs of Renfrew, but more especially in Pollockshaws. He entered into a long
tirade as to the population, to statistics of crime,

drunkenness, and the "lairge" increase in the amount of the poor rate and in the number of paupers. The analogy of all these subjects to Pawnbroking reform is very difficult to trace, except in the highly imaginative and bigotted mind of the witness. He ascribed all the evils that affected the locality as being due to the establishment of Pawnbroking. In 1835 there was not one shop in Pollockshaws, and now there were 12,* and in all the county there were 43. The pawning system was carried on very largely in the district; he calculated that the shops received quite 4000 pledges each per month. He calculated that the number of pledges made in Scotland, yearly, would amount 18,720,000 !† He believed that Pawnbroking had materially increased distress and crime; for it was difficult for him to understand how thieves could dispose of the articles they stole if there were no Pawnbrokers' shops. The witness here read several letters he had received from husbands who complained of their wives having raised goods on credit and pledged them. The Chairman inquired if witness thought or expected the Legislature to convert bad, drunken women into model members of society? The witness, who appeared to be highly astonished at the question, lamely replied that he had no such expectation. He then proceeded to say that he thought a halfpenny stamp should be put on all pawn-tickets, and it would realise about £250,000, which would go to remedy some of the evils caused by Pawnbroking. The witness did not say who was to pay for the stamps, but it

---

* In the return made by Government officials at the request of the Committee, and published as an Appendix to the Minutes of Evidence, the number is given as 2. Probably the witness included "Wee Pawns."

† It will be remembered Chief Constable McCall thought 5½ millions, and Mr. McKay about 7 millions.

may safely be assumed that he intended it should
be the Pawnbroker.   Mr. Frederick Williamson,
superintendent of the Detective Police of the Metropolis, also gave evidence—of course from a policeman's
experience point of view, and with the usual official bias.
He stated that he had been 20 years in the force and
had seen how Pawnbrokers carried on their business;
they were generally a respectable class of men, but
they did not carry on the business as strictly as
they ought. A large quantity of stolen goods went
to the Pawnbrokers, but they, as a rule, gave
facilities for inquiries; he had never known of a
search warrant being required.   He would like to
see Pawnbroking more under the observation of the
police, but would not go so far as they did in Glasgow.
He did not think they were receivers of stolen goods;
nor did he think freedom of contract would be desirable; he was also of opinion that wearing apparel
should not be kept as long as other goods.

The sensation of the whole inquiry was, however,
caused by the examination of Mr. John Morritt
Walter, of Aldersgate-street, London, Pawnbroker.
The hostility of this witness was known to be intense
in its bitterness, but those present were hardly prepared for the lavish recklessness in his distortion of
facts; the impotence of his logic, or the complete
confession of his own lawlessness. There was nothing
remarkable at the commencement of his evidence, for
he was in favour of the Irish rate; he objected to
farthings; was in favour of three books; thought
H and L absurd and unnecessary; had one lot of
tickets printed with H, and another lot with L, and
considered that cleared him of the Act. He never
asked a person whether he was a householder, or a
lodger; never had done it, and never intended to do
it unless compelled by penalties. Several Members
repeatedly asked him if they understood him to

say he deliberately infringed the law, and he as repeatedly answered in the affirmative. As for the names and addresses, he told the Committee he never asked a pledger where he lived, or the number of the house; they put any address that came into their heads; he considered to ask for such particulars was all moonshine; it was nonsense. Here, he said he would show the Committee the A B C of the business, and produced his books, but whether it was he found the Committee anything but apt scholars, or his own patience defective, he certainly from these or some other causes, became very excited. When this episode was passed, matters went on more quietly again. The witness said he did not object to making unlawful pawning a penal offence; he did not think however that a Pawnbroker should be compelled to give a person into custody, as he might be liable to legal proceedings. After severely criticising several clauses of the old Bill, the witness came to clause 17, which provided for the six months' forfeiture. To this he protested strongly; he asserted as a Pawnbroker, that the public would be much aggrieved, and he said to them, as a conservative Pawnbroker, it would do more harm than good. The Trade did not want it, and he had received letters which would prove that. Altogether he had received 108 letters, and some of them simply said "Stop the Bill." He had not so very many objecting to six months. How many had he received? Well he had selected 13, but he had more. Change of fashion was all nonsense; Pawnbrokers wanted to lend money; he wanted to lend more than he was doing. He sold his forfeited goods according to the Act. He had never put up a table of profits since he commenced business. During this examination, two or three members had been attentively turning over Mr. Walter's books, and one gentleman discovered the entry of a pledge for £2 2s. for which one

shilling per month had been charged, and another for
several reams of paper pledged for £2 16s. for
which 1s. 6d. a month was charged. On what principle, he was asked, did he consider himself entitled
to make special agreements for such sums? He
replied, by the use of a sixpenny stamp. A long
and exciting scene here took place, for the Chairman
pointed out that the practices were all illegal. The
witness rose from his chair, pacing up and down the con-
tracted space in which he had to move; and in answer
to one gentleman he said, "Do you know what
space four reams of paper would occupy?" and
then described how they would be four feet high,
and weigh about 5 or 6 cwt., and he was not going
to "lug" that up stairs for 8d. a month, as it would
not pay him. The witness reiterated time after
time that if he put on a sixpenny stamp the document would be legal. He had talked to lawyers
about it, and some said he was right and others said
he was wrong. The Chairman in a quiet aside, said,
"We should like to see the lawyer that said you
were right." The subject of dealing in duffing
jewellery was then touched upon, and after a few
questions, Mr. Walter rose in a great state of
excitement, and the feelings of members and
spectators became so intense that the Chairman
ordered the room to be cleared. On the re-admis-
sion of the public it was announced that no further evidence would be taken that day.

Mr. Walter resumed on the following Monday, but
the proceedings were conducted in a more decorous
manner, while the remainder of the evidence was
given calmly and collectedly. He made many more
objections to the Act and the Bill; asserted, boldly
and unabashed, that he took his interest "long";
ignored fractions and objected to freedom of contract,
but he made special agreements down to 30s., *but*

always used a sixpenny stamp. Mr. Alderman Carter
put a question, the answer to which could leave no
doubt. "To speak honestly, is not your mode of
doing business an evasion of the Act of Parliament?"
The reply was "Not in my opinion; but lawyers
differ." This evidence, although intended to express
the bitterest opposition, had, *de facto* and all unconsciously, considerably strengthened the cause of the
promoters.

The *Fidus Achates* of the preceding witness was
a diminutive fellow named William Shaw, who was
employed as a messenger in the House of Commons,
and proved a worthy Sancho Panza to the Don
Quixote who had instigated him to give evidence.
During his perigrinations about the precincts of
the House, Mr. Walter appears to have become
acquainted with the fact that this benighted creature
had once been a Pawnbroker. But, like his leader,
he considerably over-acted his part. He began his
evidence by deploring the passing of the Police Act of
1840, which had exterminated that social pest—the
informer; he characterized the Halfpenny Act as
one-sided and selfish legislation; he knew of "leaving
shops" in the "Dials;" when he was an assistant he
was compelled to take in soiled garments and had
taken a shirt full of fleas. A flat-iron pawned for
4d. would fetch 10d. when forfeited; eight-tenths of
the pledges, except at Mr. Attenborough's, were below
2s. He knew pledges to be split to get more ticket
money; farthings were useful and should be used;
he objected to special contracts. The poor people
would have liquor, especially at Easter and Whitsun;
when a man began with a Pawnbroker he never got
clear. He did not consider the business was demoralising, but Mr. Orr Ewing opined that witness
would have little difficulty, after all his admissions,
in coming to the conclusion that it was. Witness

P

would allow a man to pawn for 6d.; *had known a
pledge as low as a halfpenny;* he thought the rate of
interest as it stood was ample, and a splendid consideration for money lent.

The evidence which followed paled into ineffectual
verbiage compared to the brilliant veraciousness of
Mr. Shaw, as Sir Thomas Henry was mild in
his denunciations; Mr. Robert Attenborough, deprecated any effort being made to disturb his
highly-remunerative and aristocratic business, and
suggested that the term " Silverbroker " should be
applied to those who conducted high-class trades,
as the term " Pawnbroker " was rather objectionable.

Then there came more Scotch evidence of the same
bigoted, narrow-minded character as that previously
given, from Mr. McDonald, a writer to the Signet
at Edinburgh, and Mr. Robert Bruce Johnson, of
the same profession and a Procurator-Fiscal.

Mr. George Attenborough, of Fleet-street, was the
concluding witness. He made a vigorous on-slaught
upon the Bill, and the evidence given in its support.
He objected to any increase in either interest or
ticket money; he did not ask for more, nor did half
the Pawnbrokers in London. He dwelt upon the
large increase which would ensue if the proposed
rate of profit was adopted, and he selected as
examples the sums of 2s. 3d., 4s. 3d., 6s. 3d., &c.,
the charges on which would come to 41½ per cent.
The last question of the Inquiry, put by the Chairman (John Whitwell, Esq.), was, " Has not your
calculation been based upon extreme points, that is
to say the worst aspect of the step process ? " The
reply was, " Yes, I admit that," and these are the
last words in the Blue-book relative to the giving of
evidence.

Thus after twelve days of patient and exhaustive
inquiry, the examination of 36 witnesses, the pro-

ceedings closed. The next day the Secretary returned to Liverpool after an absence of 9 weeks and
4 days. Then animated by feelings hovering between
hope and fear, for nearly 13 months the whole Trade
was "Waiting for the Verdict."

CHAPTER XXXII

The Executive Committee held a meeting at Derby, on the 26th October, 1870, when a report was presented from the Parliamentary Sub-Committee, detailing all that had transpired—and the proceedings were of the highest importance—from the previous March. The Financial Secretary produced a balance sheet showing that the sum of £1549 had been received on account of the calls made upon the guarantors, and £169 had been paid in by subscribers. After the customary votes of thanks had been passed to the little band who had worked in London all through the Inquiry, a resolution was passed, that a deputation consisting of the same gentlemen should wait upon the Chairman of the Select Committee and endeavour to ascertain whether or not it was his intention to re-open the Inquiry next Session, and take further evidence. The interview took place on November 29th, when the deputation was informed, that the Committee had no intention of taking any additional evidence, but that they would meet as early as convenient in the next year to consider and agree upon their report.

The Houses of Parliament assembled on February 9th, 1871 ; and the Parliamentary Committee obtained information that the Report might be expected by Easter. On the 21st of the month Mr. Ayrton moved that the Select Committee should be re-elected, but proposed 15 names only. The two omitted were Mr. Serjeant Simon, whose professional engagements were too numerous to allow him time to attend to the duties; and Mr. Sidebottom, the member for Stalybridge, who had died since the closing of the previous session. The first sitting took place on March 9th; when an adjournment to the 23rd was made. Meanwhile the Secretary to the Reform Association compiled an elaborate document, which was an analysis or review of the evidence given by witnesses favourably disposed. Folio 1 was entitled "Days of Grace"; 2 "Forfeiture of Pledges"; 3 "Freedom of Contract"; 4 "Profits of Pawnbrokers"; 5 "Pawnbrokers and Pauperism." This paper was circulated to all members of the Select Committee, and a large number of M.P.'s who were known to be friendly towards the cause.

On the 23rd, the date to which the Committee had adjourned, they met and consulted with closed doors; the Parliamentary Committee was in attendance in the lobby, and were several times admitted, and referred to for information, on some cloudy or doubtful points. After this there ensued a long delay, which was the cause of much anxiety to the Committee. On May 2nd, Sir William Bagge (Member for West Norfolk) was induced to ask in the House, the First Commissioner of Works, the Rt. Hon. A. S. Ayrton, when the Report of the Committee on Pawnbrokers would be laid upon the table. In reply Mr. Ayrton said he could not answer the question because the Committee had not made a report. As soon as it was completed it would be laid upon the table. There was no urgent necessity for its early production, as no legis-

lation would take place during the present
session. This announcement caused great disappointment to the promoters, as this was the third year
of their operations and that was fast approaching
the completion of its first moiety of time. In July
Mr. Ayrton was seen at the House, when he promised
immediate action. His time, he explained to the
Parliamentary Sub-Committee, had been very much
occupied, but, he said, "next week we shall be free."

He so far kept his word, that the Report, bearing
date 4th August, 1871, was laid upon the table of
the House; in a few days it was distributed to all
the officers of the Association, and as early as possible, it was published to the Trade generally. The
result was a victory for the promoters "all along
the line," and next to the Act itself is the most important Parliamentary paper ever issued in connection with the Trade. It commenced with a short
preamble as follows:—"The Select Committee appointed to inquire into the state of the Law affecting
the Pawnbroking Trades, with a view to its consolidation and amendment;—Have considered the matters
to them referred, and have agreed to the following
Report;—

"Before considering the evidence taken by the
Committee in the last session on the subject referred to your Committee, and already reported to
the House,* they would observe, that the laws relating to Pawnbrokers originated in a policy which
has long ceased to be recognised or enforced in this
country."

The Report then gives a descriptive account of
the various laws which had regulated Usury and
Pawnbroking, all of which have been referred to in
some of the earlier chapters of this History. Then

* In a short paragraph prefixed to the Minutes of Evidence.

follow the recommendations, which we may briefly
summarize. The first states that;—"It appears to
your Committee that whilst all persons are free to
buy and sell goods, and to lend money upon them
for such terms as they mutually think best, subject
to the general provisions of the law, any restraint
upon the business of Pawnbroking should be kept
within the narrowest limits which the necessity of
the case may demand. Your Committee regret to
think that from the necessities, as also the reckless
and improvident habits of considerable numbers of
people, it is desirable that the small advances which
they may obtain from Pawnbrokers should still be
regulated by statute, so that they may not be subject to imposition from not knowing, or sufficiently.
understanding, the conditions under which their
goods are pledged; but as this reason does not extend to transactions of considerable amount, there
is now no ground for interfering with the freedom
of contract in such dealings. It is not easy to determine the sum at which free contract should take the
place of statutory regulation; but your Committee
are of opinion that the limit should not exceed £2,
and that all dealings above that amount should be
left to the discretion of the parties. As, however,
the public has long been accustomed to consider the
business of Pawnbroking regulated by law to the
extent of £10, your Committee would recommend
that where no special contract is made, the law relating to dealings should be the measure of the implied contract between the parties, and govern the
transaction.

"With regard to loans under £2, your Committee think it desirable, that instead of the
present complex table of charges, which it is
difficult and sometimes impracticable to apply to
current dealings, the following simple scale, which

could be readily understood and applied, should
be introduced:—The charge for interest should be
one halfpenny per month for every 2s. or any fraction
thereof advanced, and the charge for duplicates should
be one halfpenny for advances not exceeding 10s., and
one penny for advances above 10s."

The report then enters into the question of days
of grace for redemption free of charge, and states
that the Committee are of opinion that no days of
grace should be allowed, and that for every fraction
of a month less than half a month, the charge for
half a month should be taken.

The period of forfeiture is the next subject considered, and the paragraph concludes by saying:—
"Your Committee are of opinion that the period now
allowed should be reduced to six months, and that
only a week's grace should be granted to guard the
customers against errors or accidents in computing
the time for redemption." The Committee then recommended that all goods under 10s. in value unredeemed at the end of six months and a week should
be *absolutely forfeited*, and goods for 10s. and upwards,
should be redeemable until sold, after which the
Pawnbroker should be required, *during one year*, to
account for the surplus, if any, deducting therefrom a
per centage for the expense of sale. "These rates,"
the report continued, "together with the rates for
forfeiting, selling, and accounting for the pledge,
should be comprised in a convenient form as a statutory schedule, which should be printed on the duplicate
for all advances above that amount, when no other
contract is made."

The entries of householder and lodger were next
referred to, and it did not appear to the Committee
that any advantage resulted from those compulsory
provisions, but that it would be sufficient to provide
that the name and address should be entered, unless

the pledger declined to give either name or address, when the refusal should be entered instead. Also as regarded the endorsement of the amount of profit on the duplicate, the Committee thought it entailed unnecessary trouble without any corresponding advantages and might be dispensed with; but the Pawnbroker when required should give a receipt for the amount paid to him, like other persons in trade.

The liability of a Pawnbroker to make good the value of the pledge above the amount lent in case of fire, was the next subject treated, and resulted in the following recommendation : — " Your Committee are of opinion that the Pawnbroker should be absolutely liable within the time of redemption, to return the pledge or pay its estimated value, and to guard against undue claims on him, he should be at liberty to fix the value of the pledge, and state it on the face of the duplicate, and that he should be entitled to insure the whole of his liability." After this came a paragraph relative to declarations, and the Committee recommended that the Pawnbroker should be released from liability whenever the pledge is delivered by order of a justice of the peace, provided no actual or implied notice had been given to the Pawnbroker that the order has been fraudulently obtained.

The subject of restriction of the hours during which Pawnbrokers should conduct their business was next dealt with, and the Committee did not think it would be possible to enforce any law so much at variance with the ordinary idea of right on the part of the people to dispose of their own property; the Committee recommended " that all restrictions on keeping open Pawnbrokers' shops should be repealed and that they should be left to those principles of mutual interest and convenience of trader and customer, which regulate the conduct of other tradesmen in keeping open their shops."

A long review then followed, occupying nearly one
whole page, quoting the various sections of the Pawnbrokers' Acts, the Metropolitan Police Acts, &c., on the
subject of dealing with stolen property. The Committee came to the conclusion that the best security to
the public would be found in the mere liability of
the receiver of goods stolen or wrongfully obtained
to restore them without compensation. The Committee was also of opinion that there should be one
general law applicable to the whole kingdom, for
regulating the conditions under which goods should
be searched for, seized and restored to the lawful
owner; but to prevent injustice the value of the
goods should be paid by the owner when it appears
they have been unlawfully disposed of through his
own negligence. The next paragraph of the Report
directed attention to the offence of forging a duplicate; and the Committee thought that the general
commercial law was sufficiently comprehensive and
that special provision was unnecessary. The licence
duty next occupied attention and the Committee
recommended that the duty be £7 10s. throughout
the kingdom. Also that certificates should be granted
by justices; "but persons now carrying on the
business of Pawnbrokers should be entitled to receive their certificates without question." On
the subject of Pawnbrokers rendering assistance to
the police for the detection of crime, the Committee
were of opinion that police constables should not be
permitted to intrude themselves into the business of
a Pawnbroker without the written authority of a
duly qualified superior officer, and that when Pawnbrokers did afford assistance, provision should be
made to indemnify them for the loss of time they
might thereby entail upon themselves. The Report
concluded: "The Acts of which the chief defects
have now been noticed, are in such an unsatisfactory

form, that your Committee recommend that they should be wholly repealed, and that one general Act for the United Kingdom should be passed regulating the business of Pawnbroking *as suggested by this Report*, and that another general law should be passed regulating the summary jurisdiction of justices, respecting the illegal disposition of the several classes of goods, for which special provision is now made in the Pawnbrokers' Acts, the Metropolitan and other Police Acts."

Attached to the Report are "The proceedings of the Committee," and it is interesting to note, by what majorities some of the "Recommendations" were carried. At the first meeting there was "Motion made and question put: That there ought to be no statutory restraint upon the liberty of borrowing or lending money on the security of goods, except with certain limitations hereafter to be defined" (the Chairman). The Committee divided; for the motion, Ayes 5, Noes 2. Mr. Plimsoll then moved, in the same formal manner, "That it is expedient to preserve the statutory regulations to define the implied terms of dealing with Pawnbrokers; but that such regulations should not deprive the public of the liberty of making express contracts for such dealings." Amendment proposed, at the end of the question to add the words "above two pounds" (Mr. Orr Ewing). For the motion, as altered, there were 7 Ayes, and 2 Noes. Mr. Plimsoll then moved, "That the public should not be prohibited from selling goods upon an implied or express contract to repurchase them in any way they may think fit." This was negatived by 6 Noes to 3 Ayes.

Alderman Carter moved, "That the charge for licences to Pawnbrokers should be made uniform." Put and agreed to.

Mr. Thomas Hughes moved, "That the licence

should be granted by a local authority and not
by the Inland Revenue." Ayes, 5. Noes, 4. Mr.
Orr Ewing then moved, "That the local authority
be the justices of the peace, who shall have power
to revoke the licence upon cause shown." Ayes, 6;.
Noes, 3.

On the third of these sittings there were no less
than eleven members present, a larger number than
had previously attended, including Mr. Whitwell
—who was already regarded as the firm friend of the
Trade.

Mr. Mills proposed, "That the charge for the
licences should be received by the local authority,.
and applied in aid of the Local Police Fund." Mr.
Whitwell moved an amendment, to leave out from the
word "received" to the end of the question, in order
to add the words, "and paid for as usual." The
amendment was carried by 7 votes to 2.

Mr. Alderman Carter proposed that the licence
duty be £5. Mr. Hambro moved an amendment that
the duty be £7 10s. Amendment carried by 7 votes
to 2.

Mr. Thos. Hughes moved, "That the regulations
defining the terms and conditions of the dealings
should be contained in the Schedule in such a form
as to be readily understood, and exhibited in print in
every Pawnbroker's shop." Agreed to without a
division.

Then came Mr. Orr Ewing's champion resolution,
"That no article be taken in pawn upon which a less
sum is advanced than half-a-crown." He suffered a
crushing defeat, however, the voting being, Aye 1
(Mr. Orr Ewing himself), Noes 9. The next was a
motion made by Mr. Whitwell, "That it is expedient
that the rate of interest shall be one halfpenny per
month for every sum of two shillings, or any part
thereof, but that no change should be made in the

rate now charged for duplicates." Mr. Ridley moved, as an amendment, that all the words from "but that" be left out, in order to add the words, "the rate now charged for duplicates between 10s. and 20s. should be extended to 40s." Amendment was carried by 6 votes to 3.

The remaining motions were for the six months' forfeiture, by Mr. Thos. Hughes, and that the rate of charge and period of redemption be stated on the duplicate, by Mr. Whitwell, both being adopted without a division.

In the House of Commons, on August 4th, it was *ordered*, "That the Committee have power to report their observations to the House."

So terminated that great ordeal, long craved for by many, and dreaded by most. It was an undoubted justification of the reform programme, and left the promoters well defined land marks by which to steer their future course.

CHAPTER XXXIII

The reception of the Report of the Select Committee by the London and Provincial press, from *The Times* downwards, was not, in the aggregate, of the most approving or encouraging character; nor did the criticisms betray much profundity of knowledge on what to most of the writers was an occult subject. There was a plentiful supply of mawdling sentiment for the protection of the poor; pious horror at the thought of increasing the already too usurious interest taken by the Pawnbroker; the document was one-sided, oppressive, illogical; a six months' forfeiture would bring misery and degradation upon the poor pawner, whose goods would become forfeited and sold before he had time to turn round. A good feather bed, highly prized by the family, or a valuable clock handed down by former generations, would be surrendered *to become the absolute property of the Pawnbroker*. Poor pawner, indeed, to have such valuable goods and chattels so handy. One paper alone appeared to understand the principle which lay at the bottom of the report, and it said:—"We are by no means certain that if all Pawnbroking laws were abolished the Trade would not pass into much

better hands. We always underrate the shrewdness
of the poor. Would it not be better to try a compromise, and leave the Trade alone, provided the
Pawnbroker published his rates of charge clearly in
his shop window?"*

The Executive Committee took little note of what
transpired in the outside world, but resolutely and
at once endeavoured to put to practical test the
recommendations of the Select Committee. A meeting was held in Liverpool on 28th September, under
the presidency of Mr. Heys, Mr. Attenborough being
unable to be present. A short report from the Sub-
Committee was submitted and adopted. The report
of the Select Committee was then discussed, and
several modifications—notably in the paragraph referring to the insurance of the pawner's interest—
and other desirable amendments, and the Sub-Committee were instructed to devote attention to them
in the hope of securing their adoption. It was also
decided that a deputation should wait upon Mr.
Winterbotham and endeavour to ascertain his intentions, or those of the Government, with regard to the
introduction of a Bill on behalf of the Pawnbrokers.
As usual, delays took place; it was the recess; members were out of town, and so time dribbled away
until the 8th December. On that date an interview
was obtained through the kindly offices of Mr. Alderman Carter. Mr. Ayrton, Chairman of the Select
Committee, was by request present, as was Mr. Lush-
ington, Home Office Counsel. A long and exhaustive
examination of the subject took place, Mr. Ayrton
explaining the opinions of the Select Committee, while
the Pawnbrokers elucidated matters thoroughly understood by themselves, but which appeared to be very
puzzling to the Under Secretary. The deputation left

* *The Spectator.*

with the assurance that at an early date the decision
of the Government with regard to their drawing a Bill,
would be made known.

The eventful year, 1872, was three weeks old before
any intimation was received, when under date of
January 21st the Hon. Secretary received a letter, of
which the following is a copy, omitting the official
heading:—

"Sir,—I have given attention to the subject of legislation
with reference to Pawnbrokers, since I received your deputation last month.

"While I admit there is much force in the reasons you urge
in support of the changes in the law recommended by the Select
Committee last year, I cannot but think the evidence taken
before that Committee is deficient as to the effect of those
changes on the habits and interests of the poor. I desire not to
be understood as expressing any official opinion on this point,
and if a Bill, embodying the recommendations of the Select
Committee be introduced, the Government will not oppose the
second reading, if the Bill is referred to a Select Committee,
when further evidence can, if necessary, be taken.

"The Government do not feel able themselves to undertake
to bring in a measure on the subject. I am sorry I have not
been able to announce to you sooner the conclusion at which I
have been compelled to arrive.

"I am, Sir, your obedient servant,

"HENRY WINTERBOTHAM."

Immediately on the receipt of this letter, the Parliamentary Committee was called to meet in London,
when it was unhesitatingly and unanimously determined to prepare a Bill, which should be drawn
strictly on the recommendations of the Select Committee. Mr. Ayrton and Mr. Winterbotham were
both consulted relative to this decision, and the latter
gentleman stated that when the Bill was in draft, he
would judge it on its merits, and if approved, the
Government would not oppose the second reading.
A Sub-Committee, consisting of John Dicker, John
Ashbridge Telfer, and Alfred Hardaker, was appointed,
to whose hands was assigned the duty of preparing
instructions for the draughtsman. This was on the

XXXIII THE NEW BILL—SECOND READING 241

27th January, or six days after the receipt of the Under Secretary's letter.

The difficulties in the way of "Bill making" were not now so difficult as on a former occasion, for the Report of the Select Committee was a well defined chart for the guidance of the Sub-Committee, the Solicitor, and the draughtsman. Mr. Freeman, Solicitor, of Cheapside—a gentleman well known and much respected by members of the London Trade—was entrusted to convey the Sub-Committee's instructions to Mr. Reilly, the Parliamentary draftsman, and the work proceeded fairly satisfactorily. But unaccountable delays occurred; the end of March was reached before the first draft was presented, and this, on perusal, was found to be so crude and deficient, that its revision and amendment occupied some considerable time. Then Mr. Reilly said it would be desirable to have some cross references worked up, not only as to the sections of the old Act, but as to various decisions which had been given at various times on disputed points. The Sub-Committee suggested Mr. Francis Turner, Barrister, as a gentleman of greater experience on such matters than any other within their knowledge. This suggestion Mr. Reilly was good enough to accept, and the two learned gentlemen occupied until 27th April—exactly three months from the appointment of the Sub-Committee—before the completed draft was placed in their hands. No time was lost in having copies of the Bill printed and circulated to members of the Select Committee and other friends and sympathisers. Mr. Whitwell, under date April 30, acknowledged his copy by saying:—"I am pleased to find that the Pawnbrokers have drawn their New Bill. I shall read it with great attention. Pray send me another copy, as I want to send it to a gentleman who will be able to give an opinion, and one to whom you look." On the following day, May 1, a letter from

Mr. Ayrton was received, and it concluded with the
satisfactory assurance that "Mr. Ayrton thinks that
the drawing of it (the Bill) has been carried out, with
few comparatively trifling exceptions, quite in accordance with the Report."

All was now, once more, in a state of activity; the
House was visited nightly and interviews obtained!
with nearly every member of the late Select Committee, to whom the promoters had now become well
known. Mr. Whitwell was entreated to take charge
of the Bill, but he was very cautious as to committing
himself. An appointment was made with him at his
house, Chapel-place, Duke-street, Westminster, on May
6th, and he was earnestly appealed to to introduce the
Bill, and he did not appear altogether unwilling;
but he would like first to ascertain the opinions of
Members of the Select Committee, what the nature
of Mr. Winterbotham's corrections were to be, then
he would give his final answer.

On the 8th May Mr. Whitwell wrote to the Hon. Sec.:
—"Mr. Winterbotham has placed the Bill in the
hands of a professional gentleman for examination.
It is a question whether it should await his report
or be introduced now. I had a conversation with
Mr. Orr Ewing early this morning (one o'clock), and
I think our Bill must look for criticism, if not opposition from him. I did not get your note that
evening until I was leaving, else I would have come
to speak to you. (This note was to inform Mr.
Whitwell who had been seen, and the result). I
think you ought to see Sir Thos. Henry, and I
should wish to hear his report to-morrow; if it is
intended to introduce the Bill before the holidays
notice must be given to-morrow. If you are down
I should like to see you."

A letter was at once addressed to Sir Thos. Henry
at Bow-street asking for an appointment, and the

following day a reply was received, fixing the next Saturday at eleven o'clock to receive the deputation.

In the evening the Sub-Committee attended at the House and saw Mr. Whitwell and Col. Beresford, who from being an opponent was now willing to back the Bill. At the close of the interview Mr. Whitwell formally consented to take charge of the Bill. During the evening Mr. Whitwell placed the following notice on the papers of the House:—"In Committee of the whole House to move for leave to bring in a Bill for Consolidating with Amendments the Acts relating to Pawnbrokers in Great Britain."

Up to this time, May 10th, the Sub-Committee had been anxiously awaiting a promised list of corrections and emendations from the Home Office. A Member therefore attended at the House, and after considerable delay succeeded in seeing Mr. Winterbotham. He said a memorandum was being prepared and would be forwarded in a few days. "I may tell you shortly," he said, "that I think you have made out a very good case, but there are two or three points, *such as the term of forfeiture* and the rate of interest, upon which, I think, evidence should be taken on the other side. The Government will accede to the second reading of the Bill if it is referred on these matters. On being informed that the Pawnbrokers were about to see Sir Thos. Henry, he said, "I think you are quite right. Why not introduce the Bill at once, before the holidays?" He was told it was down for the first reading that night, when he replied, "Then you may get it through this Session." He repeated two or three times the words: "I think you have made a very good case, but we must give the opportunity to the other side to give evidence on the points stated." That same night the Sub-Committee attended at the House to hear that the Bill had been read a first time, but were subjected

Q 2

to one more disappointment by the House being
counted out at twenty minutes past seven o'clock.

On Saturday, May 11th, the deputation waited upon
Sir Thos. Henry at Bow-street. It consisted of Mr.
Geo. Attenborough, the Chairman ; Messrs. Dicker,
Telfer, Layman, and the Hon. Secretary, and a most
satisfactory interview ensued. The Committee were
gratified to learn from Sir Thomas that he wished
it to be understood, that he was in no wise opposed
to the Pawnbrokers, and that he had only given such
evidence before the Select Committee as he believed
to be correct. The subject was then entered into
very fully. Mr. Layman produced statistics of a
valuable character, showing at what discount or profit
he had purchased Pawnbrokers' forfeited goods for
upwards of twenty years.　　　　　　　　　　　．

The questions of profit, forfeiture, &c., were for
the hundredth time discussed, and Sir Thomas gave
the Secretary a list of minor amendments which he
thought the Bill required. He objected strongly to
the 55th clause, which was at that time drawn as
follows: "It shall not be lawful for a constable to
enter into a Pawnbrokers' shop, or to there interfere
with or inquire into the conduct of the Pawnbrokers'
business without the Pawnbrokers' consent, except
with the written authority of the Superintendent of
Police, or Chief Constable of the district, county,
parish, or place for which the constable acts, but
nothing in this section shall apply to a constable
acting in pursuance of a search warrant granted
under this Act." Prior to this time the Committee
themselves had viewed this clause with some anxiety,
and the draftsman had been approached and asked to
define the meaning and extent of the word "interfere,"
when he came to the conclusion it had better be struck
out; it was, therefore, with some satisfaction that
the deputation heard Sir Thomas Henry advise the

withdrawal of the clause altogether. They had also
the satisfaction of receiving an assurance from Sir
Thomas that he should not act in any way as an
opponent during the progress of the Bill.   When
Mr. Whitwell was apprised of Sir Thomas Henry's
disapproval of the "55th," or as it was known, the
"police clause," he advised the Secretary to go there
and then, direct from his house, to Scotland Yard
and see Col. Henderson on the subject.   Col. Henderson was absent, so the Secretary was introduced to
Lieut.-Col. Labalmondière, to whom was read the
clause, and his opinion solicited on the subject.
After a little reflection, he said he decidedly objected
to the clause.   "On what ground?" the Secretary
diffidently enquired.   "Because it is a restriction
on the powers of the police."   "Would you then
prefer the arrangement as at present existing?'
"We should, decidedly."   The Col. was then asked,
if, in the event of the Bill being introduced, the
police authorities would take steps to get any
additional powers inserted.   He replied. "No; he
did not think they would; but, personally, he was
in favour of the clause proposed by Lord Kimberley
in the 'Habitual Criminals Bill.'"   The Secretary,
retiring, murmured that there was a vast difference
of opinion between the Pawnbrokers and the Col.
on that subject.   The clause was ultimately withdrawn, much to the regret of Mr. Whitwell, who
believed it was a protection to the Pawnbrokers.

On Monday, May 27th, the House re-assembled
after the recess, and, the Bill having been amended
by Mr. Whitwell, Sir Thomas Henry, and others,
was pronounced ready for introduction.   On that
night Mr. Whitwell rose and said, "Mr. Speaker, Sir,
I beg to move that the House go into Committee."
Motion agreed to; the Speaker left the Chair.   Mr.
Bonham Carter, Chairman of Committees, presided.

Mr. Whitwell: "Mr. Bonham Carter, I beg to move
that you be directed to move the House that leave
be given to bring in a Bill for consolidating, with
amendments, the Acts relating to Pawnbrokers in
Great Britain." Motion agreed to, and the House
resumed. On the motion of Mr. Bonham Carter
leave was taken to bring in the Bill, and it was
brought in and read a first time. On it becoming
known that the Bill was actually in the House, the
Fire Offices Committee (representing all tariff
Insurance Companies) headed by H. R. Tomkinson,
Esq., took exception to the Insurance Clause; and,
at one time, strenuous opposition was feared. Modifications and amendments were made in the clause
so as ultimately to become acceptable.

On June 7th Mr. Whitwell moved the second
reading of the Bill. He said, "Mr. Speaker, I rise
to ask the House to read this Bill a second time now.
There is no opposition to it, and the only
difference with regard to it relates to the subject
of one clause referring to the sale of pledges, and
another with regard to the insurance of pledges,
which this Bill introduces for the first time. The
measure is based upon the report of the Committee
which sat last year upon the subject of Pawnbroking,
and I trust it may be found that it generally carries
out the report. If I succeed in getting the Bill read
a second time, I intend to refer it to a Select Committee, and therefore beg to move that it be read a
second time." Mr. Winterbotham: "On behalf of the
Government I may say that they have no objection to
the second reading of the Bill, on the understanding
that it will be referred to a Select Committee, not
with reference to one clause only, but generally; the
object of further inquiry being to test more fully than
was done last year the probable effect of the proposed
changes and facilities of the system upon the habits

of the people who use the pawnshops, and in reference
to which my hon. friend is aware, some doubts have
been expressed by Magistrates and others." Mr. Pim
(Dublin): "I should like to ask whether it ought not
to be considered by the Select Committee with refer-
ence to Ireland." There was no response. The Bill
was then read a second time. On the 15th June, the
new Select Committee was nominated as follows:—
Messrs. Winterbotham, Sclater-Booth, Thos. Hughes,
Lord George Hamilton, Sir Thos. Chambers, Sir Wm.
Bagge, Alderman Carter, Orr Ewing, Anderson,
Arkwright, Plimsoll, Guest, Grieve, Mills, and
Whitwell. On the motion of Mr. Whitwell, in the
House, it was " *Ordered*, That the report and evidence
laid before Parliament by the Select Committee on
Pawnbrokers in Session, 1871, and the report of Dr.
Hancock on the laws of Pawnbroking in Ireland, be
referred to the Select Committee on the Bill."

About this period the Sub-Committee were honoured
by a visit from Mr. J. M. Walter, accompanied by a
gentleman whose name did not transpire. It was
understood they were the emissaries from some of the
West-end capitalists who objected to the six months'
forfeiture. If that obnoxious feature of the Bill could
be eliminated, the opposition would withdraw. The
Sub-Committee, in reply, stated that they had no
authority to enter into such a compromise, and they
could not think of presuming to act antagonistically
to the large body of guarantors and subscribers who
desired the short term of forfeiture. On hearing this
decision, Mr. Walter metaphorically threw down the
gauntlet, and declared his intention to do his best to
wreck the Bill.

A meeting of the London Trade was held, and a
resolution was proposed that every effort should be
used to oppose the Bill. After a long, invertebrate,
and listless discussion, Mr. George Attenborough

moved that the word "oppose" be struck out, and the word "support" inserted in its place. *Majority for the amendment*, 14 !

CHAPTER XXXIV

It was only reasonable to suppose that after the
exhaustive inquiry and well considered Report of
the Select Committee, the subject of Pawnbroking
Law had been sifted and riddled and so minutely
examined, as to leave no doubt in the minds of
Members of Parliament, or any other rational human
beings in whose minds " Reasons comparing, balance
rules the whole," in which direction amendment
should be made as regarded the period of forfeiture.
In Mr. Winterbotham, however, we had a weak,
well intentioned man, who had a conscientious
dread of inflicting any unjust—as he thought—or
unendurable burden upon the poor. Although a
Liberal in politics, he appeared not to entertain the
broad free trade opinions of Mr. Ayrton. He was
timid but tried hard to be just—hence he hesitated
to agree with the six months' forfeiture; he wished
for further information and went for it to the most
impracticable body of men—the City Missionaries.
His doubts and fears and timidity were increased by
the whiles and unscrupulous " wire-pulling " of those
members of our own Trade, who had so indecently
threatened " to wreck the Bill," and who were

working incessantly, secretly and recklessly, to effect
their malignant object. Hence more evidence was
required and a new Committee elected as already detailed. The members sat for the first time on Friday,
21st of June, when Mr. Whitwell was elected Chairman.
On the 28th they commenced to take evidence, and
the first witness called was Mr. Geo. Henry Gillman,
who described himself as a London City Missionary,
and had been in that capacity for 14 years. His
experience was obtained partly in Drury-lane and
partly in Peckham. Sir Thos. Chambers conducted
the examination in chief, and said the Committee
were desirous to obtain any information with regard
to any change in the law as to Pawnbrokers that
might be desirable *in the interest of the poor* who
pledge their goods; first, with regard to the time
during which pledges should remain redeemable. At
present the time was twelve months with three
months' grace, and it was proposed to alter that
period and fix six months instead of twelve, with
one week's grace. Had the witness any information
to give the Committee as to the desirability, or the
reverse, of such change in the *interest of the poor?*
The information which the witness had to impart
was that *he thought,* as far as the poor were concerned, the longer the time, the better, and twelve
months would be more advantageous than six; they
would have a greater opportunity of paying the
money; the longer the time the more opportunity
of getting the things out; they could save up till
they had money enough. He had frequently heard
the people speak on the subject and they certainly
approved of a longer period of redemption. The poor
talked much about these things, but the witness
did not think they gave attention to the law; they
merely went to pledge things at the shops. From
his observation he should suppose that the greater

portion of goods pledged were redeemed. It was
within his knowledge that a poor man at the end of
the winter would pledge part of his clothes for the
purpose of raising money to buy suitable clothes for
the summer; they liked to redeem their goods; when
work was plentiful and wages pretty fair, they would
make an effort to redeem their things. Witness had
been in Drury-lane three years and Peckham ten
years. The principal of the people he went among
were the labouring classes, as navvies, bricklayers,
labourers, gardeners and so on. They were always
on the shift, sometimes a family would stay three
months and then go; sometimes six months, it was
uncertain. When they got into the habit of using
the pawnshop they could not very well leave off;
they never seemed to earn enough money to redeem
all their pledges; there were three pawnshops in
Peckham, but generally he found people would go
far afield to pledge; they would pledge more in the
winter time than in the summer; pressure would
begin with the frost about November; they generally
pledged clothing, not often furniture. His knowledge for the amounts would be for sums under 5s.;
they often pledged for 2s. or 3s.; had known cases
as low as 4d. or 3d. for an article. The class of
labourers about Drury-lane were a bad lot altogether; a good many of them would be beggars;
most of the people would be fallen women and
thieves; or persons getting a living by the coster
business, trading in the streets and so on; pawning was
more practised among the poorer people; it was a little
among those above the poorer class, but generally
speaking the shopkeepers did not pledge unless
driven into very bad circumstances. The Pawnbrokers did not very frequently advance sums as
large as £10. As to making open bargains above
£2, the witness thought it would be a matter of

competition; it was so then very often; if they
could not get a good bargain at one place they
would go to another. He thought that six months'
forfeiture would be better for the Pawnbroker, but
twelve months would be better for the poor people;
of course they could renew; he thought a Pawnbroker *must* renew if asked; he thought when people
found that they would have to redeem in six months
they would make an extra effort to get their pledges
back, but thought it would be sinking them deeper into
their difficulties. The witness knew of the existence
of a class of illegal pawnshops in the neighbourhoods
he had spoken of; they charged more than the
regular Pawnbroker; people who frequented them
were those who went for very small sums, 2d. or
3d., which the Pawnbroker would not lend; the
smaller shops would take articles from drunken
people, or thieves, or any one else, and ask no questions, whereas a Pawnbroker would not take a pledge
from · a disreputable person. He should say that
Pawnbroking paid under the present terms; he knew
of no complaints against the law by the pawning
class; they were quite content with the terms.
They relied on the honesty of the Pawnbroker, as to
what they ought to pay; he admitted that it would
be desirable in the interest of the public to have a
charge so simple that a person would know what
he had to pay. Mr. Orr Ewing wished particularly
to know whether the law of Pawnbroking was for
the advantage of the working classes, but the witness replied that he considered it was a matter of
business between the Pawnbroker and the people.
Pressed again by the question as to whether or not
he thought Pawnbroking was a healthy business, the
witness replied that he thought Pawnbroking as
defined by the old Act was a healthy business—
we presume morally—*and that Pawnbrokers, as a*

body, were an honest class of men, doing their duty.
He thought that sometimes goods were pledged
for drink, but not at all times; he did not think
.that restriction on pledging articles, such as
blankets or wearing apparel, would alter the case;
if they could not get money in one way they
would get it in another. As to freedom of contract,
if the pawner found that he was in any way over-
·charged, or taken in, he would go to another Pawnbroker, and the better Pawnbroker would get a
name for respectability; there could be no such
thing as combination, it would be a matter of competition among the Pawnbrokers. Those who lent
money at the lowest rate would, of course, be known
.and they would get more custom. Free trade would
be as good in protection for the borrower as the
protection now given him by the regular law.

Mr. Wm. Holford was the next witness, and he also
described himself as a City Missionary in Leather-
lane, Holborn. He informed the Committee that he
had written an article in a magazine, entitled, "A
Sketch of the Domestic Habits of the Families of a
Poor District." He agreed with what had been said
by the previous witness, generally; he thought
most Pawnbrokers were respectable. They all looked
out for number one, of course, and they would
make the best bargains for themselves; he thought
competition among the Pawnbrokers would be as
good security against excessive interest as the present
law which limited it. He believed that competition
would operate that way, and the witness explained a
case in illustration, the recital of which caused some
amusement. He said: — "People in that neighbourhood are so used to pawning that they know to a
T which house to go to. A person I knew pawned a
pair of trousers in Gray's Inn-road, last week, for
2s. 6d., and then went to Mr. Solomon. The pledge

was taken out of the first shop because it was not
the most that could be got. It was taken to Mr..
Solomon where 5s. was obtained upon it. "Oh, Solomon's is the house to go to,' they say; hence Solomon
does a large trade among the poorer classes in that
neighbourhood because he gives most money for the
goods." Another narrative which appeared to
interest the Committee, was in proof of what the
pawners thought of the proposed increase in the
charges. "I know an habitual pawner," said the witness, who complained of three things in the pawning
system; one was having to pay for a ticket, when the
article was pawned. 'Now,' said the man, 'during
the whole of this winter I have pawned my blanket
in the morning and taken it out again in the evening,
and I have had to pay a halfpenny for the ticket in
the morning as well as for interest at night, which
was very hard upon me.' That was one grief.
Another grief was this: he spoke very strongly
against one of the proposed alterations that had got
scent in the district. The report is spread about;
I suppose some of the assistants have been telling
the customers that the law was about to be altered
from twelve months to six. They are aware also
of the argument concerning the fashions; they know
that fashion changes in so many months; a coat or
a dress for instance. Of course, if an article is not
redeemed its value is less as old-fashioned clothes.
"Oh, but," says the man, "a watch will not change as
soon as that, nor will knives and forks, and things
of that kind, so that we must look to it if it is to
be altered from twelve months to six.'" His third
point was the increase of interest; but another
man had said to witness that he hoped they would
raise the interest from twenty to sixty per cent.,
as it would put an extinguisher on pawning, and it
would be done away with. The witness agreed with

that; he thought it was the opinion of the people. In their despair, when they are up to the neck in difficulties, they wished there was no Pawnbroker;. he found a large number of people who really wished they had not the facility of pledging goods.

Yet another city missionary was called—a Mr. James Clifford Parker—who had had experience in Paddington, Kensal New Town, Marylebone, St. George's, Hanover Square, and Chelsea. His evidence was mainly in support of that given by the previous witnesses. His objection to the six months' forfeiture varied somewhat from their views, and was not a little ingenious. He objected to any period less than twelve months, he said, because there were many people who could not get their things out of pawn in six months; it would depend on the time of the year, or perhaps on the length of a husband's illness. It would be a very good thing for the intemperate, *but there were very many who were not intemperate,.* who go to the pawn-shops when they are under pressure from sickness or loss of work, and he would like these persons to be studied. When the poor have, from sickness and other causes, been long out of work, they feel every 6d. or 1s. to be a pressure. His experience was not among the lowest class; he served an apprenticeship to a silver engraver, and then he worked for many Pawnbrokers; he was in and out of their shops during the day and he saw a great deal of decent people and small tradesmen, who employed two or three men, bringing watches and other things to pawn, to pay their wages. He objected to freedom of contract, as the Pawnbroker would make a contract to suit his own end, in the long run, and the pawner and he would not be on equal terms.

The concluding witness in this short enquiry was Mr. Thomas James Arnold, Police Magistrate, of over twenty-five years' experience at Worship Street and

Westminster. He was pretty well acquainted with
the habits of the poorer classes. It struck him that
the proposed Act would produce a very great
revolution in the system of Pawnbroking. He
should think it would be a very long time before the
poorer classes would get acquainted with it. They had
been going on for over seventy years, either personally
or traditionally in the then present state of things, and
they would have great difficulty in understanding
such great changes. He did not think the time a Pawnbroker kept open his shop was of any consequence,
as he would not find it to his interest to receive
property improperly come by. The witness thought
the alterations in the law were all in favour of the
Pawnbroker and against the interest of the poor. As
to reducing the period of forfeiture, he could conceive
a very large class would be interfered with; he
constantly had people coming before him, even after the
fifteen months, finding they were just a day too late,
and wanting to know if they had any redress against
the Pawnbroker. Witness had heard that some
Pawnbrokers, who, at the end of the year, when
pawners went to extend the period of the pawn,
*insisted on having the twelve months' interest paid before
they would allow the ticket to be backed for three months.**
It was not legal, but it was not everything that a Pawnbroker did that was legal. The witness was not in
favour of freedom of contract, nor did he agree with
absolute forfeiture below 10s.; he also thought that
Pawnbrokers should ascertain whether persons were
householders or lodgers; a great number of petty
thefts came before him where lodgers had pawned
the landlord's sheets and blankets. In many cases

---

* This expression of opinion exposes Mr. Arnold's ignorance
of the subject which he is trying to educate the Committee
upon. Paying the twelve months' interest would be a renewal
in itself; therefore, no backing would be required.

they did it for drink, and it was the facilities which
the Pawnbroker offers them of making away with the
landlord's property, which enables them first to
get into habits of intemperance and then fall into a
career of other crimes. Mr. Winterbotham here
interposed with the remark :—" That seems rather
like De Quincey's criminal, from murder, through
lying, to want of punctuality." "No one begins," the
witness replied, " by being an habitual criminal." Mr.
Arnold then went on to say that if a Pawnbroker did
not ask proper questions and make proper entries
in his books, he should forfeit his lien. He thought
the clause imposing the compulsory insurance of
the pawner's goods, rather hard on the Pawnbroker.
He thought the age for persons pledging should be
raised to 16 years throughout the country; twelve
he considered too young. He should say on the whole
it was for the advantage of the poor to be able to
borrow small sums; he did not think it was impossible for Pawnbrokers to obtain real names and
addresses. He would enlarge the powers for, Pawnbrokers. He considered the Act was giving great
advantages to the Pawnbroker, "if he is to have that
increase of interest and to be at liberty to put an end
to the contract at an earlier period than he was then
allowed to do, and to have an absolute forfeiture of
the pledge without sale; those were large advantages."

This concluded the evidence, and "the Committee
deliberated." They took the Bill clause by clause,
and the most serious defeat was experienced by the
promoters when clause 17 was reached, an amendment
being carried to insert the word "twelve" instead of
"six" as the term of forfeiture. This adverse decision
was carried by 7 votes to 4. Five of the seven members
were not on the first Committee, those being Messrs
Winterbotham, Anderson, Sclater-Booth, Sir Thos.
Chambers, and Lord George Hamilton. Of course

R

the majority was swelled by the votes of Mr. Orr
Ewing and Mr. Mills.   So through this disastrous
result, partly brought about by the efforts of Members
of our own Trade, the six months' forfeiture was lost.
Other matters were gone into, such as the Fire
Insurance clause, when the 25 per cent. limit was
agreed upon; the substitution of three years for one,
in the application for overplus; the alteration to 20
per cent. above 40s.; and a limit to the hours of
business which was, however, afterwards rejected
by the House.

CHAPTER XXXV

IN COMMITTEE OF THE WHOLE HOUSE

On July the 8th the second Select Committee's report and minutes of evidence were brought up and reported to the House of Commons, and the Bill, as amended, was ordered to be printed. On the 12th Mr. Whitwell cleverly carried a motion that the House go into Committee to consider the clauses of the Bill, for it was necessary that it should once more undergo a sort of refining process—as the old poet expresses it—"So doth the fire the drossy gold refine," and Bills in Parliament pass through a similar fire of criticism. Owing, however, to the lateness of the hour nothing further than the consent could be proceeded with. Progress was by this quick move assured, as the Bill was practically in Committee and that stage could not now be disputed. On Monday, 15th, at a quarter to three o'clock in the morning (really Tuesday), the House went into Committee and Mr. Bonham Carter, the Chairman, called " Clause 1 " for consideration. This brought up Mr. Orr Ewing — who kept sleepless watch upon the Bill—who appealed to the House not to proceed, for he did not think it was convenient at that late hour of the night. The Bill was really one of the most important it was possible to con-

ceive. He moved that the Chairman report progress.
Mr. Whitwell promptly rose and addressing the
Chairman said : "I trust the hon. gentleman will
withdraw his motion. The Bill emanates from one
Select Committee and it has been considered by
another, and a large number of hon. members have
come down to consider it to-night." But Mr. Orr
Ewing was not in a conciliatory humour, so he
returned to the attack. The Bill, he said, had only
been in the hands of Members since Friday and
they could not have had time to study it. During
the sitting of the previous Select Committee, and
the Committee which had considered the Bill, they
had only before them a strong body of rich Pawnbrokers, but they had no representative of the poor
people who pawned their goods, and who, under that
Bill, would have to pay an enormous addition to the
sum they had hitherto been accustomed to pay. It
was, he said, really impossible to go on with the
Bill at that time of night. Then, unexpectedly, Mr.
Winterbotham became a champion of the Trade and
said : "Before the commencement of the present
Session, I may say that I shared the opinions which
have just been expressed by the hon. gentleman,
but I have read the report of last year's Committee,
and that together with what I know of the proceedings of this year's Committee, has led me to change
my opinion. It is true that the principal evidence
last year was given by Pawnbrokers, and it did occur
to me that it was to be regretted that evidence had
not been taken from the pawners, who are specially
concerned in this matter, and it was for that purpose alone that the Bill was referred to a Select
Committee again this year. In that Committee we
took evidence exclusively from those who represented the interests of the poor. I came to the
distinct conclusion, and so did the whole Committee,

with the exception of the hon. gentleman, that the Bill and the reforms proposed by it were as much in the interests of tho poor who have dealings with the Pawnbrokers, as they were in the interests of the Trade itself. Every clause in the Bill was carefully considered by the Committee and there are no amendments of importance on the notice paper, with the exception of a few put down by those who are promoting the measure. The Bill will not take up much time—it is generally accepted by both sides of the House—and therefore, I trust, the hon. gentleman will allow us to proceed with it."

But Mr. Orr Ewing was not, as we have said, in a conciliatory mood. He exclaimed: "I am much surprised to hear the remarks which have just been made by the hon. gentleman, the Under Secretary for the Home Department, as to the effect of the evidence which was given upstairs. We had only four witnesses, three of whom were Missionaries, but I differ entirely from the hon. gentleman's view as to the nature of the evidence given. It was against Pawnbroking altogether, and I think you will find that the evidence given by those witnesses has not yet been presented to the House,* so that it is not possible for hon. members to know what it was. I differ entirely from the views the hon. gentleman has just expressed; they were perfectly opposed to this legislation, and the only thing they were in favour of was a point in reference to loans above 40s." After elucidating to the House that a weekly pledge of one shilling would pay 433 per cent., and other "monstrous" features, he concluded by saying: "We can wait another year; the delay will not hurt the Bill

* The evidence was presented to the House on July 8th, and the hon. gentleman was speaking on the 15th.

much, and it is better that we should do that than
that we should pass a Bill which is oppressive upon
the poor, and which is entirely in the interests of
the rich Pawnbrokers. I must insist .on pressing
my motion." Mr. Candlish thought that as the Bill
was acceptable to the House, it would lose nothing
by being postponed; it was unreasonable that a Bill
of 60 clauses should be taken at three o'clock in the
morning. Mr. Anderson (Glasgow), said, as a member of the Select Committee, he thought it was a
good Bill and he hoped they would go through with it.
Two other hon. members spoke, and then the division
was called; the voting resulted in their being 22
for reporting progress, and 71 against, or a majority
of 49 in favour of proceeding. Colonel Barttelot followed with another motion for reporting progress on
account of the lateness of the hour. Mr. Whitwell
then consented and the motion for Committee "was
by leave withdrawn and the further consideration of
the Bill postponed until to-morrow."

Early on Tuesday morning, July 16th, the Parliamentary Sub-Committee sent out an urgent "whip"
to a large number of Members of the House of
Commons, earnestly requesting them to be in attendance and to vote against the amendment of which
Mr. Orr Ewing had given notice. There was
a large number present, but at one period of
the evening there was a narrow escape of a
"count out." Shortly after midnight, however,
the House got into Committee. Clauses 1 to 13
were agreed to without discussion. On clause 14, which
provided that every Pawnbroker, on taking a pledge
in pawn, should give a pawnticket to the pawner,
Mr. Orr Ewing rose and moved as an amendment
the following addition to the clause :—" But no article
shall be taken in pawn on which a less sum than two
shillings shall be advanced, and no wearing apparel.

*bed, or bed clothing, shall be taken in pawn without a
certificate being delivered to the Pawnbroker, signed by
the relieving officer of the district in which the person
pawning such article resides, or by a respectable householder residing in such district, setting forth that the
owner of such articles can pawn the same without injury
to the health or serious inconvenience of himself or any
member of his family; and any Pawnbroker taking such
pledge without such certificate, and any person who shall
give a false certificate, shall be guilty of an offence under
this Act."* After this astounding proposal Mr. Orr
Ewing entered upon a long rambling exposition of
his views, and quoted lengthy extracts from the
evidence which had been given by the Scotch and
Missionary witnesses. He said the Bill was evidently a
Pawnbrokers' Bill, initiated by one section of the Trade,
and there was another section which was against any
legislation at all, because they feared very much that
if the subject came before the House, they might not
be treated so well as they desired. This was evidently
the hon. gentleman's estimate of the motives of the
opposition. He then proceeded to say that all the
evidence which was laid before the Select Committee
was entirely brought forward by Pawnbrokers. He
had ventured to suggest the names of one or two
witnesses from Scotland, and they came before the
Committee and gave *some* evidence.* He then quoted
Mr. Hector, and related a few of the harrowing stories
of drunken wives, with which that witness had
beguiled the time of the Committee withal. Then
came copious quotations from Mr. Arnold, and Mr.
Holford, delivered amid loud cries of "move," "divide,"

---

* Mark the modesty : *some evidence.* The real facts were that
no less than 1,569 questions were answered by the Scotch and
non-Pawnbroking witnesses. Fully 30 per cent of evidence was
given by persons over whom the promoters had no control.

"oh, oh," and laughter. In an exasperated tone the speaker cried "I know very well that I have not the least chance of carrying my motion, *for you are all pledged to the Pawnbrokers.*" At this there were yells of laughter, but the hon. gentleman was not in the least disconcerted, but set on to the luckless Under Secretary. "Now the hon. gentleman told us last night," he said, "that until that evidence was laid before him he shared my opinion, that the Bill was against the interests of the poor people, but that he had changed his mind. If that is so, I really am surprised at the construction of his mind." There was great laughter at this sally. Mr. Orr Ewing then rambled off to the laws of France, and amid cries of "divide" he concluded by saying, " I tell you again that I will speak my mind on this subject, because I know there are many Hon. Members here who have sat for two nights for nothing else but to support the Pawn-brokers. But I say that this system of Pawnbroking for these small sums is a black spot upon our social system. It is degrading and demoralising to the people who deal in it; it does not limit any suffering; it only increases those gross passions which we all wish to see improved. I believe, if the House will agree to my amendment, they will do more to stop dissipation and benefit the working classes than by passing all your Licensing Bills or your Permissive Bills."

Mr. Hambro—a member of the Select Committee—appealed in strong terms to Mr. Orr Ewing to with-draw his amendment. Mr. Hambro said the hon. member had brought up his motion in the form of a clause, but he was constantly defeated upon it, and was always in a minority of one. The opinion of the Committee was that it was very "hard lines" on a poor man that he should not have the opportunity of borrowing a shilling if he wanted one. At the same time Mr. Hambro said he felt very strongly about the Bill; it was brought in by one class, and he wanted to know if those hon. gentlemen who supported it, were not injuring the interests of the poorer classes. Those classes were hardly able to take care of themselves, and there was no evidence from them, but only from the Pawnbrokers and rich men. He should certainly oppose the progress of the Bill through the House.

The Committee then divided, with the following result :—

For the amendment   1
Against   88
—
Majority against Mr. Orr Ewing   87

The announcement of the result was received with derisive laughter and loud cheers. The clause was ordered to stand part of the Bill. Clauses 15 to 29 were agreed to without a division, or even discussion. On clause 30 Mr. Russell Gurney moved the omission of the words, "and profit," where a magistrate should order the amount lent to be repaid, in consequence of the conduct of the owner. Mr. Whitwell called attention to the fact that the clause simply gave the Court of Summary Jurisdiction "discretion" in the matter. The objection was withdrawn, but at a later stage the words were eliminated and the section in the Act only mentions "the amount of the loan," and does not name the profit. On clause 32, providing general restrictions on Pawnbrokers, Mr. Whitwell proposed the addition of a new sub-section, as follows :—"Takes any article in pawn before seven o'clock in the forenoon, or after seven o'clock in the afternoon, except only until eleven o'clock of the evening next before a day mentioned in the last foregoing paragraph of this sub-section." The exception referred to Sunday, Good Friday and Christmas Day. Messrs. Anderson and Winterbotham

strongly opposed the amendment; Messrs. Dalrymple
and Orr Ewing supported it.   Seeing, however,
that the idea did not meet with general accept-
ance, Mr. Whitwell ended the discussion by saying,
"As there is a possibility of this amendment not
being carried, I will not press it any further.   I
therefore beg to withdraw it." Amendment, by leave,
withdrawn, and the clause agreed to.

The remaining clauses and schedules were
ultimately passed, with many verbal amendments;
Mr. J. Lowther, Mr. Monk, Mr. Crawford, and Mr.
Dalrymple, taking part in the discussions.   On the
preamble of the Bill, which was taken last, Mr.
Dalrymple, said, "I shall raise the question about the
25 per cent profit (Fire Insurance Clause) on the
report of the amendments."   Mr. Hambro: I have
already stated my strong objection to this Bill, and
I now give notice that on the report, I shall
move that the report of amendments be considered on
that day three months.   The preamble was then
agreed to and the Bill ordered to be reported, with
amendments, to the House.   The Chairman left the
chair and the House resumed at nearly three o'clock
in the morning.

Mr. Hambro kept his word.   From the 16th July
to the 27th no progress could be made in consequence
of the notice of his amendment being on the proceedings day after day.   By order of the House no
opposed order could be taken after half-past twelve
o'clock; therefore, the Bill was effectually "blocked,"
and although the Parliamentary Sub-Committee
attended nightly in the hope of seeing the order
reached before the prohibited time, no step forward
was made.   A feeling of settled and hopeless despair
prevailed once more in the minds of the workers, at
the prospect of failure, when victory seemed to be so
nearly within their reach.

CHAPTER XXXVI

The gloom and despondency had, by the 26th of July, become intensified, for it was already announced that the Session would terminate about the 10th of August, and there appeared to be no hope that the "block" to the Bill would be removed. Every effort had been made which the ingenuity of the promoters could invent, to induce Mr. Hambro to withdraw his opposition and allow the Bill to proceed. A deputation waited upon him at his hotel; he was seen and spoken to on several occasions in the lobby of the House of Commons; yet he remained obdurate. At length it was discovered that there was a Pawn-broker at Weymouth who was a constituent of Mr. Hambro's. This gentleman was telegraphed to and urged to communicate with his representative, without delay, and press upon him as strongly as possible how important it was to the Pawnbroking body that the Bill should be passed that Session, and to implore Mr. Hambro to allow it to proceed. The plan succeeded, and the amendment in that gentleman's name was removed from the papers, but not—as the Sub-Committee speedily discovered—before he had made arrangements with Mr. Orr Ewing to put his name to a similar amendment against the progress of the Bill.

Attention was now concentrated upon their old
foe. Every conceivable means were exerted to induce
him to relax the bitterness of his opposition, but he
was implacable; his obstinacy defied all attempts at
conciliation. The most influential member on his own
side of the House—including, it was said, the future
Prime Minister—and the Conservative whip, tried
persuasion, but in vain, and the only course which
appeared practicable to Mr. Whitwell was to try and
get the order placed higher on the paper in the hope
that it might be reached before half-past twelve, and
risk defeating the amendment on a division. The
situation was truly desperate. A copy of a memorial
was drawn up, and a large number written by the
law writers and forwarded to hundreds of constituencies, with instructions to obtain signatures,
and as rapidly as possible forward them to the
Members of Parliament. The memorial prayed that
each member would use his influence with Mr. Glyn
—now Lord Wolverton—the Liberal whip, to give the
order for the report a better position on the proceedings. Mr. Orr Ewing was appealed to, and
shown the serious loss the non-passage of the Bill
would be to the promoters, who had laboured over
four years, and spent three thousand pounds, to
attain their long desired amelioration. But it
had but little effect, for he replied to their appeal
by saying, "Why do you not accept my amendment,
and then your Bill will get through?" In return he
was assured that such a regulation would be most
disastrous to the poor, would originate and encourage
illicit trade, while a wholesale and profitable traffic
would be created by householders .giving bogus
certificates (for a consideration) which would thus be
no proof of the bonâ fides of the pledger. He then
modified his proposal and suggested, "Suppose the
limit was fixed at 2s. and the certificates abandoned,

would the Pawnbrokers accept?" To this an un-
conditional and unhesitating negative was given. A
few days later he expressed himself willing to limit
the amount to 1s. without the certificate, and gave
the promoters a few hours for consideration. The offer
of such a compromise, which might save the Bill,
had in it very great temptation; but, after discussing
the subject, it was decided that such a condition
was entirely antagonistic to sound commercial polity,
the liberty of the subject, the objects of the promoters,
and would be injurious to thousands of the necessitons
poor. Before, however, giving a definite reply to
Mr. Orr Ewing it was considered desirable to make
one more effort to convince him of the hardship
such a regulation would inflict upon the needy
pledger. In the hope of compassing his conversion
to more lenient views and sentiments, several
"low" pledge books were borrowed from Pawnbrokers
in Drury-lane and other districts, and, by an arrangement with Mr. Whitwell, they were placed
in a small apartment, called at that time, a
conference, or newspaper room. An appointment
was then made with Mr. Orr Ewing, to inspect the
entries in those books so that he might assure himself on what days of the week pledgings for the
smallest sums took place. The entries indisputably
proved that the largest number of transactions below
one shilling took place on a Friday; a day, probably,
in the whole week on which there is the least indulgence or intemperance. It was thus shown to
the satisfaction of any reasonable mind, that necessity
and not vice or dissipation was the reason for those
small pledgings towards the end of the week.

The attempt, however, to convince Mr. Orr Ewing
was, as on other occasions, an utter failure, as he
spurned such evidence as being unreliable, but if
it was it proved his view of the matter, for he could

not believe that threepences and fourpences and six-
pences could be for any other purpose than the
purchasing of drink.

Having by this time utterly exhausted all their
resources the Committee were reduced to the lowest
extreme of despondency. Hope and courage and
strength were fast draining out. Mr. G. Attenborough, the Chairman, had to retire from the battle
on account of failing health, and so departed, with
his family, to the more bracing climate of North
Wales. Thus the 26th of July had arrived and yet
no prospect of being able to proceed, as the deadlock
continued. At a late hour, the Committee, weary
with waiting, were in conference with Mr. Whitwell, as to there being any escape from their desperate
condition, when Mr. Charles Forster—afterwards Sir
Charles, and but recently deceased—came upon the
scene. This gentleman, for many years the respected
Member for Walsall, was little known outside the
House, but he was a power within. He was Chairman of the Petitions Committee and recognised as
a deputy but unofficial whip on private bills. He
was an acknowledged authority on procedure, was
a general favourite, and familiarly known in the
precincts of the House as " Charley" Foster. It had
been announced by Mr. Gladstone, the Prime Minister,
a day or two previously, that a morning sitting had
been arranged to take the Licensed Victualler's Bill
in Committee, and it was to take place the next day,
Saturday. When Mr. Foster approached, he said,
"Well, no luck, Whitwell?" "No," replied Mr.
Whitwell, "We appear to be at a deadlock; what
would you advise?" "Put it down for to-morrow;
G——" (the party Whip) "won't like it you know,
but put it down, take the risk."

This advice brought a peculiarly grim smile upon
Mr. Whitwell's face, and his eyes had a far off look

as though his thoughts were absorbed in other than
present subjects. He neither dissented nor acquiesced
from or with the advice. He left the Committee in
an absorbed manner, and quite ignorant of what
course he would pursue. Many old Members to whom
the matter was mentioned ominously shook their
heads and thought the day was entirely at the disposal of the Government and that no private member's order would be allowed on the paper.

To the intense joy and satisfaction of the Sub-
Committee, however, they found on the delivery of
the Parliamentary proceedings for the day, that the
third item was printed thus : " 3.   Pawnbroker's
Bill; Report."

The morning sitting, it had been stated in the
House, would not extend over two hours—from two
to four o'clock. The second item was the Autumn
Manœuvres Bill, 3rd Reading, for which the House
had to resume, and being a Government measure did
not occupy many seconds before the Speaker declared
that the "Ayes have it." The Speaker next read
out the order, "Pawnbrokers' Bill, Report," when
Mr. Whitwell rose and said : "Mr. Speaker, I move
that this report be now considered." Then up rose
the ever watchful Mr. Orr Ewing, who said : "Mr.
Speaker, I beg to protest against this Bill being
proceeded with now. I look upon it as a breach of
faith for any member of the Government to insist
on going on with the business to-day after four
o'clock. I know very well that there are many
gentlemen who are in favour of my amendment, that
the report be considered on this day three months,
and who would certainly support it if they were
present, but I do not see them here now. I am
not aware whether there are any present or not,
but I say it is a most unusual thing for Her
Majesty's Government to be a party to any such

proceedings as this.   I beg, sir, to protest against
it, and I beg to move that you do now report progress—(roars of laughter)—that is to say,
I beg to move that the House do now adjourn."
     The Speaker, "Does any honourable member
second that motion?"   There being no response, the
Speaker again rose and said; "As no hon. gentleman
seconds the motion for adjournment, it cannot be put;
the question before the House, therefore, is that this
Bill, as amended, be now considered."   Mr. Orr Ewing
then rose and proposed that the Bill be considered, as
amended, on that day three months.   The Speaker,
addressing the hon. gentleman said, "You have
already spoken in this debate and cannot speak again."
After the laughter, which this retort aroused, had
subsided, Mr. Legh addressed the House and said:
"Mr. Speaker, I should like to ask a question of the
right hon. gentleman, the Secretary of State for the
Home Department.   I should like to ask if he has well
considered this Bill, which is being carried through
the House rather rapidly?   I am told that it is a Bill
greatly in favour of the Pawnbrokers, and consequently
very much against the poor unfortunate people who
go to Pawnbrokers' shops.   All that I want to know
is that this Bill has been well considered, and that it
is not a Bill in favour of Pawnbrokers."
     Mr. Secretary Bruce: "I can assure my hon. friend
that I believe the interests of all parties who are at
all affected by this Bill, have been well and fairly
considered."
     The Speaker then put the question and the report of
amendments was considered and agreed to.   Then
followed a curious, unusual and quite unexpected
episode.   Mr. T. Collins rose and said : "Mr. Speaker,
I beg to move that the Bill be now read a third time."
Sir J. Elphinstone begged to second the motion.
This unexpected move brought up Mr. Orr Ewing

once more, but this time on a question of procedure.
"Mr. Speaker," he gasped out, "I wish to ask whether
it is in order that a Bill can be considered on the
report, and read a third time on the same day?"

Mr. Secretary Bruce: "Under ordinary circumstances such a proceeding would be very unusual,
and it would never be permitted, unless there was an
almost unanimous feeling in favour of the measure.
I believe that the unanimity to-day is only disturbed
by the hon. gentleman opposite, and under the circumstances, I hope he will feel that it is not his duty
to persevere in this opposition to the Bill?"

Mr. Jas. Lowther: "If I might throw out a suggestion, it would be that the hon. member for Dumbartonshire should withdraw his opposition to the Bill,
because there are very serious objections to reading
an opposed Bill on the same day, when it has been
considered on the report of amendments. I hope my
hon. friend will obviate the necessity for that, by
withdrawing his opposition, for I think it would be
very undesirable that such a bad precedent should be
set. I hope he will bow to the unanimous wish of
the House."

Mr. Thos. Hughes: "I join in that appeal to my
hon. friend; I have sat for two years with him in
Committee on this Bill. He fought his case very
well there, but he was in a minority of one upon the
Committee, and now he is in a minority of one here
to-day. I can confirm what has been said by the
right hon. gentleman, the Home Secretary, as to the
careful consideration which has been bestowed upon
the Bill. The subject was before a Select Committee
one year and then it was referred back to them a
second year. I hope my hon. friend will withdraw
his opposition to the Bill."

The Speaker: "I may say that it is a very unusual
thing to read an opposed Bill a third time on the

s

day when the report of amendments has been considered. Of course, if it is the pleasure of the House
to read the Bill a third time to-day, the House is
free to proceed in that matter; but I am bound to
say that where any opposition arises it is contrary
to the practice of the House, to take two stages
of a Bill on the same day, except in cases of
emergency."

Mr. Secretary Bruce: "I appeal to the hon. member for Dumbartonshire not to put himself in the
invidious position of opposing the feeling of the
whole House—otherwise I admit this would be unusual and not according to precedent."

Mr. Orr Ewing: "I have no wish to oppose the
general feeling of the House, but I can assure the
right hon. gentleman that I do not stand alone, and
if I had time to go into the whole matter to-day, and
to show the nature of the evidence of the Scotch
witnesses, and the strong feeling of Scotchmen against
the Bill, I could show that in a practical light. But
I have no wish to continue to oppose the Bill in this
House, as an evil precedent might be brought in
by the extraordinary act of reading an opposed Bill
a third time on the day it has gone through the
report. I had much rather pledge myself to offer
no opposition, so that the House may keep itself
in order, and therefore, if the third reading is
pressed, I shall withdraw my opposition."

Mr. James Lowther: "I thank my hon. friend for
the course he has adopted. It is quite understood
that it is by consent, that the Bill is read a third
time now?"

Mr. T. Collins: "Under the circumstances, I withdraw my motion for the third reading." Motion by
leave, withdrawn.

Mr. Whitwell: "I fix the third reading for Monday next."

On Monday morning, following this eventful day, the Parliamentary papers were eagerly scanned by the Sub-Committee. To their intense pleasure and satisfaction the order for the third reading of the Pawnbrokers' Bill, appeared without the little a (a) which always signifies an amendment, or in other words a block. So on Monday, July 29th, in the early hours of the morning, the Bill was reached as an unopposed measure, read a third time, and passed.

CHAPTER XXXVII

THE STRUGGLE THROUGH THE LORDS

On Tuesday, July 30th, the Bill was read a first time in the House of Lords as a matter of course. It is not necessary that a Bill brought up from the Commons should have a sponsor for its introduction and first reading; but some noble Lord must undertake to move the second reading and to explain the objects and purposes of the proposed legislation. The small Parliamentary Sub-Committee had been so absorbed with their troubles, difficulties and desire to overcome the menacing obstacles in the lower House, that their thought of imminent need had not travelled as quickly as events. The second reading of the Bill was to be taken on Thursday, the 1st August, so that there only remained some 48 hours to procure the required agency from among the Peers. In this new and pressing emergency, Lord Sandon, then one of the members for Liverpool, was applied to, and in response to the earnest appeals made to him, promised to endeavour to prevail upon his father, the Earl of Harrowby, then very far advanced in years, to undertake the duty of proposing the second reading of the Bill. Little time remained, when the assent of the noble Lord had been obtained, to give his Lordship the necessary instruction and information to enable him to perform his duty. It was arranged with Lord Sandon, that the Secretary should attend at the Earl's residence, 39, Grosvenor-square, and from blue books, statistics and other available matter instruct him so that he might construct a speech which would convey intelligibly, the objects, history and progress of the measure, before the noble Lords assembled. The interview extended over some two hours, and although there are a few palpable misconceptions, easily detected by those persons well acquainted with the subject, the address and the scheme were delivered and unfolded in a clear and concise manner.

The labour at this period was severely exacting and incessant. The broiling heat of the early August days, told upon the toiling trio with terrible effect. Like weary travellers in the desert they hardly possessed strength to reach the goal which was within sight. They had become so thoroughly mentally and physically depressed and overworked, that their very courage seemed—like Bob Acre's—to be oozing out of the palms of their hands. The restless and inevitable Scotchmen were as busy as a certain disreputable personage is said to be in a gale of wind. The air was thick, as it were, with amendments. Many of these Mr. Whitwell modified and agreed to, and with so much patching and mending and siftings many important matters were eliminated, about this time, and it was with immense difficulty that they were re-inserted. The members of the Sub-Committee, when in attendance at the House, were frequently called upon to copy amendments which must be put in before the House rose, so, that the work became so bewildering and exhausting that it was felt it had become an absolute necessity to invoke additional help. Consequently, Mr. H. E. Kidson, the Financial Secretary, readily consented to give all the assistance in his power, and went from

Liverpool, and plunged into the fight with such fresh-
ness and vigour, as to infuse new courage and life
into the well-nigh exhausted and now veteran trio.

On Thursday, August 1st, the Earl of Harrowby
moved the second reading of the Bill. In his address
to the House he said that as that was the first
appearancce of the measure before their Lordships,
he must trouble them with a few observations, for
the purpose of stating the object of it. He alluded
to the long period the old Act had been in existence,
and the little legislation on the subject which had
taken place since the year 1800. It had been for some
time desirable that a reconsideration of the whole
laws upon Pawnbroking should take place—hence a
Select Committee had been appointed in the House
of Commons in 1870 and a variety of evidence
taken. That Committee reported to the House in
1871 and recommended many changes as being
desirable to be made. His Lordship concluded : " I
believe also, on the part of her Majesty's Government, the Secretary of State for the Home Department is quite satisfied that the interests of all
parties are properly provided for in this Bill, and I
therefore find it unnecessary to detain your Lordships with any further details, but if necessary, I
shall be quite willing to go into them when the Bill
is in Committee and when there will be an ample
opportunity for doing so. At present I shall only
ask your Lordship's acquiescence in the second
reading of the Bill, upon the ground that the
measure is the result of a very full investigation by
two Committees of the other House of Parliament
and that it has received the support of all parties
in the House of Commons. I have no doubt that
my noble friend opposite (the Earl of Morley) who
represents the Home Department in this House, will
be able to confirm my statement, and I therefore

ask your Lordships now to read the Bill a second time."

Some considerable alarm was caused by the un-expected uprising of Lord Stanley, of Alderley, in the character of a hostile critic. He commenced his remarks very mildly by drawing attention to the increase in the rate of interest, but he thought that increase was compensated for by the reduction charged for pawn-tickets; but he objected to the reduction in the charge made for licences, because it would increase the number of Pawnbroking estab-lishments in the Metropolis and make them less respectable. He should propose, as an amendment in Committee, that no such reduction be made. His Lordship's concluding remarks were as follows: "I shall also propose another amendment of which I beg leave to give notice, and that is that the second proviso in the fourth schedule shall be omitted. By that proviso, whenever the charge shall amount to one farthing, the Pawnbrokers are allowed to charge a half-penny; and whenever it amounts to three-farthings, they are allowed to charge a penny. There seems to be very great objection to that; because it puts an unnecessary burden on the poorer classes. I trust this amendment will meet with the accept-ance of those who promote the Bill."

The fate of the Bill appeared to be trembling in the balance, when the Marquis of Salisbury began a spirited attack upon it. "My lords," he said, "I cannot help calling the attention of the noble Earl opposite (the Earl of Morley), and of the Govern-ment, to the practice of passing through Bills at this time of the Session, when we cannot possibly inquire into them. If a Bill came up here, prepared by her Majesty's Government, and prepared under their responsibility, of course it would be a very different matter; but this Bill was prepared by a

private member, and then brought before a Select
Committee, and I do not believe that there is any
responsibility attaching to it at all. It is brought up
to us at a time when we cannot possibly examine it;
and I hope that before it is allowed to pass a second
reading your Lordships will look at the schedules
and see what it is that it does. It begins by repealing a statute of the time of James the First,
the effect of which is to enable persons whose property has been stolen and pawned in a Pawnbroker's
shop, to recover the same. Then, again, the schedule
deals with the very long Act of the 39th and 40th
years of George III., for amending the law of Pawnbroking, and with a number of subsidiary laws which
have been passed since. I will not undertake to say
all that it does or does not do; but there is one
thing which I find it does do, and that is that it
interferes very considerably *with the right of free
trade* between the Pawnbroker and those who go to
him. It increases the rates which the Pawnbroker
may charge, without—so far as I know—anyone
having been heard in defence of the rights of those
who are the customers of the Pawnbroker. I am
told that the Pawnbrokers are in favour of this Bill,
and I dare say they are, for it enables them to
charge 25 per cent. where before they were only
allowed to charge 20. No doubt it reduces the price
of the pawn-ticket; but the small sum which they
can charge for that pawn-ticket has this effect—
that on a month's loan it increases the 25 to 50 per
cent. I believe it is perfectly true that with the
Pawnbrokers of London small loans of two or three
shillings form a very large portion—I may say an
enormous share—of the number of loans which go
to form their business. Now, my lords, it does not
seem to me to be fair that, without more inquiry
than we are now able to give to the matter, we

should alter the law on a point which so vitally
affects the poorer classes, who have less chance
than any other set of people, of making their voices
heard. We ought not to pass a Bill of this kind
without further inquiry and the exercise of more
care; and I confess that I dislike very much this
subject being handled, at all, otherwise than by the
responsible ministers of the Crown. This Pawnbroking legislation is the remnant of an older state
of things; it is a kind of boulder that has wandered
from an old formation, and is found resting on the
new. It is a remnant of the old usury laws, left
existing in the middle of all our free trade principles.
I have no objection to let the matter rest for the
present; we need be in no hurry, and we might
give the Government time to digest it and take it
up. When it is so taken up it can only be dealt
with in one sense, and that is in the sense of *perfect
freedom of trade between the Pawnbroker and those who
go to him.* No doubt in such a Trade as this you
must have precautions in the interest of criminal
justice; but the great object you have in view is
to establish perfect freedom of trade. But the danger
is that if you now consider the whole of this legislation and give *pledges* to this particular *trade*, you
may have just such a difficulty as you have lately
had in the licensed victuallers—you may have vested
interests to deal with. In whatsoever point of view,
therefore, you look at this Bill, I feel that it is not
right to deal with the subject at such a season of
the year without more examination. The Bill is one
which affects the interests of classes who cannot now
be heard here and *it perpetuates a remnant of the
usury laws contrary to the principles of modern legislation.* My only subject of regret is, that I should
have to oppose my noble friend upon the cross
benches in this matter: but I confess that I must

oppose him, and therefore I move that the Bill be
read a second time on this day three months."

The feelings of perturbation which held possession
of the Sub-Committee during the delivery of the
foregoing speech and its concluding motion, we shall
not attempt to describe.   Utter defeat, ruin, rout
and disgrace appeared inevitable and imminent.
All hope of future progress and success seemed
shattered at a blow.

The words of the Earl of Morley, who followed,
sounded weak and ineffective in their ears.   He, however, appealed to the noble Marquis to remember
what scrutiny the Bill had passed through.   The
narratives about the Select Committees were repeated and particular stress was laid on the fact
that the Bill had received the most careful consideration of the Home Secretary.   It had besides been
agreed to by all parties, and that when an attempt
was made to obstruct its progress only one hon.
member was found to oppose that progress.   The
speaker hoped that when it was remembered the time
the measure had occupied in the House of Commons,
and the general opinion which existed in its favour
on all sides, their lordships would agree to give it
a second reading.

The Earl of Harrowby briefly replied.   He reminded
the Marquis of Salisbury that the Bill contained a
nearer approximation to free trade than the existing
law.   After a few further observations, the Marquis
signified that he did not intend to press his amendment, and to the intense relief and satisfaction of the
Sub-Committee *the Bill was read a second time!*

The House was up immediately, the foregoing
order being the last item on the papers.   The Marquis of Salisbury was approached in the corridor,
and he graciously consented to receive the promoters on the following Saturday at his house, 20,

Arlington-street. Mr. Dicker, Mr. Telfer and the Hon. Sec. attended, and the conversation occupied quite an hour, his lordship entering fully and freely into his objections to the Bill. The deputation left with a confident feeling that all danger from that quarter had been averted. He had, however, as the leader of the Opposition, uttered his protest, but the main object appeared to be to flout the Government. It was also deemed advisable to seek an interview with Lord Stanley of Alderley. He was found at the Langham Hotel, and received the gentlemen with courtesy and patience. In a few minutes' conversation it became evident that there was nothing dangerous in him, his principal "craze" being on the question of what he termed "disfranchising the farthing." On other points he had no decided opinions, and he became so far friendly as to take charge of the Bill and pilot it through its remaining stages, as the Earl of Harrowby had been called away from town.

The Bill was taken in Committee of the whole House on Tuesday, August 6th, leaving just a sufficient number of days to work through before the prorogation on the following Saturday. On going into Committee Lord Stanley explained that in the absence of the Earl of Harrowby, he had undertaken the conduct of the Bill. The Marquis of Salisbury, although he had given his assurance to the deputation, that he had no design upon the measure, still had another fling at the Government. He could not help fearing, he said, that at a later period, when Her Majesty's Government should find leisure to take the matter up for themselves, they would find that there was no real issue from the difficulties of the Pawnbroking trade except by the adoption of a system of genuine free trade. At present they had hampered the Trade and the customers by a series of trade regulations, but they did not do what a thoroughly paternal Government might do to protect the poor man altogether from the temptation of pawning small articles of property, which if the paternal theory were to be accepted, would be the wisest use to which it could be put. But, on the other hand they did not adopt free trade. He knew the objection taken to free trade in relation to that Bill, was that a Pawnbroker's trade is peculiarly liable to abuse, in consequence of its being made use of by those who dreaded the criminal law, and who wanted to dispose of articles which they had stolen. Perhaps his experience of the administration of the criminal law had not been very long or very wide, but he had never heard that any articles which thieves had pilfered, were in the least degree difficult to get rid of *without applying for the aid of the Pawnbroker.* Thieves knew very well that the Pawnbrokers' shops were under the supervision of the police, and they knew that if they went to a Pawnbroker to get rid of their stolen goods, those goods would be handed over to the police in a very short time. They, therefore, find buyers of another kind, and they never have any difficulty in doing so. His Lordship concluded in the following terms: " All the restrictions that you impose upon the Pawnbrokers do not enable you to lay your hands on a thief with any greater certainty than would be the case if Pawnbroking were a perfectly free trade. I do not wish to detain your lordships, because, as I have already said, I do not intend to bring this matter to a practical issue to-day; but I do wish, if it is of any use, to enter my protest against this Bill, and against the constitution of any vested interest which may be adverse to any future reform, or any future legislation in the Trade."

The Earl of Morley made a few remarks, after

which the House went into Committee upon the Bill, Lord Redesdale in the chair.

The Duke of Argyl desired to observe, in reply to the noble Marquis, that the Bill created no vested interest.

Lord Stanley, of Alderley, said that in the absence of the Earl of Harrowby, he had a number of amendments to move. They were all verbal and did not require any explanation.

Some twenty amendments were moved and agreed to *en bloc*. Many of them were of slight consequence, but others were of greater — indeed almost vital importance, and it was fortunate they did not attract greater attention. One instance may be related. Clause 38 was originally drawn to include the words, "If a Pawnbroker is convicted on indictment" for receiving stolen goods, his licence should be forfeited. In the second Select Committee the words "on indictment" were struck out. It was some time before this important elimination was discovered, but from the moment it was, every possible effort was made to get the words re-inserted. If the clause had been passed with these protecting words omitted, every Pawnbroker to-day, would be at the mercy of any lay or stipendiary magistrate throughout the country, and his licence liable to forfeiture for any trivial offence the justices might magnify as being deserving of conviction. Happily the full importance of the matter did not attract attention and the amendment passed through with the rest. In the hurry to get through, several blunders were committed. Among the rest an alteration was made in the wording of the example of the C ticket in schedule 3. It applies to loans above forty shillings, and was hastily copied from the form of the B ticket, and it was not noticed that the words "for the sum of eleven shillings" had been left standing, and appear so in the Act now.

Lord Stanley then carried his amendment about the farthings and the Bill passed through Committee.

On Wednesday, August 7th—the only Wednesday sitting in the House of Lords during the Session— the Bill was reported as amended, and on Thursday, the 8th, it was read a third time. It went down to the Commons at a quarter to four o'clock on Friday morning and the Lords' amendments were agreed to.

There only remained one more ceremony to be performed — and that was "THE CROWNING OF THE EDIFICE."

CHAPTER XXXVIII

After the intense strain and prolonged excitement, extending over many months, it was a curious—indeed, almost painful—sensation which the Sub-Committee experienced on the morning of Saturday, August 10th, to find their occupation had suddenly gone and that there was no further work for them to perform. After the violent and continuous storm with which they had battled through many anxious and exhausting days and nights, a dead calm had ensued. The reaction was depressing: as it was difficult to realise that nothing more could be done. They had time now to reflect on the past, and to see that whatever defects and shortcomings their fellow-tradesmen might detect in the finished work, there was no opportunity for anything to be amended. In a few hours the Bill would become an Act, and be the law of the land, whether its effect would be for either good or bad.

How closely the race against time had been contested, will be seen from the first paragraph in the following letter from Mr. Whitwell, now, for the first time, made public. Although it was dated the 9th, it was written in the small hours of Saturday morning:—

"St. James Lodge, Chapel Place,
"Duke St., Westminster, S.W.
"August 9th, 1872.

"Dear Sir,—It was five minutes to four o'clock this morning when I moved that the House agree with the Lords' amendments, which were passed. The work is, therefore, completed, and I trust that the Bill may help to maintain the character of the Trade it is intended to govern.

"A great sacrifice of time and convenience has been required from those who have had to carry the measure to a successful termination.

"For myself, I do not say that I should have refused my assistance, had I foreknown the labour—because I was convinced of the need of legislation, and I knew that so important a Bill could not be carried by a private member without trouble, time and perseverance—but I might, nevertheless, have shrunk from the attempt. I must confess that when I saw Government bills, and those of eminent private individuals, falling on the right hand and the left, I could sometimes only hope against hope. The delay in the introduction of the measure, consequent on waiting for the answer of the Government, placed the Bill at great disadvantage, and had we not 'got *into* Committee' by stealing a march upon Mr. Orr Ewing, or had we not put it down on the Saturday, contrary to the opinion of many experienced and official members, we should have been shipwrecked.

"I have now to congratulate you and the Committee on success, and I wish in the plainest and fullest terms to express my thorough appreciation of the unremitting zeal and ability of the gentlemen of the Committee, through whose exertions this has been accomplished, and without which no Member of Parliament could have been successful. I hope you will convey this to Mr. Geo. Attenborough and your colleagues.

"I will say nothing of the opposition in the Trade, which opened the way for much of our difficulties coming in, but one thing I will add, that during the three years' campaign I have learned to place unhesitating reliance on the statements of the gentlemen who have communicated with me, whether made for or against the case.

"I did not mention to you that at the two last stages in the Lords there were fresh attempts made from Scotland to introduce new matter into the Bill.

"I am, yours truly,
"JOHN WHITWELL.

"A. Hardaker, Esq."

To this letter the Committee replied, expressing as strongly as the medium would allow, their sincere gratitude for the generous and devoted services Mr. Whitwell had rendered to the whole Trade. Through-

XXXVIII   VICTORY—DISSOLUTION—REWARDS   289

out the difficult task of conducting the measure
through Parliament he had displayed great determination and strongly defined purpose, together
with a knowledge of the forms of the House which
aroused the admiration of the Committee. He was
always accessible, and the Hon. Secretary had morning
.audiences at his house during many weeks as to the
business of the day, while his fertility of resource and
quick appreciation of the position in any emergency,
·enabled him to carry the largest work of a private
member to a successful issue during the Session of
1872. Many other Members were also specially
thanked for their support and assistance, including
Lord Sandon, now the Earl of Harrowby, Mr.—later,
Sir—Chas. Foster, Mr. Plimsoll, Sir James Elphinstone, Mr. Glyn, now Lord Wolverton, Mr. Alderman
Carter, and the then Earl of Harrowby.

At two o'clock on the eventful day on which the
Bill was to receive the Royal Assent, the Members of
the Sub-Committee went over to the House and were
just in time to see Mr. Inspector Denning—for many
years a familiar figure in the precincts of the House—
heading a small procession consisting of the Usher of
the Black Rod and a few other dignitaries, who were
on their way to the Commons with a message from
the Lords for the Speaker to attend. In a few minutes
the procession returned, and was considerably aug-
mented by the addition of the Speaker, Mace Bearer,
Sergeant at Arms and others. The Speaker's train was
borne by an official in Court dress, tie wig, silk stockings,
sword, &c. After these followed a crowd of Members,
among whom were Mr. Winterbotham, Mr. Whitwell,
Mr. Plimsoll, Mr. Mundella, Col. Beresford, and several
others who had befriended the Trade. The remnant
of the Sub-Committee joined in the tail of the procession and soon found themselves in the "gilded
chamber," with the Speaker standing in front of them.

T

On the woolsack were seated five odd-looking figures
who resembled a section of Madame Tussaud's famous
wax-work exhibition. These seedy looking individuals
were habited, some in crimson robes, trimmed with
tarnished gold lace; the Lord Chancellor in a black
robe; the Bishop of London had on an ermine tippet
and wore a college cap, while the other four wore
antiquated, not to say dilapidated cocked hats. The
Lord Chancellor handed the Royal Commission to
the Clerk, Sir John Lefevre, who immediately read
the document, which in the most circumlocutory
language imaginable conferred the necessary powers
upon the five noble lords to represent Her Majesty,
and give the Royal Assent to Bills and prorogue
Parliament.

The ceremony of giving the Royal Assent is a
quaint one. The Clerk to the House takes up a Bill,
bows low to the automata sitting on the woolsack
and reads out the title. The Royal Commissioners
raise their hats and bow in return. The Clerk then
turns about and faces the Speaker and Members of
the Commons, and exclaims "La Reigne le veult,"
which is old Norman French for *the Queen wills it,*
and the Bill is thenceforth the law of the land.

Time passed, and Bill after Bill became law, till
our fears were excited that perhaps after all, the
Pawnbrokers' Bill had been mislaid. Such a calamity
seemed to be within possibility, for we had been
entertained a day or two before, by the recital of a
legend that in "the reign of James the Second," as
they sing in "Trial by Jury," a Bill had been lost in
transit from the Commons to the Lords, and had
never since been found. We were relieved at last,
however, by the Clerk reading the title :—"A Bill
for consolidating, with amendments, the Acts relating to Pawnbrokers in Great Britain." Then came
the profound obeisance to the five titled occupants

of the woolsack, who in turn bowed and raised their hats, and the Clerk once more faced the Speaker and with "La Reigne le veult," the Royal Assent was given, and for the first time in the history of Pawnbroking a complete Act was passed regulating the Trade. The struggle had been a protracted, tedious and severe one, but tenacity had conquered the numerous forms of hostility and opposition, and secured victory at last.

On that day, "big with the fate" of future Pawnbroking, and which should in the ordinary estimate of human emotions have been the most festive the Committee had ever yet enjoyed, those three dejected and spiritless individuals, suddenly finding their occupation gone, were plunged into the lowest depths of despair. After having been so closely connected during the long campaign of four years and four months—in daily communion almost—it was suddenly apparent to each one's consciousness that on that day they must part. The tension which had been continuous for years, snapped so suddenly, that the situation was difficult to realize, and the last and greatest "notch" was celebrated in a dull and dismal stupour which it would be impossible either to be imagined by the reader or described by the writer.

It was soon, however, discovered that there was still some work to be done, but it was not in the Parliamentary groove. The Executive were called together, reports and accounts submitted, and arrangements made for the dissolution of the Association. It was decided to convene a final meeting of the guarantors and subscribers, to be held in Manchester. The date fixed was Thursday, November 28th, 1872, and the place of meeting the Clarence Hotel, an old and famous establishment many years ago, but since swept away for improvements. So large was the attendance that it became apparent

T 2

there would be insufficient accommodation. Fortunately, the Memorial Hall in Albert-square happened to be available, which was secured and the meeting held there. Mr. George Attenborough presided, and after an introductory speech of congratulation to the members, the Hon. Sec. read reports from the Executive, Parliamentary and Sub-Committees. The Financial Secretary produced a balance sheet which showed the total receipts to have been £3,137 6s. 4d., and the total expenditure to be £2,954 7s. 8d., leaving a balance in hand of £182 18s. 8d.

A series of resolutions was passed in the midst of the greatest enthusiasm. The first being on the motion of the Chairman, seconded by Mr. Cooper (Staleybridge):—"That the report and cash account now read be received, adopted, printed, and circulated amongst the guarantors and subscribers." The second was on the motion of Mr. John Grantham, seconded by Mr. Blakey (Leeds):—"That the balance of money remaining in hand after the discharging of all liabilities, be placed in the hands of Mr. Little, treasurer of the Committee which has been formed at Liverpool, for the purpose of presenting Mr. Hardaker with a national recognition of the valuable services he has rendered to the Trade." The third was moved by Mr. John Dicker and seconded by Mr. Brook (Halifax): — "That the best thanks of the Pawnbrokers of Great Britain are due, and are hereby most gratefully tendered, to John Whitwell, Esq., M.P., for his kindness in having undertaken the conduct of the Pawnbrokers' Bill, and still more for the great zeal, devotion and practical acquaintance with the forms of the House displayed by him on all occasions, without which it would have been impossible to have obtained the passing of so important a measure as the Pawnbrokers' Act, 1872." The next was a resolution moved by Mr. Beesley, and seconded

by Mr. John Eaton (Sheffield):—" That a copy of the
foregoing resolution be suitably engrossed, signed by
every member of the Executive Committee, and forwarded to Mr. Whitwell by the Hon. Sec. Another resolution was proposed by Mr. J. A. Telfer, and seconded
by Mr. McKay, " That the cordial thanks of the Pawnbrokers of Great Britain are due, and hereby respectfully
tendered, to Mr. Alderman Carter, M.P., Samuel
Plimsoll, Esq., M.P., and Chas. Foster, Esq., M.P., for
the efficient assistance given by them to the cause of
Pawnbroking Reform, and the constant and unvarying
kindness shown by them to the Members of the
Parliamentary Committee." Then, on the motion of
Mr. Councillor Fairhurst, seconded by Mr. A. Porter
(Manchester), it was resolved, " That this meeting
desires to recognise, with much gratitude, the eminent
services rendered to the Trade in the procuring of
the Pawnbrokers' Act, 1872, by the Executive Committee, and hereby tender to the Secretary and each
of those gentlemen, the best and most sincere thanks
of this Meeting." Then a resolution was adopted, on
the motion of Mr. Dickinson, seconded by Mr. Aber-
crombie (Liverpool), "That the Liverpool Association
be requested to take charge of the various books and
documents, and that the materials be presented to
the Hon. Sec." Then Mr. Heys moved, and Mr.
Walker (Macclesfield), seconded, " That the Pawnbroking Parliamentary Reform Association, having
completed the purpose for which it was instituted, be
and is hereby dissolved." A long and complex resolution was adopted, on the motion of Mr. John Tatton,
the late and lamented Hon. Sec. of the Manchester
Association, seconded by Mr. Starling, recognising the
laborious efforts of certain gentlemen upon whom the
principal part of the work had devolved, namely,
Messrs. G. Attenborough, Heys, Dickinson, Dicker,
Telfer, and Kidson, and the meeting felt that some

memento should be presented to them, and recommended that the London and Liverpool Committees should undertake the matter in conjunction with the Hardaker Testimonial Fund. The concluding resolutions were that the hours of business should be voluntarily restricted, and that the London and Liverpool Committees should continue their efforts to obtain a satisfactory solution of the insurance question. A vote of thanks, carried by acclamation in a most enthusiastic manner, to the Chairman, closed the proceedings of the last meeting of the Reform Association, which had first seen light at Nottingham in April, 1868.

Before dismissing this business portion of our narrative, it will be not a little interesting to record the positions held by large towns as to their contributions to the funds of the Association. We give, therefore, a list of the seven cities and towns from which contributions of over £100 were made. Thus London stood at the head of the list with £558 10s., but can barely claim pre-eminence for it was closely followed by Manchester and Salford with £535 18s. 6d. Then came Liverpool with £366 13s. 6d.; Glasgow, £177 17s.; Leeds, £155 19s.; Sheffield, £132 19s. 6d.; and Nottingham, £113 17s. This last amount was contributed by only twenty business houses, which speaks well for the enthusiasm of the "birth place" of the cause of Reform.

The last scene of all in this strange eventful history, was enacted at Liverpool, on the 6th of August, 1873. For the previous nine months there had been working, in the most devoted and slavish manner, a determined little body, at Liverpool, known as the Testimonial Committee. Mr. Councillor Fairhurst was the Chairman, and the Hon. Sec. was Mr. Wm. Guyler, who laboured with such incessant and unselfish devotion as to make the recipients entertain lasting feelings of gratitude to him. The result of this devotion and labour was a sum closely approaching £2,000. Of this was awarded to the Honorary Secretary £1,000 and a gold watch, chain, and a timepiece; to Mr. John Dicker, a full service of silver plate; to Mr. Geo. Attenborough, drawing and dining-room clocks, vases, and silver dessert service; to Mr. John Ashbridge Telfer, a gold watch and chain, lady's diamond *suite*, and illuminated record of the event; to Mr. Henry E. Kidson, a gold watch, chain, diamond ring and pin; to Mr. Dickinson, richly chased silver salver, and *suite* of silver dinner and dessert service; and to Mr. Edward Heys, a library of standard and scientific books.

On the 6th August a Banquet was given at the Adelphi Hotel, Liverpool, Mr. Fairhurst presiding, when the above valuable testimonials were presented. · Among those present were Mr. Alderman Carter, M.P. (Leeds), Mr. H. Bremner, Solicitor, Mr. Folkard, Mr. Alfred George (who acted as Secretary to the Testimonial Fund in London), Mr. Child, Mr. Bullworthy, Mr. Layman, the last five gentlemen being from London, and a large number of Pawnbrokers from all parts of the country.

Such were the honours by which the conquerors were decorated. This was the last, but brilliant scene, in the drama of Pawnbroking Reform; "Which, being finished, here the story ends."

CHAPTER XXXIX

When the new Act came into operation on the first
day of January, 1873, expressions of satisfaction and
congratulation were to be heard from all quarters.
A new era, it was supposed, had dawned for the
Pawnbroking Trade, and it was felt that those who
were workers within its ranks could breathe freely
and "look the whole world in the face," for they
could act legally and uprightly and yet profitably,
without resorting to violations or evasions of the
law, as had been done, under the old, but now defunct
Act.

After many years of agitation, labour, dissatisfac-
tion and turmoil, there was now peace; litigation
was to be unknown; the Act was so clear and simple
that disputed questions of law could not arise; nay,
it was even soberly and sincerely believed by many,
that all necessity for Protective and Defensive Associations had passed away, and there seemed no·
reason why—

> " Peace,
> Dear nurse of arts, plenties, and joyful births,
> Should not in this best garden of the world,"

be of long, unbroken continuance. For some time,

our own Trade organ, the *Pawnbrokers' Gazette*,
had little to chronicle but the proceedings of uneventful meetings of different Associations, and could
give space enough to record the progress made by
those two admirable and beneficent Institutions, the
"Charitable" and the Journeymen's "Benevolent."
The honour and credit of supporting these organiza-
tions—to say nothing of the large number of similar
but smaller Associations dotted all over the Kingdom—might excite admiration in a community of
double the number than that of which the Pawnbroking body is composed; while the large amounts
dispensed yearly, reflect the highest honour upon
all concerned for the humanity, charity and benevo-
lence displayed.

The first of these Institutions called the "Charitable," was established as far back as 1823, and is
said to have been the first Trade Charity established
in London. It was instituted in the first instance
to relieve the necessities of the Assistants only. It
was ushered to the Pawnbroking world in a prospectus of a highly florid description of composition,
which Mr. Hows considered so valuable as a scarce
historical record as to quote it in full. Our space,
being limited, our readers must be content with a
few specimen extracts. It begins with rather a bold
assertion as to the completeness of the human feeling
which pervades us as a Nation, and says:—"It is a
peculiar characteristic of the era in which we live
that the wide wings of charity overshadow the
world; and justly pre-eminent is our nation in this—
that distress can scarcely present itself in any shape
without finding a heart to console or a hand to
relieve it." Alluding to what had been done by the
"opulent members" of other professions, the document goes on to give some reasons why the
Pawnbrokers should imitate such good examples, as

thus:—"In many businesses the moral character of
the man is looked upon as a matter of minor consideration. If he be but strong it is not minded that
he is uncivil; if he returns to his work punctually
and soberly in the morning, it is not objected to him
that he was seen inebriated or in mean company after
he had left it at night. But a Pawnbroker's servant
must conform to stricter rules. He must be scrupu-
lously sober and honest; he must be cleanly, civil
and respectful; he must observe good hours, want
no holidays, and when to these all the other decencies
of life are joined, they have but the weight of
negative qualities, for which, alone, no one would
keep him. He must superadd intelligence, activity
and habitual industry, or all his excellencies are
nothing worth. Tied by his profession to the counter,
forbidden any intimacy with the customers, he can
form no connexions, has no chance of other pursuits,
and the best friendship he can hope to acquire is
that of the master who retains him. If he grow
rich in such service his integrity may be questioned!
If any accident happens to his sight he is useless!
If he marry, it is a great chance whether he can
keep his place or any other master will employ
him."

If the foregoing is a true sketch—and the men
who composed it were men of experience—of the
Pawnbrokers' Assistant of the period, his lot, to say
the least, was not a happy one, nor his prospects
of the brightest. This is followed by the *raison
d'être* for practical sympathy being extended to him,
and the "prospectus" proceeds:

"Serving under these disadvantages, who would
neglect such men in their extremities; or, when they
have lived to old age in our service, abandon them
to the world? Nature revolts at the idea! A man
of ordinary feeling will not turn loose upon its mercy

a worn-out horse or dog; and shall we treat that
human being with less commiseration who has lived
under the same roof with us for years—in sickness
has been the object of our solicitude—in health, the
creature to whom our property is confided—and who
has acquired that confidence and merited those at-
tentions by sharing in our disquietudes, rejoicing in
our successes, considering our interests as his own,
and promoting our fortunes to the utmost of his
abilities? Who that reflects on this will venture to
affirm, they have not irresistible claims on our
generosity and justice, in despite of the slight faults
by which their lustre is tarnished?"

The last sentence is decidedly enveloped in rhe-
torical fog, for it is not explained in what the
"slight faults" consist.   There would be little
"lustre," we venture to think, in sleeping on the
counter, working unreasonable and inhumanly long
hours, with recreation for a short period only, on two
or three nights in the week. This was the treatment
of the Assistant seventy years ago; he of our day may
be thankful he lives within a measurable distance
of the twentieth century. This remarkable address,
in another paragraph, indulges in prophecy; whether,
or not, it has been realised, we leave to the knowledge and experience of our readers. It says, after
speaking of the successful establishment of a
charity :—

"This once established, ask yourselves, will your
servants quit you now, as heretofore, on every
pettish whim or idle speculation? No. Taught by
those instances of kindness to respect you, you will
acquire an ascendency over them which the heart
rarely yields to interested motives; and it may be
hoped they will think of quitting you with that feeling
of reluctance, which a son endures in separating from
his parental abode.

"It has been but too much objected to us already, probably by those who know us least, that parsimonious habits and cold maxims of prudence, operating on an acquaintance with human wretchedness, have rendered us callous to the miseries of life ; and although a just inquiry would have ascertained that where parochial distress or national calamity have claimed the aid of those who earned their bread, such liberal contributions have scarcely been found in any branch of trade; yet it remains with us still more forcibly to rebut the charge, by thus generously providing for those who have been worn out in well-doing in our service; and our rejoicing will be, if we, who are supposed to be so cold and cautious—earning wealth with so much pains, and hoarding it with so much care—can communicate warmth to gentler natures, and induce other trades to go and do like-wise to those who have similar claims on them, and: whose claims are equally urgent."

Without quoting further from this somewhat re- markable prospectus, we may state that the Institution was inaugurated, and it came into partial operation, but ten years elapsed before the funds were made available for the relief of decayed Masters. From year to year it gradually progressed, and about 1840 the idea of building the Alms-Houses was promulgated. Many leading Members of the Trade, including Mr. Neate, who acted as Honorary Secretary,. took up the cause with great enthusiasm, and worked with unflagging energy, and finally the promoters attained their object. The foundation stone was laid amid much display and rejoicing in 1849 by Sir James Duke, Bart., M.P. In April, 1850, a meeting of Members of the Institution was called to pass the revised rules. On the motion of Mr. Neate, it was resolved that the following address, which is a brief epitome of the Institution's progress, should be adopted:—

"This Institution was established in 1823, for the relief of sick and decayed Journeymen Pawnbrokers; in the year 1834 it was renovated by extending the sphere of its usefulness to decayed Masters, and the widows and children of all Members of the Trade; in 1840 it was further enlarged by granting pensions to deserving Pawnbrokers in their old age; and in 1850 Alms-Houses were built at West Ham, Essex, for their occupation." In January of that year a grand Ball was held in the Queen's Rooms, Hanover-square, under the patronage of Sir James Duke, Bart., M.P., and the Sheriff of London, Donald Nicoll, Esq., in aid of the Building fund. On June 21st, 1850, a grand festival was held in the new building, which was that day opened by Sir James Duke, and the first four inmates were elected. The Hon. Sec. read out a list of subscriptions received, amounting to £800, which included one donation of £50 from J. C. Dexter, Esq., a Member of the Trade, and a member of the Festival Committee. The investment of the funds of the Institution, so as to produce the largest available sum to be devoted to the alleviation of the necessities of worthy applicants is by many Members of the Trade thought not to be the most profitable or productive, in consequence of the large amount being sunk for ever in land and buildings, which produce nothing for their own maintenance. In these later times it is considered more profitable, thus creating larger means for the comfort of the indigent, that liquid capital, judiciously and safely invested, leaving no loophole for risk or leakage, is the sounder principle than if it is parted with for ever, in creating a limited number of dwellings, which are insufficient to accommodate all who apply for them. It is fortunate, however, that the land purchased nearly half-a-century ago, has, in consequence of the development of the neighbour-

hood by increased railway facilities and other reasons,
become so valuable as to bring increasing prices for
leases, &c., which will ultimately produce such an
income, as we may hope will be ample for all the
charitable demands made upon it.

Somewhere about the year 1836, we learn from a
contribution made recently to the *Pawnbrokers'
Gazette*, at the instance of Mr. Cocks and a few others,
a meeting of Assistants was held, and it was decided
to found a Journeymen's Benevolent Society. The
first regular meeting was held in Mr. Johnson's
Auction Rooms, in Gracechurch Street, when Mr.
Cocks moved, "That a Society be now formed to be
called the Benevolent Society of Journeymen Pawnbrokers, for the relief of sick and decayed journeymen."
From this period the Society has made regular and
prosperous progress, as may be instanced by the fact
that at the first Annual Meeting it was reported that
the Society had 107 donors, and subscribers to the
amount of £51. The relief to applicants was £7 10s.,
and after the incidental expenses for the year had been
defrayed, the Treasurer had a balance of £46 6s. 5d.
Then coming to the Third Annual Supper, held at the
Queen's Arms, in Newgate Street, the host of which
was appropriately named "Mr. Balls," the donations
only amounted to £8 17s. 6d.; while in brilliant contrast
in the last year of grace, under the presidency of Mr.
Ruston, the contributions, at the Fifty-fifth Annual
Dinner, amounted to no less a sum than £153 8s. 2d. In
addition to this the same occasion witnessed the inception and development of the "Benevolent Day," the first
being appropriately held on the 85th birthday of Mr.
Robert Cocks, the sole surviving Founder, when a sum
of nearly £200 was collected, which will enable the
Executive to declare additional pensions and thus
extend the beneficent and charitable objects of the
Society. It has now reached a degree of popularity

and prosperity that, with its funds safely and judiciously invested, its usefulness should continue to be extended, a fact which, we should suppose, would induce every Assistant in the Metropolitan district to be proud of such an Institution, and consider it not only a duty but an honour to have his name emblazoned on its roll call.

There are numerous Benevolent Societies throughout the country, some of which have been marvellously successful. In Manchester, Liverpool, Leeds, Bradford, Nottingham, Sheffield, Bristol, Dublin, and other places, these organisations have taken root and flourished. Not only have the Assistants been instrumental in relieving the distress of their colleagues who were unfortunate enough to require assistance, but they have promoted social intercourse and rational enjoyment, as the reports of their meetings, dinners, &c., testify, and altogether reflect the highest honour on the Trade which such institutions cannot but adorn.

Gradually these "piping times of peace" began to be ruffled and disturbed by differences of opinion regarding the proper interpretation of the licence clauses of the Act. These clauses were *entirely* drawn by the legal officers at Somerset House, as those drawn by Mr. Reilly and which appeared in the early revises of the Bill, were pronounced entirely unsuitable. Yet the Inland Revenue administration did not seem capable of deciding on the meaning of their own clauses. Thus Mr. Bate, a London Pawn-broker, who required no certificate, opened a branch establishment in Lambeth, but the Authorities refused to grant a licence without a certificate. Mr. Bate tendered the money, which was refused, and he began business in defiance of them; then legal proceedings were commenced against him, and the Commissioners of Inland Revenue *were defeated*, as they have been on several other occasions since.

Suddenly an alarm was sounded which spread dismay throughout the length and breadth of the land. Mr. Alfred A. George, of the Strand, wrote to the *Pawnbrokers' Gazette*, under date of April 11th, 1881, and warned the Trade that there was hostile and injurious legislation contemplated for Pawnbrokers, as the Lord Chancellor (Selborne) had obtained leave to introduce a Bill into the House of Lords to amend the law relating to the recovery of stolen articles. Mr. George had procured a copy of the Bill and found, amongst other obnoxious provisions, several which related to licences, giving power to a Magistrate to endorse a Pawnbroker's licence for a first offence, and for a second, power *to deprive him of his licence altogether and for ever.* As a Member of the Metropolitan Pawnbrokers' Protection Society, Mr. George wrote, he thought the matter offered an opportunity to prove the value of the Society to the Trade at large by taking immediate action, in conjunction with their provincial friends, without delay.

This warning shot roused the country thoroughly, and not many days elapsed before an army of defence was organised and in the field, strong and united, animated with an earnest spirit of determination to repulse the invader.

CHAPTER XL

From the time the warning was given, not a
moment was lost before the Trade all over the
country met hastily in council. The day after the
publication of the *Gazette*, containing Mr. George's
letter and a leader from the Editor on the same
alarming subject, a special Committee Meeting was
called of the Metropolitan Protection Society, Mr.
H. A. Attenborough presiding. In opening the proceedings he said they met under most extraordinary
circumstances. They had all seen that a new Bill
was before the Legislature which proposed to exercise a most important influence upon the future
prospects of the Trade. Somewhere about the beginning of January, 1880, Mr. Howard Vincent, the
Director of the Criminal Investigation Department,
Scotland Yard, had expressed a desire to meet and
confer with certain influential members of the Trade,
in order to consider whether they could not devise
an improved system of arranging the police lists of
stolen and lost property. An interview took place
between Mr. Vincent and a deputation from the
Committee of the Society. Many suggestions were

U

made and had since been acted upon. Mr. Vincent
expressed his grateful sense of the assistance which
the deputation had given him in improving the list,
and they had parted with such marks of cordiality
on his part, that they had certainly expected better
treatment from him than they were now meeting
with. Since that time several communications had
been addressed to the Committee from Scotland
Yard, but there had been nothing in them to which
the Committee thought they ought to make any
categorical reply.* The object of these proceedings
on the part of the Director of Criminal Investigations, and the objects he had in view, would be fully
carried out in the Bill then before them. The Chairman then went carefully and exhaustively through
the clauses and explained the effect they would have
upon the Trade, if they were passed. In addition to
this exposition, there was read a long detailed and
lucid report, which had been drawn up by Mr. John
Attenborough, the well known Solicitor to the Association. After the report had been read it was
resolved that a Sub-Committee be appointed consisting of the Chairman, Hon. Sec. and Messrs. Mel-
huish, Sprunt and Telfer, to make arrangements for
a General Meeting of the whole Trade. Letters
were read from the Secretaries of various Provincial
Associations, including Birmingham, Liverpool, Leeds,
Stoke, and many other places, which were all unanimous in expressing the determination of the local
Committees to resist the passing of the Bill to the
last extremity. It was also agreed to arrange for a
special issue of the *Pawnbrokers' Gazette*, at the expense of the London Society, containing the reports

---

* The author thought, at the time, that it was a mistake to
leave these letters unanswered. Mr. Vincent doubtless hoped
for some such assistance as was afterwards rendered by the
Defence Association.—See Chap. XLIV.

and resolutions, and this was done the following day
(Wednesday), thus placing valuable information before
all provincial readers, and enabling Country Societies
to fully realise the police intentions.

One of the most important, as well as the largest
and most unanimous General Meetings in the history
of the Trade, was held on Wednesday, April 10th, 1881,
at the Albion Tavern, Aldersgate-street, London. It
was estimated that this gathering of London and
Provincial Pawnbrokers numbered nearly five hundred
determined and resolute men, called together " to
consider the best means of defending their Trade
against the oppressive clauses of the Lord Chancellor's
' Stolen Goods Bill.'"   Mr. Richard Attenborough was
unanimously called upon to preside. A series of
resolutions had been prepared, the first of which was
proposed by Mr. J. A. Russell, and ran as follows :
"'That the Bill presented to the House of Lords by
the Lord Chancellor, intituled 'The Stolen Goods Bill,
1881,' be opposed." It was seconded by Mr. Mayfield
(Hull), and, after considerable discussion, caused by an
amendment being proposed to add the words "as far
as it applies to Pawnbroking," was carried almost
unanimously.

Mr. J. A. Telfer next proposed the establishment of
one General Association of the Pawnbrokers of London
and the Country, which was immediately adopted. It
was then decided to elect an Executive, consisting of a
President, Vice-President, Treasurer, Hon. Sec., and
thirteen Members of Committee, with power to add
to their numbers, and that London be represented by
five Members. The election of officers was then
proceeded with, with the following result, viz. : Mr.
Richard Attenborough, Chairman ; Mr. John Grantham (Manchester), Vice-Chairman ; Mr. J. A. Russell,
Treasurer ; Mr. A. Hardaker, Hon. Sec. ; with the
following Executive, partly elected at the Meeting and

by additions afterwards made, Mr. John Tatton (Man-
chester), Mr. Frederick Green (Liverpool), Mr. Dixon
(Birmingham), Mr. John Eaton (Sheffield), Mr. Alfred
Fletcher (Nottingham), Mr. Layman, Mr. Lawley, Mr.
Telfer, and Mr. Sprunt (all of London), Mr. J. K.
Wilkes (Darlington), Mr. A. A. Lyddon (Bristol), Mr.
Carryer (Burslem), Mr. Morley (Bradford), Mr. G.
Walter (Northampton), Mr. Walker (Leeds), Mr.
Hollins (Dudley), Mr. Ballantyne (Glasgow), and Mr.
J. O. Garland (Leith). Then came the question of how
the sinews of war were to be provided. After many
differences of opinion had been expressed, it was
resolved, "That after the conclusion of the Meeting
the Association, now formed, shall consist only of such
Members of the Trade as shall either guarantee a sum
of not less than two pounds, or who shall subscribe a
sum of not less than one pound."

The new Executive met the next day, and, among
other business done, was the election of a Sub-Committee—as the Executive was much too large a body
to remain long in London—consisting of the Chairman,
Treasurer, Hon. Sec., and Messrs. Telfer and Eaton.
In a few days an office was secured in Palace Chambers,
Bridge-street, Westminster, and the work of defence
was earnestly and at once commenced.

The author or instigator of this attempted mischievous and obnoxious legislation is a somewhat
remarkable man, of whose career it may be interesting
to give a brief sketch. Chas. Edward Howard Vincent,
C.B., was born in the year 1849, and was, at the time
of the introduction of the Stolen Goods Bill, just
thirty-two years of age. He is the son of the Rev. Sir
Frederick Vincent, eleventh baronet, and was educated
at Westminster and Sandhurst. He entered the Royal
Welsh Fusiliers in 1868, and retired as Lieutenant
in 1873. He was Captain in the Royal Berkshire
Militia, 1873 to 1875; Lieutenant of the Central London

Rangers, and became afterwards and is still Colonel of
the Queen's Westminster Volunteers. He was called to
the Bar at the Inner Temple in 1876. Mr. Vincent
went to the South-Eastern Circuit, and practised in
the Probate and Divorce Divisions of the High Court
of Justice. He entered at the French Bar in 1877.
About 1878 a great discovery of fraud and corruption
was made in Scotland Yard, which resulted in the
trial and conviction of such prominent members of the
detective force, as Meiklejohn, Druscovitch, and several
others. This gang entered into a gigantic conspiracy
to defraud a French Countess, from whom they succeeded in extorting fabulous sums of money, and were
tried and sentenced to long periods of penal servitude.

Whether or not the Chief Police Authorities considered that in Mr. Howard Vincent a Hercules
to cleanse their "Augean Stable" was to be
found, we know not, but in March of the
above named year, he was placed at the head of a
newly created department, with the imposing title
of the Director of Criminal Investigations. Anxious
no doubt to justify his appointment, he worked like
the newest of new brooms, and it may be that he
found pigeon-holed in his office the rejected clauses
of the Habitual Criminals Bill, which some years
previously had excited the admiration of Colonel
Labalmondier, one of his chiefs. If so, he went considerably beyond the severity and rigour of those
clauses in his Stolen Goods Bill.

His subsequent career may be summarised
briefly. In 1882 he married an heiress, and about two
years after retired from the police, after which he and
his wife made a tour round the world, and on his return
to this country he became a convert to toryism. In
1885 he was returned by a majority of 903 for the
Sheffield Central Division, and again in 1886 by an increased majority of 1,196. His wife, as well as being

daughter of a millionaire, displayed considerable
literary ability, and wrote a book entitled " Forty
thousand miles over land and water."

Such is the man who essayed to place the whole
body of Pawnbrokers under the ban of the police.

The Stolen Goods Bill, in the first draft, consisted of 32 clauses, and two schedules. The provisions were of the most stringent character, bristling
with penalties to be inflicted upon offenders, while
they conferred powers of the most dangerous elasticity
and amplitude upon the police officers. These wary
and astute individuals, with that keen instinct which
the race possesses for promotion, had only to state
that they had reason to believe, and did believe, that
certain articles were in some premises named by them,
" although such officer does not specify any particular
reason for his belief," and the Court was to grant a special
search warrant. Armed with this authority and with
such assistance as might be necessary, the officer could
enter the premises mentioned in the warrant, and
there search for, seize and take away all articles there
found *which appeared to him to have been stolen*, and
take the same before the Court. Then on *primâ
facie* evidence to show that the articles had been
stolen, the Court could order the same to be detained
till the true owner had been found ; and if the person
in whose possession the goods were found, had reasonable cause to suspect they were stolen, and failed to
give information, he was to be liable, for a first offence,
to a penalty of five pounds; for a second offence, twenty
pounds ; and for the third £50, or a month's imprisonment with or without hard labour. Similar delightful,
but unprofitable fines were to be inflicted when a
person failed to give information, or concealed, melted,
defaced, or altered any stolen articles. Then if a
person bought any old gold or silver or other precious
metal, or second-hand watches, or jewellery, he was

not to alter or melt the same within seventy-two
hours; he must keep a book and enter all particulars
of such purchases; a constable was to be allowed to
examine the book, and if the purchaser refused this
privilege, he might be fined five pounds, or fifty
pounds. If a person offering an article for sale, or
in pawn, should be unable or refuse to give a
satisfactory account of how he became possessed of
the article, he would be subject to the penalty of
twenty pounds, and if the Court should consider there
was sufficient *primâ facie* evidence to show it was
stolen, then imprisonment for a month with or without hard labour.

It was also to be enacted that when a police notice,
as provided by the Act, had been given to a Pawnbroker, relating to a stolen article, he should render
assistance without unnecessary delay, by giving information to the chief officer of police, with a description
of the person from whom the same was received, and
the name and address of such person, and should
permit a constable, specially authorised, to inspect all
articles of a similar description, or the aforesaid
penalties would be inflicted.

Clause 15 was one of the most severe and dangerous
in the Bill. It provided that "Where a Pawnbroker
is convicted of an offence punishable under the
Pawnbrokers' Act, 1872, or this Act, and has
previously been convicted of the same, or any other
offence under the Pawnbrokers' Act or this Act *
* * the court before whom he is convicted may
direct his licence and his certificate (if any) *to be
endorsed with a record of his conviction,* and if any
conviction has been endorsed on the licence or certificate within five years previously, *may direct his licence
and certificate to be forfeited.* Where a licence or
certificate is directed to be forfeited, *the then existing
licence shall be void.*"

Under the above enlightened provisions, if a Pawnbroker happened to be fined for taking goods from
children, serving a drunken person, or by any inad-
vertence committed the smallest offence against
either Act, there would be endorsement and ultimately
forfeiture of the licence. Under such a law it was
felt Pawnbroking could not exist.

Then there were supplemental provisions as to endorsing licences; another clause was that if a Pawnbroker
should be convicted of any offence against the Act of
1872 "or this Act," the Court might direct that he
should be registered *at the office of the Chief Officer of
Police for the district*. The registration of a Pawnbroker should be in force for a period not exceeding
three years, but should he commit another offence
within that period the Court might order a further
period of registration. Next we had a clause of eight
paragraphs giving the *effect* of registration. A Pawnbroker so registered should not remove or open new
premises without giving notice to the police; he
should enter in a book particulars with respect to all
articles he became possessed of, or sold, or disposed of;
he should *not* take in pawn, purchase, or receive, sell,
or deliver any article before the hour of nine in the
morning, or after six in the evening ; he should, when
required, produce his books to the police, and any
article in his possession, and permit the officer to
examine the same. He should keep all articles taken
in pawn, purchased, or received by him, for a period of
seventy-two hours without changing the form or
disposing of them in any way. The penalties for any
offence named in this clause were : first, £5 ; second,
£20; third, £50, or one month's imprisonment; and in
failing to give notice of opening new premises, ten
shillings a day for the time he carried on the business.

Then there was a trap laid for Managers and
Assistants. Fearing the employer might escape

punishment by pleading that certain offences were committed without his knowledge, it was provided that agents or servants of Pawnbrokers and second-hand dealers should be liable to the same punishment as the Pawnbroker or secondhand dealer.   The Pawn-broker should be entitled upon information duly laid by him to have the person (servant or agent) he charged as the actual offender, brought before the Court at the time appointed for hearing the charge, and if the Pawnbroker proved to the satisfaction of the Court that he had used due diligence to enforce the execution of the Act, and that the said other person committed the offence in question without his know-ledge, consent, or connivance, the said other person should be summarily convicted of the offence and the Pawnbroker should be exempt from any punishment.

It is difficult to speculate as to the effect the above provisions might have had upon the future supply of Pawnbrokers' Assistants; but a reasonable inference would be that young men would avoid entering a business so dangerous, and would prefer a trade in which they were not liable to pains and penalties, and free from the probability of one month's imprisonment with or without hard labour.   But this is only one instance of the impracticable and tyrannical character of the Bill.

There were other clauses providing for police notices: specially authorized constable; definitions of Pawn-brokers and secondhand dealers; definition of stolen property, which was to include " embezzled," " fraudu-lently obtained," &c.   We have, however, shown in the brief summary of the measure that no Pawnbroker could exist under its provisions, and that the struggle just commenced was to free himself from the in-tolerable despotism of the police.

CHAPTER XLI

The Sub-Committee of the newly organized "Pawnbrokers' Defence Association," lost no time in getting steadily and earnestly to work. An office was taken in Palace-chambers, Bridge-street, Westminster, directly opposite Palace-yard and the entrance to the Houses of Parliament, and in five days after their election the small Committee commenced work and were in daily attendance. On the 28th April a stirring appeal, signed by the Chairman and Hon. Secretary was circulated to nearly 4,000 Pawnbrokers in Great Britain and Ireland, and resulted up to May 17th in guarantees and subscriptions amounting to £1,089 being in the Treasurer's hands. It was evident that the Trade was thoroughly aroused and determined to defend itself against the police attack. Some estimate of the amount of work which suddenly devolved on the Sub-Committee may be formed from the fact that soon after the address had been in the hands of all Pawnbrokers who could be reached, there were not less than 181 letters received by the morning's delivery, and others followed by every post throughout the day. Copies of the Bill accompanied by ex-

planatory letters were sent to Lord Sandon, the Marquis of Salisbury, Earl Dalhousie, and many other
peers, and a large number of Members of Parliament,
while letters of introduction were received daily from
all parts of the country.

Tho Hon. Secretary prepared a statement for the
defence of the Trade against the passing of the Bill.
It dealt categorically with every clause and explained
the difficulties and dangers which would result therefrom and the degradations such a measure would
inflict upon a body of respectable and upright Tradesmen.   When completed this document with some
valuable statistics appended, under the title of
"Observations and Reasons" upon and against the
Bill, was printed and circulated largely to Peers,
Members of Parliament and influential friends who
had promised assistance and introductions.   It was
also forwarded, previous to interviews, to the Lord
Chancellor, Marquis of Salisbury, Earl of Shaftesbury,
and many others who were likely to be interested in
the subject.

The Lord Chancellor was then written to, asking his
lordship to be good enough to receive a deputation
from the Pawnbrokers, and to kindly name an early
day for so doing, as the time for the second reading of
tho Bill was fast approaching.   A courteous reply was
received fixing Wednesday, May 11th, when his Lordship would see them, and suggesting that the number
should be limited to twelve or fifteen.

On the day named the following gentlemen repaired
to the Lord Chancellor's room in the House of Lords :—
Messrs. Richard Attenborough, Russell, Grantham,
Telfer, Eaton, Lawley, and Hardaker, representing the
English Trade; Messrs. McKay, Garland, and Brown,
Scotland; and Messrs. Chaffey, and Bentley, of Dublin.
Lord Dalhousie and Mr. Howard Vincent were present
with the Lord Chancellor.

The Hon. Secretary opened the proceedings and made enquiry if the Committee's statement had been received by his Lordship, and was answered in the affirmative, with the assurance that it had been read and notes made on the points to which attention had been drawn. The Hon. Secretary then urged the withdrawal of the Bill as it affected them seriously, not only as Pawnbrokers, but also as dealers in second-hand goods, besides which there was no proof that such a measure was at all necessary. There appeared to be some misunderstanding as to the meaning of the terms "Brokers" and "Pawnbrokers," as they were used in the Bill. If such a Bill were passed into law, a Pawn-broking business would become valueless in the market and the means of earning a livelihood would be denied to those who were embarked in it.

Mr. Attenborough followed with a long and clear criticism of the Bill, showing how hardly it would apply in instances of goods of similar patterns being taken away, very much to the annoyance of the legitimate owner, and the exposure of his circum-stances. The person, too, whose circumstances might be thus revealed, might, in many instances, belong to the upper classes of society, both in this country and on the continent. One clause would also introduce a very inconvenient extension of the definition of "Stolen Goods," which would embrace many trans-actions not of a criminal character.

Mr. J. A. Telfer drew attention to the fact that already in the Pawnbrokers' Act of 1872, a Pawn-broker might be deprived of his licence if he were "convicted on indictment," for fraud in his business. In the new Bill the licence might be forfeited by the successive commission of three trivial offences—per-haps of an involuntary character—thus placing the Pawnbroker's capability of pursuing his calling in such jeopardy as would render his business almost valueless and would prevent respectable persons devoting themselves to the practice of so precarious an employment.

Mr. Lawley strongly urged the withdrawal of the Bill as the respectability of the Trade rendered it quite unnecessary.

Mr. John Grantham said he represented an important section of the Trade—that of Manchester. He had an extensive knowledge of it, as he had been Hon. Secretary to the local Association upwards of 16 years, and he could say with every confidence, that he did not know of any necessity for such a Bill, as the police already possessed sufficient power to enable them to recover any property which had been stolen and found its way into the hands of a Pawnbroker. The Trade felt the humiliation at the fact that their business should be inserted in a Bill having for its object the recovery of stolen property.

Mr. Eaton supported what had been said by previous speakers, and that he knew it was a common practice in the provincial trade to carry on the sale business in shops forming part of the Pawnbroking premises. He pleaded that the new Bill should not be imposed upon them without a full inquiry before a Select Committee.

Mr. Bentley on behalf of the Dublin Trade said there existed no need to include them in the Bill, as the Irish Act already provided for the satisfactory inspection of the books, stocks, etc. Mr. McKay said although it was not the custom for Scotch Pawnbrokers to buy and sell over the counter, they were willing to stand by their English friends in resisting such a Bill.

After a few other remarks from members of the deputation, the Lord Chancellor replied that he would give every attention to what he had heard, but he could not help thinking there was a good deal of

unnecessary alarm expressed. At any rate, no harsh-
ness was intended towards Pawnbrokers, and perhaps
some alteration might be necessary to remove such
alarm. He should also have no objection to refer the
Bill to a Select Committee of the House, and, of
course, evidence would be taken. The customary form
of thanks was expressed to his Lordship as the
deputation withdrew, the interview having lasted
exactly an hour and a half.

On the day following, through the intercession of
Lord Sandon, the Chairman, Hon. Secretary and Mr.
Telfer, obtained an interview with the Marquis of
Salisbury. A copy of the "Observations and Reasons"
was in his Lordship's possession, and he informed the
deputation that he had carefully read it. A descriptive criticism of the various objectionable clauses of
the Bill was entered into, and the disastrous results
were pointed out which might be expected both to
the public and the Pawnbrokers should the Bill
become law.

Lord Salisbury in reply said two points appeared to
strike him; the first was that *the Bill was the outcome
of police desires*, and he thought it very unusual to
introduce such a Bill without inquiry. The second was
that it looked like an attempt to introduce some
of the features of the French system, which he thought
was not required in this country. The interview closed
in a friendly conversation, and his Lordship expressed
his willingness to see the gentlemen again should it
be thought necessary.

On the afternoon of the same day, Thursday, May
12th, the Lord Chancellor moved the second reading of
the Bill. In the course of his speech he said the Bill
was intended to increase the power now possessed by
the police to recover stolen goods, and to make several
provisions calculated to discourage the receivers of
stolen property. The police authorities had com-

municated with the different branches of the police
established in various parts of the country, to ascertain
their opinion as to the necessity for further legislation;
the general opinion was that further legislation *was*
necessary, and would be likely to check the evil.*
He was told the authorities, the chief magistrates *and
police officers,* all concur that there is a great difficulty
in tracing stolen goods, as there is nothing to show the
officers where to search. It was with some surprise
that he learned that the members of an exceedingly
respectable trade of the country, the Pawnbrokers,
were alarmed as if it were a measure especially against
them. When he stated the provisions to their Lordships, they would find there was no ground for those
suppositions. He found it stated that one of the
reasons against the Bill was that Pawnbrokers and
receivers of stolen property were identified in it. That
was a matter he had tried to rectify. No one could
be more sensible than he was of the very great and
high respect due to the Pawnbrokers, therefore, to
confound those two together was an error which no
one of sense would be guilty of. But it was certain
that even the most upright and honest Pawnbrokers
were sometimes induced to take goods that had been
stolen; and while there were Pawnbrokers with the
greatest standing and integrity, *there were others who
were by no means so scrupulous as they ought to be.*

The Lord Chancellor then proceeded to expound the
provisions of the Bill, and concluded by saying that
he thought it was entirely in the public interest, and
by no means threw restrictions upon the Trade, and as
it was going into a Select Committee he would not
trouble their Lordships further.

---

* We presume this always has been and always will be the
opinion of every policeman, because he is puzzled to know
where stolen property goes to.

The Marquis of Salisbury was the only other speaker in the debate—if it could be so called—and we give his words verbatim as they were specially reported at the time. His Lordship said:—" The Bill which my noble and learned friend has laid before your Lordships' House, and asked your Lordships to read a second time, has been accurately described by him, as a Bill similar in many respects to a Bill which he is about to bring forward presently, to increase the power of one class of her Majesty's subjects, and, of course, by increasing the power of one class in certain directions you necessarily restrict the rights and liberties of certain other classes of her Majesty's subjects.* There is no doubt but that all parties in the State are persuaded that the law respecting the recovery of stolen goods should be amended, but when it is proposed that the powers which are provided by this Bill should be entrusted to police officers, then I think it is the duty of your Lordships to watch very vigilantly these proposals, since they have not been subject to any public or parliamentary scrutiny. My learned noble friend *relies almost entirely on the evidence of the police.* I have great respect for the police as a body, but I think that when such a Bill as this is framed other opinions besides those of the police require to be taken. The Bill as it stands is one which has created much alarm amongst a respectable class of traders—the Pawnbrokers—and the alarm has had its effect upon the mind of my noble and learned friend. If it were attempted now to push this Bill through this House without further enquiry, in my opinion its provisions would require the most careful scrutiny. But it has entered the judicial mind of my noble and learned friend that the Bill, as it stands, requires amendment, and he has intimated in what

* The Criminal Code Bill: police.

manner he proposes to amend some of the most
objectional clauses. If these are not satisfactory, then
the noble and learned Lord has promised to send it to
a Select Committee. I believe that is the wisest
course that can be adopted." The Bill was then
formally read a second time.

From this time the Sub-Committee were busily
engaged in the preparation of evidence, collection and
arrangement of statistics, in anticipation of the first
sitting of the new Select Committee. Several
modifications had been made in the Bill, the most
important of which was the withdrawal of the registration clauses, so far as regarded the Pawnbrokers; but
what the Defence Association most sought for was
entire exemption from its provisions, and the Lord
Chancellor was written to, to concede this before the
Select Committee was appointed; had he done so
the campaign would have ended, and the tedious and
expensive labour of going through Committee would
have been saved. A letter was received from Mr.
Kenneth Muir Mackenzie, principal Secretary to the
Lord Chancellor, which said, "I am directed by the
Lord Chancellor to acknowledge the receipt of your
letter of the 27th inst., and to say that the Bill cannot
be further altered before going to the Select Committee to which it was agreed that it should be
referred, but that it will be open to any one of the
Members of that Committee to move such an amendment as you propose, while it is under their consideration."

The pressing Parliamentary duties of the Sub-
Committee were, soon after this time, somewhat
relaxed by the Whitsuntide recess, which extended
over ten days; but the uncertainty as to how soon
the Select Committee might be appointed, made it
necessary for those who remained in London to be
incessantly at work. Upwards of one thousand forms
w

to be filled in with statistics were sent direct from the London office, while Manchester, Liverpool, Leeds, and other important centres, circulated forms specially prepared for their own Members, a large portion of which were duly filled in and returned to the Sub-Committee.

It was not until the 20th of June that there appeared upon the Parliamentary papers a notice of the Select Committee to be named.   On the 21st a list of the Peers selected was published as follows : The Lord Chancellor, Earl Waldegrave, Earl Morley, Earl Beauchamp, Earl Cairns, Viscount Sherbrooke, Lord Aberdare (the Mr. Bruce, Home Secretary of 1872), Lord Winmarleigh, and Lord Ramsey (Earl Dalhousie), with a notification that the Committee would sit for the first time on Friday, June 24th.

The work at that period for the Sub-Committee became of the most exacting character, involving unceasing attention for many hours each day. Statistics, from all parts of the country, arrived in considerable quantities, which were carefully tabulated for future use.

Two important points had been gained by getting the Bill referred to a Select Committee; first, *time*, which is a most important factor in all parliamentary strategy; and second, the opportunity of hearing the indictment against the Trade which Mr. Howard Vincent had drawn, and to which the Pawnbrokers had to prepare their defence.

CHAPTER XLII

On the 24th of June the Select Committee sat for the first time and appointed their Chairman, which was, of course, the Lord Chancellor, who practically held the brief on behalf of the police, as was apparent from his speech on moving the second reading of the Bill, and he now almost assumed the position of a judge. During the short sitting, a messenger was sent out of the room, to say the Lord Chancellor would speak with the Hon. Secretary. His Lordship informed the Secretary that it had been decided to take the evidence of the police first, which would commence on Monday, July 4th, and he wished to know how many witnesses the Pawnbrokers proposed to call. Some half-dozen, probably, was the reply. His Lordship said nothing could be more reasonable; he requested that a list of the witnesses should be prepared and sent in to the Committee clerk not later than the following Wednesday. On Friday, July 1st, the Committee sat again for a short time in private to arrange order of procedure. A message was again sent out to the Sub-Committee who were in attendance, to say that the Committee would sit to take evidence and

w 2

that no persons would be admitted but those gentlemen whose names had been sent in as witnesses.

The battle began in earnest on Monday, July 4th,
when the enemy unmasked his batteries and opened
fire. The attack in the first instance was of somewhat
feeble character, the first witness being Sir James
Taylor Ingham, then the Chief Metropolitan Police
Magistrate. The state of the law, this witness said,
with regard to tracing stolen property was not satisfactory. The powers contained in the Metropolitan
Act were inadequate. He would point out one thing
particularly. There was a clause which enabled
constables to stop persons in the streets who were
carrying suspected articles, and the constable might
take them before a magistrate, who, after inquiry,
might inflict a fine or commit the person to prison
for two months. The magistrates formerly imagined
that the warehouse, or premises of such persons,
might be searched, and if any suspected articles
were found, the possessor of the articles might
be brought before the magistrate, who could deal
with them. But there was a decision of the courts
of law which showed the magistrates that they were
wrong, and the decision materially abridged their
power of dealing with receivers of stolen goods.
They (the police) wanted power to search premises,
and the witness thought it desirable that the powers
of the magistrates should be extended. Under the
Pawnbrokers' Act if the court is satisfied on oath
that there is reasonable cause to suspect, a warrant
may be granted, but in all these cases the language
of the statute is such as to throw upon the magistrate
a greater burden, at least, to make him think it was
his duty to require a greater burden of *primâ facia*
proof, *than is consistent with the object of the inquiry
in that stage.* It may, perhaps, be instructive to point
out that the replies here given were actually only

assents to elaborate and leading queries periphras-
tically put by the Lord Chancellor. The replies
generally were "Yes," "Certainly," "I think so."
In fact, the whole evidence given by Sir James
Ingham consisted of expressions of opinion. As an
instance, taken hap-hazard, as we are looking through
the "Minutes of Evidence" for our extracts to record
here, we come upon question No. 46, which the Lord
Chancellor put to the witness thus: "Then we come
to the 6th clause, and that raises the question to
which you were addressing yourself before, of the
time in which a dealer in precious or other metals,
shall not melt or alter the form until after that time
(72 hours) has expired. You were about to make an
observation, I think, upon the time?" To this the
witness said: "*I have no practical acquaintance with
this matter*, but I should certainly think 72 hours
*a very short time; I should propose at least seven
days*." It will be seen from this single extract that
the evidence was of no practical value: the witness
would suggest a longer period than was drawn in the
Bill, for no other reason, logically, than that he knew
nothing whatever about the subject. So he thought
the police should have greater facilities for search,
because they had not the ability to discover what
became of stolen property, but assumed that all goods
that could not be found must be in the possession
of Pawnbrokers. He thought that authorized
constables should have power to examine goods
themselves if they were not satisfied with the mode
in which the Pawnbroker examined. A person
intending to cheat would make an illusory examination; a "slippery Pawnbroker" would make an
illusory search. The witness thought also that
Pawnbrokers should close at ten o'clock on Saturday
nights. "My own opinion," added the witness, "is
not worth anything upon that point; I can only say

that I am an advocate for closing Pawnbrokers' shops
at the earliest possible hour." In reply to Lord
Aberdare, the witness thought that goods pawned at
night were always pawned for drink. In the
concluding portion of the evidence the Lord Chancellor, addressing the witness, said: " It has been
pressed upon me by very respectable members of the
Pawnbroking business that it would be safe to exempt
them altogether from the Bill; I collect that that is
not your opinion." "Most certainly not," was the
reply. "There are in that Trade," continued the
Chairman, answering the question himself, "persons
very unlike the principal and very respectable
members of it who are among those that do receive
stolen goods?" The witness replied that he was
glad of the opportunity of bearing testimony to the
great respectability of many of the Pawnbrokers,
and to the services they rendered to the public in
bringing persons before the magistrates when they
had offered suspicious articles. "At the same time,
I must say that there are some Pawnbrokers *who are
nothing better than receivers of stolen goods*, and I think
it would be a scandal if some effort were not made to
check the practice of these Pawnbrokers."

Let the reader note that throughout the entire
evidence, not one word of *proof* was uttered to justify
either the Lord Chancellor or Sir James Ingham in
the defamatory and opprobrious language they used,
or the conclusions and beliefs they expressed, in regard to the Trade of Pawnbroking.

Now entered the hero of the hour, Mr. C. E.
Howard Vincent, who took his seat as the next
witness. The usual preliminary queries as to position, profession, &c., were gone through, and then
the Director's opinions were elicited. His duty, he
said, was constantly directed to the means of tracing
stolen property; it was his opinion that the powers

of the existing law were certainly not sufficient for
the purpose. The Bill introduced was prepared
under his superintendence; he had communicated
with the police authorities in other parts of the
country, and he found that 69 chief officers of police
in counties, and 166 chief officers of cities and
boroughs, making a total of 235 chief officers, were
in favour of the Bill. It was drawn upon the
same lines as regarded stolen goods as the Glasgow
Police Act; there were also numerous local Acts
which provided for the objects contemplated by the
Bill. Mr. Vincent described the method of
search then existing, varying little from the opinion
expressed by Sir James Ingham. He added that for
want of power of search, it was an absolute impossibility to trace stolen property. The clauses of
the Bill were discussed by the Lord Chancellor,
Lord Aberdare, and the witness, until the 7th and
8th sections were reached. These required from
Pawnbrokers,* the examination of their books, and
the production of articles upon proper inquiry being
made, and the witness found that as the law stood
there had been frequent difficulty in obtaining information, where afterwards it was proved that the
articles were in the hands of the persons from
whom inquiry had been made. There were many
respectable Pawnbrokers, but there was the utmost
difficulty in obtaining information in answer to inquiries. He had numberless instances—innumerable
instances—but he would produce *seven*, which were
perhaps a little worse than the others. In answer
to a subsequent question (No. 207), Mr. Vincent said
he had in all 59 other cases, therefore it was, to say
the least, mild exaggeration to say they were "numberless," when he had himself enumerated them.

* The Bill mentioned "and second-hand dealers," but we
confine our remarks to its bearing upon Pawnbrokers only.

The seven worst cases Mr. Vincent had woven
into little narratives or storyettes, as it is the
fashion to say in these days, and he seemed to be
able to rival the lady story-teller in the *Arabian
Nights* had he the material within reach. Each
little story—or more properly fable—we propose to
give *verbatim et literatim*, so that our readers may
be acquainted with the incomparable turpitude of
which their fellow tradesmen have been accused.
We take:

Story No. 1. — "In the case of a robbery
of jewellery worth £30, the description was inserted
in the Pawnbrokers' list, and special inquiry instituted regarding it. Nothing was discovered until
the thief was apprehended, and stated where he
had pawned the things. During the trial, the
various articles were brought into court by several
Pawnbrokers' assistants, none of whom could identify
the prisoner as the person who had pawned the
articles." Non-identification is a heinous offence in
the eye of a policeman, but people with ordinary
capacities might conclude that the prisoner never
himself pledged any of the goods, which is highly
probable.

Story No. 2.—"A servant girl absconded, stealing a gold watch, the property of her master. A
constable called on Mr. D., Pawnbroker, and asked
if such a watch had been pledged with him. He
said he had not seen it, but that if he did he would
communicate with the police. Some days later the
thief was apprehended, and she told the constable
that she had pledged the watch with Mr. D., on
the day of the theft. The Pawnbrokers' book on
examination showed this to be a fact and the watch
was found. The Pawnbroker was requested to produce it at the police court, but he declined, saying
it was inconvenient to do so. He was again re-

quested to attend, but still refused, and a summons
was issued to compel his attendance. His assistant,
however, appeared in his place, and stated as a
reason for his master's refusing to appear, that he
was prevented by important business. The magistrate remarked that Mr. D.'s conduct was dis-
graceful, in treating the order of the court with
contempt, and in not giving proper information to
the police. He directed that the watch should be
given up without compensation, and requested that
the reports in this case should be kept for reference, should any further misconduct take place on
the part of the Pawnbroker." The Pawnbroker's
defence will be found in the following chapter of
this veracious history.

Story No. 3.—"A convicted thief, and receiver
of stolen property, named Elliot, pawned a number
of bank notes with Mr. B., a Pawnbroker; Mr. B.
was informed by an inspector that about 20 of such
notes had been taken in pledge at his establishment. He replied, 'Yes, I know, and I know Elliot
very well; I have heard that he is a convicted
thief.' The inspector asked Mr. B. to furnish him
with the numbers of the notes, but he declined to
do so. Particulars were then given to Mr. B. of
about 40 bank notes which had recently been stolen.
He refused to let the officer see those in his possession, but said, 'I will see if they answer the
description of those you have mentioned.' He then
left the shop for a moment and returned saying,
'I have not got any of the notes you have described.' Subsequently a Pawnbroker's duplicate was
found in Elliot's possession for a Bank of England
note for £100, pledged with Mr. B. There was not
sufficient evidence to detain the prisoner on the
charge upon which he was apprehended, but a copy
of the duplicate was taken. The inspector called the

following day and asked to see the note, but the
Pawnbroker said 'It was taken out this morning.'"
Not an unnatural proceeding for a man to take who
had just escaped from the clutches of the police.

Story No. 4.—":Two men were arrested for house-
breaking, and in their possession were found the
proceeds of a larceny committed at a certain house.
Everything was found with the exception of a
lady's gold chain, and from information received, it
was surmised that the chain had been pledged at
Mr. D.'s, on whom the inspector called, and Mr. D.
replied, 'You are always coming and annoying me
on my busy nights, you fellows are a great nuisance
to me,' and other similar remarks. He then looked
at his books, and said he had nothing of the kind
required. The inspector then left the shop, returning
later on to inquire again ,but without better result.
On the same night the ticket for the chain was
found at Dartford, showing that it had been pledged
with Mr. D. When the ticket was presented to the
Pawnbroker, the latter stated that he had found
the chain after the inspector left and had sent it to
Bow-street. On inquiry being made at the police
station, nothing was known of the fact." This
was rather a lame and impotent conclusion; the
story does not appear to have been constructed
with the author's usual ability.

Story No. 5.—"In the case of a robbery of rings,
an accurate description was given, woodcuts were
inserted in the lists, and a reward of £200 was
offered, but no information was obtained for two
months, when the thief was apprehended. The
pawn-tickets found upon him showed that seven
Pawnbrokers held portions of the articles stolen,
woodcuts of which had been supplied to them.
The thief was also in possession of another ticket
relating to a gold watch, *pledged for £10, its real*

value being £70. On inquiry it proved to be stolen, and although the owner's name was engraved upon it, no information was given on the subject by the Pawnbroker."

Story No. 6.—"Certain goods to the value of £100 being stolen, their descriptions were circulated in detail, the distinctive marks on several of the articles being given. The special attention of Pawnbrokers was called to the accurate description, but no information was obtained until the pawn-tickets were sent anonymously to the jeweller from whose shop the articles had been taken. Three tickets showed that the things had been pledged with the very Pawnbrokers, in various parts of London, *who had denied all knowledge of them.*"

Mr. Vincent appears to have overlooked the probability, that if the Pawnbrokers who had "denied all knowledge" of the stolen goods, had desired to keep possession of them—which is implied—they would not have committed the foolish act of issuing pawn-tickets at all, which are, as Mr. Telfer later on told the Select Committee, "*the best automatic detectives in the world.*"

Story No. 7 and last.—"A servant, known to a Pawnbroker, brought valuable articles to pledge and gave a name and address which *he knew to be false.* Inquiry concerning the property was made by the police, but the Pawnbroker denied all knowledge of it until the arrest and admission of the thief."

It is utterly impossible to accurately describe the deep feelings of indignation, shame, and humiliation which animated the Sub-Committee, as they, helpless and defenceless, heard these accusations. They felt that these stories were gross exaggerations, and must be capable of explanation, so that when the Select Committee rose for the day, the Hon. Secretary went at

once to Mr. Vincent and requested to be furnished with
the names and addresses of the Pawnbrokers whom
he had that day publicly pilloried for dereliction of
duty, and whose characters it was impossible to clear
until it was known who they were. He promised the
names should be sent the next day. In corroboration
of this, Mr. Attenborough, the Chairman, preferred
the same request, when Mr. Vincent replied : " Yes ;
I have promised them to Mr. Hardaker." The same
evening the Hon. Secretary wrote to Mr. Vincent
reminding him of his promise, and two days later a
reply was received in which he refused to regard that
promise. After a string of sophisms excusing his
breach of faith, the writer said: "But on further
consideration I think it inadvisable to relieve police
reports of their confidential character, or by com-
municating them to you to afford ground for any
departure from that friendly feeling the public
interest demands between the Pawnbroking Trade
and the police, and which it has been and will be
my aim to encourage and develop." The next day
the Select Committee sat, and before taking evidence, the Hon. Sec. stepped forward and informed
the Lord Chancellor what had occurred, and asked
his Lordship to be good enough to make an order
for Mr. Vincent to furnish the required information, so that rebutting evidence might be given.
This his Lordship declined to do, saying, the Select
Committee were not appointed for the purpose of
making *personal investigations;* such a course would
be altogether outside the object for which they were
appointed, and he might have added that we permit
Mr. Vincent to make *personal allegations,* but we
cannot allow the victims of his vindictiveness the
opportunity of saying one word in their own defence.

As for the rest of the evidence given in
favour of the Bill, we have little to say. There was

a Mr. W. Alexander Brown, the Procurator Fiscal
of the Lower Ward of Lanarkshire, and he was
kind enough to give *his opinion* that Legislation in
the direction of the Bill was much required for
England (in which he had had no experience), but
not in Scotland, as he thought they had most of
the powers already. Then we had our old friend
Mr. Alexander McCall, Chief Constable of Glasgow,
who appeared against the Trade in 1870. Our
limited space will not permit us to follow him, but
the general tenour of his evidence was in favour of
the Bill, but he would make it more imperative.
In Clause 9 for instance, where "a Pawnbroker may
seize and detain" a suspected person, he would
substitute "shall." Then said Lord Aberdare:
"That a little Pawnbroker should seize a big thief,
you mean?" "He would have a good excuse for
not being able to detain him," was the wily reply.
Then followed a Mr. Carpenter, of Brentford, a
retired metal merchant, who had volunteered evidence. His observations did not apply to Pawnbrokers. Mr. John Mallon, Superintendent Detective Department, of the Dublin Metropolitan Police,
who spoke of "the amicable arrangement" which
existed between the Pawnbrokers and the police,
which allowed the latter to examine the stocks when
in search of stolen goods. The Irish Act provided
that Pawnbrokers should commence business at ten
in the morning, and close at four o'clock in the
afternoon, from September to March, and ten to
seven the remainder of the year, but by "the
amicable arrangement" they were allowed to open
at 8.30 and close at 7 all the year round. In reply
to Earl Beauchamp, the witness said that it would not
be too strong an expression to say that the Pawnbrokers were under the thumb of the police. Messrs.
Claffey and Cummins, Pawnbrokers from Dublin,

had previously been examined, and pleaded that such a Bill was not required, as the police were allowed to search and examine the books if they wished. Mr. Malcom Wood, Chief Constable of Manchester, also gave evidence, which was mainly an exposition of the Manchester Police Act of 1844, and its working. The police, he said, received every facility from the Pawnbrokers.

Mr. Howard Vincent had thus opened his case against the Pawnbrokers. The indictment consisted of general charges of neglect and carelessness of members, in not giving prompt information with regard to the reception of stolen property, and seven specific charges against individual Pawnbrokers for conduct which made it necessary to place *four thousand* honest tradesmen wholly and helplessly in the power of the police.

CHAPTER XLIII

It would hardly be believed that in the enlightened and cultured days of the latter quarter of the nineteenth century, that it would be necessary to appeal, time after time, to the highest legal authority in the land, for permission to defend a man's character and reputation from insinuated charges of practices, which, if proved, were little short of criminal. Yet such was the case in 1881, when Mr. Howard Vincent was permitted, before the Select Committee, to detail serious and disreputable transactions against *individual members* of the Pawnbroking Trade, and those members were denied the common right of every prisoner in Her Majesty's dominions—that of calling evidence for the defence. The Lord Chancellor had, as we have shown previously, when applied to replied, that they were not appointed for the purpose of making *personal investigations*, and yet charges had been admitted against respectable men, who were to be judged and condemned, without one word being heard in their defence.

Smarting under the sense of this cruel injustice, two or three members of the Sub-Committee sought the advice of a nobleman of high rank, who had before given kindly assistance and counsel. The position of affairs was fully described to his Lordship, who sympathised with the Pawnbrokers' grievances. His Lordship advised that a strong statement be drawn up, detailing the matters on which the Pawnbrokers felt aggrieved, and asking for leave to give rebutting evidence. If the leave should be refused, they might then ask that the statement be allowed to be printed in the minutes of evidence. In the event of this again being refused, then the deputation might see his Lordship again, and he would decide what course to adopt. After reporting the result of the interview to the whole Sub-Committee, the Hon. Sec. was instructed to draw up such a statement as he conceived would meet the difficulty, and the following document was the result :—" Session 1881. — House of Lords. Select Committee on the Stolen Goods Bill. — To the Right Hon. the Chairman and the Members of the Select Committee. My Lords.—The Committee acting on behalf of the Pawnbrokers in Great Britain, against the Stolen Goods Bill, which threatens to so seriously interfere with the peaceful and successful working of their Trade, beg most respectfully to draw attention to the defenceless position in which they are placed, in reference to the very grave charges contained in the evidence given before your Lordships by Mr. C. E. Howard Vincent, the Director of Criminal Investigations, as follows :—

"1. Seven specific charges have been made against as many individual Pawnbrokers, of such a character as to insinuate that those persons were guilty of deliberately and wilfully obstructing the police in their efforts to detect crime. That they received stolen property and neglected to give any information thereof, in order to screen the offenders and share in the profits of the plunder, and that the provisions of the above Bill are requisite to be applied to the whole Trade, in order that the wrong doers may in future be punished.

"2. On application to Mr. Howard Vincent for the names and addresses of the offending Pawnbrokers, he refused to furnish them, although on Monday, July 4th, he promised to do so.

"3. That the undersigned believe that if such names and addresses had been supplied to them, the cases could have been investigated with the most satisfactory and convincing results.

"4. That this belief is confirmed by the fact of three cases, in which Mr. Vincent made use of initials and an address, clear proof has been adduced that the facts have been greatly distorted, and serious misstatements made as to other circumstances connected therewith.

"5. That these allegations, being nearly criminal in their character, reflect discreditably upon the whole body of Pawnbrokers, as when printed in the minutes of evidence, they will convey the impression,. not only that such transactions are possible, but are not uncommon.

"We, the undersigned, therefore beg to request:—

"1. That the names of the seven Pawnbrokers should be furnished to the Committee of the Pawnbrokers' Defence Association.

"2. In the case of such information being furnished, that the Select Committee will graciously allow each of the Pawnbrokers named to be examined in answer to the charges made by Mr. Vincent.

"The objects this Association have primarily in view are to prove to your Lordships that all the Pawnbrokers are honest men, anxious to assist in the detection of crime and the punishment of criminals.

"That it is contrary to the Pawnbroker's own interest to advance money on stolen goods, as in most cases of detection he loses the money lent, and expends much valuable time in attendances at police and other courts.

"If these statements are admitted, we earnestly appeal against being condemned, unheard, and upon the unsupported evidence of one police official, who cannot understand the difficulties of carrying on the Pawnbroking business, and who bases his conclusions solely on that aspect which the Trade presents to the police authorities.

"We honestly and sincerely believe that *all* the cases named by Mr. Vincent to the discredit of our body, are capable of satisfactory explanation, and should not be recorded in the proceedings of the Select Committee without a fair and unbiassed investigation, and the Pawnbrokers being permitted to give rebutting evidence.

"This just and equitable enquiry we pray for at your Lordships' hands."

This document, signed on behalf of the Sub-Committee by the Chairman and Secretary, was forwarded to the Lord Chancellor on July 18th, 1881. On the 22nd of the same month a reply was received from Mr. Kenneth Muir MacKenzie, the Lord Chancellor's Chief Clerk. It commenced with the usual phrase: "I am directed by the Lord Chancellor," and went on to say that in not furnishing the names and addresses of the Pawnbrokers *referred to* in certain passages of Mr. Vincent's evidence, that gentleman acted, as it was his duty to do, under the direction of the Committee, who were of opinion that it was neither necessary nor desirable for them to treat as personal charges requiring investigation before them in detail, the instances mentioned by Mr. Vincent (without names) of Pawnbrokers who had failed to give that assistance to the police in tracing stolen articles, which, in the cases referred to by him, might have led to the discovery of stolen goods. The Committee did not find anything in the letter of the 18th of sufficient reason for authorizing Mr. Vincent to give the names which were asked for, " but," the letter concluded, " as they have been informed that a Pawnbroker named Burnett is supposed to be referred to in the case mentioned by Mr. Vincent in which bank notes were pledged, the Committee propose on Monday next to have the circumstances of that case proved before them in detail by Mr. Vincent and the police officers who are able to speak to them, after which they will be prepared to hear any evidence which Mr. Burnett or those in his employment may desire to offer upon the same subject."

This partial concession—or all that could be obtained at the time—was perforce accepted, and what became known as "the bank note case," was investigated. The Sub-Committee had not, however, been idle either in this or the other cases mentioned. When they found that the names and addresses of the accused Pawnbrokers were not obtainable they adopted the plan of writing to every Pawnbroker whose name could be found in the London Directory which began with " B," " D," and so forth, so that in the course of two or three days the Sub-Committee were in possession of *all the facts in every case*, which had been dilated upon by the accomplished Director of Criminal Investigations. It was in consequence of being in possession of this information that the Sub-Committee were encouraged and emboldened to earnestly and strenuously press that the explanations of the Pawnbrokers should be heard. They had discovered that the great "bank note case " occurred in September, 1876, *five years previous to the appointment of the Select Committee*, and *two years before Mr. Vincent's own elevation*

x 2

to office. Consequently, he had not related his **own** experiences of the difficulties of obtaining assistance from Pawnbrokers; he had simply adopted the traditions of Scotland Yard, and was unable, personally, to vouch for the truth of a single statement.

When the "bank note" case was investigated **a** police inspector and a serjeant were called to give evidence in support of Mr. Vincent's narrative. Then the Pawnbroker's manager was heard. He acknowledged that he had taken bank notes in pledge from Elliott—not only a hundred pound note—but two notes for one hundred pounds each; one for fifty, and four for five pounds each, making a total of £270. This was in September, 1876, and he advanced the sum of £1 upon them. Elliott was a kind of "coster," and lived in Lambeth, and the witness had known him as a customer, both in pledging and purchasing clothing, but never heard of his being a thief, nor had he ever any reason to suspect him of being one. The reason he gave for wishing to pledge the notes was because his wife was a drunkard, and he dare not leave them at home. Witness understood Elliott to say that he had obtained the money for the sale of his business. The witness could not recollect the serjeant or the inspector coming to the shop, as it was five years previous; but he was certain he never said Elliott was a suspected person. He did not say that the man was a convicted thief, because he did not know him to be so.* When the officer applied for the numbers of the notes which were in pledge witness refused to give them, but he offered to examine what he had in pledge if the

---

* Nor was it true; for in the appendix F to the Minutes of Evidence will be found a copy of a slip, put in later by Mr. Vincent, headed: "Note. George Charles Elliot was tried and convicted at the Liverpool Sessions in March, 1878." This was nearly two years after pledging the notes, when he was described as a "convicted thief."

officer would furnish witness with the numbers of any
stolen notes. The officer then read out some numbers,
and the witness informed him that he had none of
those in pledge.

Continuing the history of the pledging of the bank
notes, the manager said that two days after they were
deposited some of the £5 notes were taken away and
those remaining were entered as a new transaction.
Again, in October all the £5 notes were redeemed; on
the 8th December, the £50 note was taken away, the
£100 note only now remained in pledge for £1. This
was finally redeemed on either the 18th or 28th
January, 1877, but the date in the Pawnbroker's book
was rather indistinctly written. The inspector was
again called forward and produced a scrap of paper
on which was written January 12th, as the date on
which Elliott was taken into custody, consequently, he,
the inspector, must have gone to the Pawnbroker's on
the 13th, when he was told the note had been redeemed. Earl Beauchamp queried curiously: "Is it
usual in the police station to have bits of paper lying
about ante-dated?" The inspector replied that it was
evidently a mistake. [By the direction of their Lordships the charge-book is sent for.]*

Later in the day, after Mr. Barnett and his son had
given evidence confirmatory of the manager's statement, the inspector appeared with the charge-book
for January, 1877. It contained particulars of the time
when Elliot was brought up by the police. The case
was No. 12, and the entry ran as follows: "No. 12, date
when brought in 10.30 p.m., 16th." The witness said,
in answer to the Chairman, that having refreshed his
memory, he was enabled to state that it was on the 16th
January that Elliot was locked up and *it must have*

---

* This is a correct copy of the parenthesis which appears on
page 210 of the Minutes of Evidence.

been on the morning of the 17*th that he went to Mr. Barnett's.* Thus the first of Mr. Howard Vincent's very bad cases " crumbled into dust." It was true that there existed the discrepancy of one day between the Pawnbroker's entry of the date of redemption, and the entry in the charge-book of the arrest of Elliot, and the subsequent visit of the inspector to the Pawnbroker's shop, but considering the blundering which had been exposed it would be difficult to decide on which side the error lay.

By dint of unceasing perseverance and the assistance of friends on the Committee, leave was obtained for another of the " Fairy Tales " to be investigated. This was story No. 5, relating to a gold watch worth £70 and only pledged for £10, and the Pawnbroker gave no information.

The Pawnbroker's manager was permitted to give his version of the story to the Select Committee, and his " plain unvarnished tale " is printed in the minutes of evidence as follows: " On the 17th July, 1880, I took in a gold lever hunting watch made by McCabe, of Cornhill, It was offered in pledge to me by a person who had the appearance of a gentleman, who asked £10 upon it, which sum I lent him. As I took the watch, I saw a crest on the back and said to him, ' Is this your own watch, because I see it has a crest upon it ? ' and he replied, ' Yes ; and if you open it you will see my name inside, Andrew Hay, on the dial, and by that you will see it was made expressly for me.' I then tried to open it, but failed owing to its having a secret spring. He then said, ' If you will allow me I will show you how to open it.' He did so, and I then saw that the name on the dial corresponded with the name he had given me. I then made out the duplicate, and he gave me the name Andrew Hay, and address 16, Princes-street, Cavendish-square. *I had examined the police lists,* as is my custom, but no such watch was mentioned as having been lost or stolen. About two months after the pledging an inspector came into the shop and produced the ticket* of the watch, and said he should require me to produce it on a certain day at Marlborough-street Police Court, and he remarked that the person who had pledged it was the same that had stolen Lady Bective's jewels. He also said that if it had not been for the prisoner attempting to destroy or burn the ticket, he should not have troubled any further about it, as he believed from prisoner's statement that it was his own. I produced the watch as desired at the Police Court and gave evidence. The magistrate remarked : 'You lent £10 upon this watch valued at about £70.' I should consider the outside value of the watch, being very old fashioned, £12—not sufficient to cover interest and commission (of sale). The prisoner was committed for trial, but I was not called upon to give evidence."

The inspector stated that the owner of the watch was a passenger on a P. & O. steamer, coming from India, and it was missed on arriving in London, but the loser thought it had been stolen on board ship. *No notice of the loss was given by the police to the Pawnbrokers.*

Some little amusement was created by the cross-examination of the Pawnbroker's Manager and the Inspector, as to the appearance of the prisoner when he pledged the watch. The Pawnbroker insisted that the man appeared to be quite a gentleman. On the other hand, the Inspector said the prisoner had the appearance of a butler, his clothing was shabby and he wore *an old white hat with a black band round it.* Every face but the Inspector's, was illuminated with a smile, as a hat of a similar description, the property of a noble Lord, was in a prominent position on a table at the opposite end

---

* " The automatic detective."—*Tyler.*

of the room. The idea seemed so thoroughly ludic-
rous that a man should be suspected of theft because he wore a style of hat which was much
affected by both Noble Lords and Members of Parliament.

One other case was investigated, but little was
proved beyond the fact that a careless assistant
who had been discharged for intemperance took in
a stolen watch and did not give notice to the police.
The employer "D," knew nothing of the case and
when requested to attend the court, he was unable
to do so because his other assistant was engaged
at the Guildhall, giving evidence against a dishonest employée, who was convicted for systematic
robberies in a large manufacturing silversmiths,
the detection and prosecution being entirely the
result of the efforts of the Pawnbroker named.
To him the firm of silversmiths wrote: "to thank
you for the prompt action you took in the matter
leading to the discovery of the robbery, and for
the assistance rendered by the attendance at the
prosecution."

The circumstances detailed in Story No. 2, took
place in January 1878, before Mr. Vincent's appointment; he knew therefore nothing whatever of the
matter, but what his trusty servitors were pleased
to tell him.

Further endeavours were made for other of the
charges to be investigated, but all progress in that
direction was abruptly terminated by Mr. Vincent
writing: "I regret to be unable to say whether I
intended to refer to them in my evidence, for I
refrained from making any mention of individuals."

We are compelled to omit notice of the evidence
for the defence given by the Hon. Sec., Mr. Alfred A.
George, Mr. Geo. Howarth, Mr. John Hepper, Auctioneer, Leeds, Mr. J. A. Telfer, Mr. Thos. Layman,

Mr. Geo. Attenborough, and Mr. Richard Attenborough, in which all spoke strongly of the disastrous
effects of the Bill upon the Trade.

CHAPTER XLIV

On the 18th of August the Bill was finally disposed of for the Session of 1881, so that for nearly six months the Trade were secure from further attack; while it was with some confidence the Committee believed that the labour expended had achieved valuable and favourable results. It was even assumed that the Director of Criminal Investigations himself was modifying his rancour, for with a view of ascertaining what he desired the London Pawnbrokers to do in aiding the police, Mr. Alfred George approached him, and after interviews and correspondence Mr. Vincent drafted seven regulations which he desired to see adopted by the Metropolitan Pawnbrokers. Mr. George lost no time in drawing the attention of the Committee of the Protection Society to the proposed rules and correspondence. That body held a meeting which was several times adjourned, and ultimately resolved to accept the regulations in spirit, but requested the Defence Association to secure their adoption by the London Trade.

The Sub-Committee were accordingly called together in London on February 15th, 1882, and after considering the communication from the Secretary of the Protection Society, they passed the following resolutions:—

"1. That the Sub-Committee of the Pawnbrokers' Defence Association are of opinion that the suggestions of Mr. C. E. Howard Vincent, dated January 17th, 1882, are such as should be adopted by the Pawnbrokers of the United Kingdom, and that the Sub-Committee will use their best endeavours to carry out the suggestions with a view to their effective adoption.

"2. That the foregoing resolution be conveyed to the Committee of the Metropolitan Pawnbrokers' Protection Society.

"3. That the above resolutions be forwarded to the members of the Executive Committee, together with a circular asking their approval of the steps taken and the course proposed."

The Protection Society Committee, in response, received the resolution with expressions of satisfaction, and thanked the Sub-Committee for having taken the matter in hand, and the whole of the Executive, with the exception of two, signed approval within a few days.

It was then decided to send to the whole of the London Trade a circular and a copy of the seven rules, accompanied by an undertaking to carry them out, the latter document to be signed by the Pawnbroker, and returned to the Secretary of the Defence Association. Before, however, adopting this plan it was thought desirable to seek an interview with Mr. Vincent, and ascertain whether or not the course proposed would receive his approval. The interview took place on February 23rd, and it was gratifying to find that the Director expressed his pleasure at the plan proposed, and thanked the Sub-Committee for the trouble they had undertaken, and in return promised to use his influence in the proper quarter, to mitigate the severity of the Stolen Goods Bill; also to obtain the appointment of respectable officers to conduct enquiries at the shops of Pawnbrokers, and, if possible, to make better arrangements for the attendance of members of the Trade at police courts and sessions houses. If the promised influence was used in the "proper quarter" after experience induced us to conclude that it was not very potent, for if anything, the severity of the Bill was rather increased than mitigated.

The Secretary was then directed to draw up a circular and an undertaking to be signed by every London Pawnbroker within the Metropolitan police district, and asking each to earnestly endeavour to faithfully carry out the following seven rules :—

"Rules to be observed for the better detection of crime, and the restoration of stolen property.

"1. Careful searching of the Daily Lists of Property Lost and Stolen, and comparison with the property recently pledged.

"2 Prompt information at the nearest police station with all particulars.

"3. Filing of the Lists and transcriptions therefrom in books of ready reference, of the principal articles, to save Pawnbrokers from loss by innocently taking the same in pledge.*

"4. Detention of any person offering in pledge an article advertised as stolen as provided by statute.

"5. The institution of close enquiry concerning any property of especial value, and possessing distinctive marks, whether advertised as stolen or not.

"6. Searching of the books and stock to see if a

_____

* Books specially designed for this purpose can be obtained at a cheap rate from the ticket printers in London and the Provinces.

stolen article has been taken in pledge, when requested by a police officer.

"7. Production of any article similar to one des-cribed as stolen for purposes of identification.

"The adoption of these few rules, added to a general desire to further the ends of justice, will promote security of property and be not less conducive to the interests of Pawnbrokers than valuable to the Public."

A strongly worded circular, a proof of which was submitted to Mr. Vincent, and approved by him, was sent out with copies of the above rules, and by the 24th April no less than 511 assents had been received. About this date Mr. Vincent wrote that he was anxiously awaiting the result as he "hoped the Stolen Goods Bill was about to be expeditiously proceeded with, and I am anxious to represent properly your action and its probable effect."

About a week later he again wrote: "I am looking forward to the early receipt of the detailed result of the appeal of the Defence Association to the London Pawnbrokers to undertake to abide by the admittedly few requirements of Justice in the conduct of their business, and was fully prepared to submit in its most favourable light this action of the Trade, and even, possibly, to use such very small influence as my humble opinion may chance to possess with those in higher authority, *for the exemption of Pawnbrokers from the Stolen Goods Bill.*" From the self deprecating tone of this letter it might be assumed that the writer had no control over the fortunes of the Bill, while, when under examination, he stated it had been drawn under his direction. This being so, and he had sufficient "small influence" to induce the Lord Chancellor to introduce it, and take charge of it in the House of Lords, one is inclined to ask why the same influence could not be exercised to withdraw the Pawn-broker from its operations?

Correspondence and interviews on the subject of
the seven rules occupied much time, after which the
Sub-Committee decided that another strong circular
should be issued to those members of the Trade who
had not yet sent in their adhesion to the rules. Eventually the signatures of 592 assenting members were
received, out of 617 requests sent out, leaving only
25 doubtful ones, while out of this small number some
were executors for businesses they little understood,
and therefore declined to accept such a responsibility.
Three indexed books containing the names and
addresses of all the Pawnbrokers who had accepted
the rules were written by an engrossing clerk, one
book was presented at an interview by the Secretary
to Mr. Vincent, when he said he complimented the
Sub-Committee very highly for the trouble they had
taken, and was pleased to find so large a majority of
the London Trade had signed. He assured the
Secretary that he would present the result to the
Lord Chancellor, and suggested that the Hon. Secretary should also write to his Lordship, detailing what
had been done. Of the two other books, one was retained by the Chairman, and the third was kept by
the Secretary, and is now in his possession.

The recommendation to communicate with the
Lord Chancellor, led to no other result than disappointment, with the accompanying sense of
humiliation to the Sub-Committee that they had
performed a useless, although onerous task, for on
the 5th June his Lordship was civil enough to say
that he would place the papers before the Select
Committee, but his Lordship must at the same time
lay before them the answer which he was awaiting
from Mr. Vincent. "The Lord Chancellor, subject
to any modification of his opinion to which he may
be led by Mr. Vincent's answer, *does not at present
see any reason why the accession of the Pawnbrokers*

to the Rules referred to should lead to any material alteration in the Bill."

Meanwhile the Stolen Goods Bill was making progress through the Lords. It had been read a first time on 21st April, a second time on the 25th, and was then referred to a Select Committee. On May 5 the Committee was named and consisted of the Lord Chancellor, Earls Waldegrave and Beauchamp, Viscount Sherbrook, and Lords Thurlow, Brodrick, Roseberry, Aberdare, and Bramwell. Four of the noble Lords were new Members, and had not heard the evidence given the previous Session, while Earl Morley, Lord Winmarleigh, Lord Ramsey and Earl Cairns, who had heard the evidence, were not again nominated.

The new Select Committee sat with closed doors on May 10th, 12th, June 7th, 14th, and 21st. On each occasion the Chairman and Hon. Sec., and sometimes other members of the Sub-Committee, attended in the lobby, but were unable to learn any particulars as to the proceedings. On the 21st, the Committee clerk stated that the sittings had that day terminated, and the same evening the Hon. Sec. wrote to Earl Beauchamp, asking for information. The next day a reply was received, and his Lordship said: "I need have no scruple in telling you that the Bill, though much altered in form, has been so far as Pawnbroking is concerned, not materially altered by the Select Committee."

The old offices in Westminster were again opened, for it was felt the struggle of opposition must be vigorously re-commenced. Copies of the Bill "as amended by the Select Committee" were obtained and forwarded to each Member of the Executive. In the meantime amendments were drawn and forwarded to Earl Beauchamp to be moved in Committee of the whole House. An appointment was

also made by his Lordship to see the Chairman and
Secretary at his own residence, 13, Belgrave Square.
Here the grave aspect of affairs was discussed, with
the result that his Lordship promised to see the
Lord Chancellor the same evening, and hoped to
get the consideration of the Bill postponed. Fortunately this move was successful, and a few days'
breathing time were obtained, which, as July had
now been reached, were of the utmost value to the
defenders; for every day that elapsed without making
progress, rendered the chance of the Bill passing
more improbable. A few days later the Marquis of
Salisbury was seen, and his Lordship promised to
give consideration to the Bill in its relation to the
public freedom and convenience, as against the proposed serious enlargement of the police powers.

The Bill, with no favourable alteration, passed
through Committee of the Lords, despite the strenuous
efforts of Earl Beauchamp, which were supported by a
strong speech by the Marquis of Salisbury. On the
13th it was read a third time and passed, and appeared on the proceedings of the House of Commons,
as "brought from the Lords, July 14th," and in that
position it remained until the close of the Session.
Thus, for the second year, the Committee of the
Defence Association had successfully defeated the
attempt made by the Lord Chancellor and Mr. Howard
Vincent, to place the Pawnbroking body under the
iron heel of police despotism. It was very naturally
thought by the Sub-Committee, that further duties
in connection with the opposition would at least
be suspended until Parliament again met. It was
arranged that there should be a winter session;
consequently a welcome respite of a few months was
eagerly anticipated. But it was not to be. Only
twelve days had elapsed when Mr. Vincent sent a
report to the Hon. Secretary detailing the particulars

of a robbery of jewellery pledges from the safe of one of the wealthiest London Pawnbrokers. Mr. Vincent desired the Sub-Committee to constitute themselves into a Court of Investigation, as there were serious allegations made against two respectable Pawnbrokers, of great carelessness, little short of actual dishonesty, in receiving property which was a portion of that 'stolen. The Sub-Committee at once met and commenced an enquiry, the result of which proved to their satisfaction that the report was a grossly exaggerated account of the transactions, and that one Inspector of Police had gravely exceeded his duty by reporting a conversation, the purport of which he gathered by unscrupulous eavesdropping. A report of the Sub-Committee's investigations was forwarded to Mr. Vincent, being for the most part a direct contradiction of the statements made by the police.

In a little more than a month, another report from Scotland Yard came to the Hon. Secretary, containing two serious charges against a Pawnbroker, for purchasing stolen property. There were grave suspicions connected with the case, and the Sub-Committee were of opinion that the Pawnbroker was not entirely free from blame. Considerable misunderstanding arose as to the mode of enquiry by the police. Two officers who were examined by the Sub-Committee, confessed that they confined their enquiries to the manager of the pledge department, while the goods were purchased by the salesman in a distinct shop. The matter was then reduced to the unsupported evidence of the salesman and one police-sergeant. The Sub-Committee considered that the Pawnbroker had not acted in accordance with the rules prepared by Mr. Vincent, circulated by the Defence Association, and accepted over his own signature. Mr. Vincent was advised of the

Sub-Committee's opinion, and two somewhat severe resolutions regarding his conduct were forwarded to the Pawnbroker.

Early in October, 1882, the Hon. Secretary wrote to Sir Wm. Harcourt, who was then Home Secretary, and asked him to receive a deputation on the subject of the Stolen Goods Bill. The Pawnbrokers' Committee, that letter said, "are quite aware that legislation is much required in the direction indicated by the Stolen Goods Bill, but they hold the opinion that its operations should be confined to the really criminal classes, such as are enumerated in the Judicial Statistics as being known thieves and receivers; and that a respectable body of tradesmen, already stringently legislated for, after careful and protracted enquiry, should not be subjected to pains and penalties ruinous in their severity, or be placed under the degrading suspicion that police surveillance is necessary for the honest conduct of the Pawnbroking Trade." The letter concluded with a hope that the Bill might be drawn, prior to its introduction next Session, in such a form as might obviate the necessity of opposition by the Pawnbrokers.

A reply was received stating the Home Secretary would receive a deputation of the Pawnbrokers; meanwhile he would be glad to receive a written statement of the views of the Association. The Hon. Secretary duly prepared another series of "Reasons and Observations" against the Bill and forwarded them to Whitehall. Several letters and telegrams were afterwards exchanged and the date for the deputation was fixed for February 12th, 1883. Several members of Parliament were invited to accompany the Pawnbrokers, but in consequence of only three days' notice being given of the exact date, only Mr. Serjeant Simon (now Sir John), the member for Dewsbury, appeared and introduced the deputation.

The interview was apparently so far favourable

as to give encouragement and hope to those who
composed the deputation, although Mr. Howard
Vincent was present. He made no remark, however,
but remained a listener only, while some of the
speakers alluded to his intentions and general attitude towards the Trade in scathing and vigorous language. On leaving the Home Office, Mr. Serjeant Simon
promised his assistance to the Pawnbrokers, and expressed himself as being perfectly willing to take the
responsibility of organising an opposition to the Bill.

In little more than an hour after the deputation had
left, a telegram was received from Mr. Vincent, stating
that he would be glad to see the Hon. Secretary the
next day, Tuesday. Of course such a wish was complied
with, and there was shown a disposition to effect some
compromise. The Director expressed his willingness
to withdraw the Pawnbrokers from the Stolen Goods
Bill, but he was told they required more; they must
have clear exemption from the operation of its clauses.
To this he agreed. He also promised to draw a
Pawnbrokers' Amendment Bill in which the power of
search should be limited to goods specifically named
in the warrant. He would do away with the police
detention, and would meet the Pawnbrokers in
any reasonable way. It was agreed that another
interview should take place on the following Thursday,
when the subject would be more matured and might
be reduced to writing. The Hon. Secretary reported
this important intelligence to the Sub-Committee,
when it was resolved that if the Committee received
positive assurance from the Home Secretary that they
were to be exempted from the Stolen Goods Bill, and
he was of opinion that the Pawnbrokers' Act, 1872,
required amendment, they would consider his suggestions. At the second interview Mr. Vincent
handed the Hon. Secretary a draft of all the proposed amendments of the Pawnbrokers' Act; they

were subsequently discussed by the Sub-Committee, printed and sent to the members of the Executive, with a circular requesting opinions to be sent back not later than March 10th. Mr. Vincent was informed of this step, and also that the subject was too important for the Sub-Committee to decide, and as soon as the opinions of the members of the Executive were known, the result would be communicated to him.

To this Mr. Vincent replied that he could not permit the circulation of the draft as he had not the sanction of the Secretary of State, nor had it been settled by Parliamentary Counsel. To this the Hon. Secretary replied, and in the last paragraph of his letter said, " Providing you propose to legislate for the Trade in a separate measure, we have no other. course left but to wait until the Bill is drawn, before deciding whether it has our approval or otherwise. I think it will be well in future, before any communication is made to us, that it should be official and have the approval of the Secretary of State, as it is useless consumption of time to discuss a subject and then receive the information that there is no authority for its being before us." For nearly a year no further communication was received from Mr. Howard Vincent. Later the Hon. Secretary wrote to the Home Secretary asking for precise information as to whether it was his intention or not to exempt the Pawnbrokers from the Stolen Goods Bill, and the following reply was elicited :—

" Whitehall, March 6, 1883.

SIR,— In reply to your letter of the 29th ult., asking whether Pawnbrokers will be exempted from the provisions of the Stolen Goods Bill, I am directed by the Secretary of State to acquaint you that the *Pawnbrokers will not be dealt with in that Bill*; but, if necessary, an Amendment of the Pawnbrokers' Act, 1872, will be introduced. I am, your obedient servant,
" A. F. O. LIDDELL."

Thus, when a meeting of the Executive was held in London, on April 11th, 1883, the Stolen Goods Bill had been practically defeated.

CHAPTER XLV

Notwithstanding the fair promise made by the Home Office, "that Pawnbrokers would not be dealt with in that Bill," the Sub-Committee did not relax their vigilance as to the progress of the Stolen Goods Bill. So that the Pawnbrokers should not be dealt with in that Bill, an exemption clause was inserted, and this was so loosely drawn, as to be practically no exemption whatever. Twice Counsel's opinion was taken upon it, and each time the clause was condemned as being ineffectual. It was finally drafted with the marginal title of "Saving Clause for Pawnbrokers, 35 and 36 Vic. cap. 93," and it went on to say that the provisions of that Act should not extend to any Pawnbroker to whom the Act applied in his business, nor to any pledge taken in the course of such business, and the sale by a Pawnbroker in pursuance of the Act, and the lawful purchase or acquisition* of his own unredeemed pledges, or of unredeemed pledges of other Pawnbrokers' and the sale by him of articles so bought or acquired, should be deemed part of the business of a Pawnbroker, and

* This word referred to pledges of ten shillings or under, which on forfeiture become the absolute property of the Pawnbroker.

should not constitute such Pawnbroker a second-
hand dealer; and the term pledge or pledges, included
every pledge whether the loan was above or below
ten pounds. This, as briefly as we can put it, was the
clause, and although we have denuded it of its legal
phrases and repetitions, it will easily be seen of what
a circumlocutory character it was. Perhaps the mind
of a Lord Chancellor is so contrived by nature, that he
could not express himself otherwise, but the manner
certainly created distrust in our minds. What the
Sub-Committee required, and which it was thought
would be effectual, was a brief and straightforward
clause to the effect that "This Bill shall not apply
to Pawnbrokers," as is the case with our own Act
of 1872, in which the second sub-section of clause 2
says, "This Act shall not extend to Ireland"; and
similar exceptions are made in many hundreds of other
Acts which are passed. But the clause as drawn was
the only way we could obtain exemption, and we were
induced to believe that it was correct and effectual.

All attention was speedily to be concentrated upon
the new Bill entitled an "Act to amend the Pawnbrokers Act, 1872." It was suddenly and unexpectedly
introduced into the House of Lords by the Lord
Chancellor, on the 5th June, 1883, and put on the
proceedings, to be read a second time on the 12th of
that month. With the promised exemption from the
Stolen Goods Bill, alarm had subsided, and it was
thought possible that Pawnbrokers would now be
forgotten. The sudden appearance of the Bill took
all by surprise. The Sub-Committee was summoned
to London at once. The Hon. Secretary appealed to
the Lord Chancellor to defer the second reading as
seven days gave no time to master the scope and
intention of the Bill. Another week was granted, and
ultimately the second reading was put off until
June 22nd.

This was time gained. The Executive Committee was next summoned, and several members of that body, who were experienced workers, came in advance and commenced vigorously and unceasingly to interview noble Lords connected with their own localities, while no opportunities were lost of seeing their Parliamentary representatives. The objections to the clauses of the Pawnbrokers' Amendment Bill were fully explained and many friends and supporters were secured.

When the Executive assembled in London the clauses of the Bill were exhaustively discussed, and many amendments were drawn, to be moved by some friendly disposed noble lord, in the event of the Bill not being defeated altogether.

Many of these amendments were accepted, and new revises or editions of the Bill were issued, on the 3rd July, and again on the 10th. The second reading and Committee were gone through quickly, and the report stage was reached on the 10th; Lord Henniker (the Lord Hartismere) as he was styled in the proceedings, who had become a strong opponent of the Bill, undertook, at the instance of the Defence Association, to move an amendment to clause 5, which provided that in addition to the entries in a Pawnbroker's books required by the Act of 1872, a further column should be adopted wherein should be entered "clear and distinctive marks as are borne by all watches or articles of plate or jewellery pawned with him and all other goods pawned with him for the sum of twenty shillings or upwards, *that is to say, any inscription, mark, initial, monogram, or crest, or in case of jewellery any peculiarity of setting, and shall otherwise so describe such articles as the more readily to secure their identification*." Lord Henniker proposed to leave out all the words after " upwards," which we have underlined. The Lord Chancellor refused to accept the amendment, consequently a division was called, with the result that there were 30 votes for it and 34 against; it was therefore lost. Still it was regarded almost as a victory, for it was no small matter to be proud of, that the friends of the Pawnbrokers did almost defeat the Government. The 34 "Contents" were Selborne (Lord Chancellor), Dukes, Bedford, Grafton and Richmond; Marquises, Lansdown and Northampton; Earls, Camperdown, Derby, Granville, Kimberley, Morley, Northbrook, Redesdale, Spencer and Sidney; Lords, Alcester, Ampthill, Boyle, Breadalbane, Brodrick, Carlingford, Carrington, Cottesloe, Digby, Kenmore, Monson, Penrhyn, Ribblesdale, Rosebery, Stanley of Alderley, Stratheden and Campbell, Sudeley and Truro. The minority or "Non-Contents" were Marquises of Bath, Hertford and Salisbury; Earls Carnarvon, Doncaster (Duke of Buccleuch), Fortescue, Lathom, Mount Edgcumbe, Ravensworth, Selkirk and Wharncliffe; Viscounts, Gough, Hawarden and Sidmouth; Lords, Amherst, Boston, Brabourne (formerly Knatchbull Huggessen), Colchester, Colville of Culross, Denman, Egerton, Foxford (Earl Limerick), Hartismere, Hopetown, Lamington, Norton, Shute, Silchester, Wemyss and Winmarleigh.

Two days after, the Bill was read a third time, and on July 13th it appeared on the proceedings of the Commons as "*brought from the Lords.*"

The Stolen Goods Bill, also in the Commons, made no progress. It was "blocked" by Mr. Wharton ("the champion blocker" he was called in the House). Mr. Hopwood, then Member for Stockport and now Recorder of Liverpool, Mr. Callan and Mr. Thomasson all placed notices of motion on the paper, "On second reading of the Stolen Goods Bill, to move, That it be read a second time upon this day three months. [Monday, 30th July]."

The Executive met in London, on August 1st, to

consider the Pawnbrokers' Amendment Bill, which had
undergone much revision and alteration, and after
carefully considering each of the amended clauses, it
was declared that the measure was still unacceptable
and must be opposed; it was felt the time had now
arrived when the Trade must show the strength of its
organization.

Arrangements were made for a "reconnaissance in
force," and the order was passed on to Mr. Alfred
George to open the movement by summoning the
various deputations which he had previously, with
astonishing success, organized in the city, borough and
county constituencies within the whole of the
Metropolitan district.   There were two Pawnbrokers
from each constituency, and their response to assemble
was prompt and hearty.   On Friday, August 3rd, these
gentlemen assembled in large numbers in St. Stephen's
Hall, and commenced to interview their various
representatives, requesting them to oppose the
Pawnbrokers' Bill.   The result was most satisfactory.
It was intended to follow up this advance movement
by Members from every provincial constituency that
could be got together, on the following Monday.   Upwards of thirty despatches of a most urgent character
had been prepared, and others were in progress,
as quickly as the writers could complete the work,
when at 4 p.m., on Saturday, August 4th, a letter was
received from Mr. Hibbert, the Under Secretary
of State for the Home Department, stating that THE
GOVERNMENT HAD DETERMINED TO WITHDRAW THE PAWN-
BROKERS' BILL FOR THAT SESSION!

The jubilation on the receipt of this intelligence was
great.   The work in progress was thrown aside, and in
a very short time upwards of forty telegrams and
letters of congratulation and thanks were dispatched,
and the Hon. Sec. wrote to Mr. Hibbert expressing
the sincere thanks of the Committee for the with-

drawal of the Bill, and stating that if the Stolen Goods
Bill was proceeded with the Pawnbrokers' Association
would not oppose its progress, providing the exemption
clause was drawn to their satisfaction; if not, *the whole
strength of the opposition would be directed against the
passing of the Bill.*

For the second time Counsel's opinion was taken
on the exemption clause, as it was still left in the
unsatisfactory condition that any goods purchased
by a Pawnbroker which had not been pledges were
liable to be searched for, seized, and taken away if
there was a suspicion that such goods were stolen. .
This was not satisfactory to the Pawnbrokers, consequently, after Counsel had amended the clause,
it was sent with other amendments to be inserted
in the Bill, and Mr. Hibbert was good enough to
accept them.

Events dribbled along until the 22nd August, when
the Sub-Committee were delighted to find on the
proceedings the following entry: "30. Stolen Goods
Bill [*Lords*].—Order for the Second Reading read, and
discharged;—Bill *withdrawn.*" Victory for the Trade
once more. During this Session the strength and
influence of the opposition had vastly increased. In
the Lords it had never been so great, and this was
owing in some measure to the invaluable assistance
rendered by Earl Wemyss, the Chairman, and other
members of the Liberty and Property Defence League.
The Marquis of Salisbury, Earl Beauchamp, Lord
Henniker, Earl Fortescue, Lord Winmarleigh and
others were unremitting in their endeavours to serve
the interests of the Trade, while in the Commons the
numbers of friends were legion.

Once more the Westminster office was closed. Not
so, however, the labour. Voluminous correspondence
was carried on, commencing in November and terminating in January, 1884, between the Hon. Secretary

and J. T. Hibbert Esq., the Under Secretary of State
for the Home Department. The Hon. Secretary
desired to know, for the information of the Committee, what the intention of the Government was
in regard to both Bills in the ensuing Session? The
reply was that the question of introducing one or
both Bills was occupying his attention, and he would
take care that the Hon. Secretary's letter should be
carefully weighed before a final decision was arrived
at. "Looking at the increased assistance," the letter
went on to say, "which the Director of Criminal
Investigations reports that the police are now receiving from the Trade, Mr. Hibbert is disposed to
abandon the Pawnbrokers' Bill, but to proceed with
the Stolen Goods Bill." In December Mr. Hibbert
forwarded copies of the five new search clauses which
it was proposed should be inserted in the Bill; two
of those did not affect Pawnbrokers. The others
were considerably softened from their tyrannical
character of 1881. It was provided that application
should be made to a Justice of the Peace for
a search warrant, and the superior officer of
the police must name the premises, and he
was to swear that he believed a robbery had
taken place and that the stolen goods were in
such premises, &c. After the reception of the
clauses the correspondence was continued until
the 15th January. Mr. Hibbert wrote, in reply to
a request for a copy of the new Bill, that the Stolen
Goods Bill, as proposed to be altered, had not yet
been printed. "As, however," the letter proceeded,
"you have already been supplied with the Bill of last
Session, the copy of the search clauses of general
application, proposed to be inserted, and the exemption promised to Pawnbrokers from the trade clauses
of the Bill which do not apply generally, Mr. Hibbert
trusts that the information afforded will be sufficient

for the purposes of your meeting on the 31st inst."
The meeting alluded to was that of the Executive
Committee which had been called together to consider
the proposals from the Home Office. After these
had been fully discussed, a resolution was proposed
by Mr. John Grantham, seconded by Mr. John Tatton,
"That the Executive Committee recommend to the
members of the Defence Association that they accept the
terms offered by the Home Office subject to the retention
of the exemption clause in the Stolen Goods Bill."

This was the beginning of the end. A General
Meeting was held in London of the guarantors and
subscribers on February 6th, 1884, and the principal
resolutions passed thereat were (1) "That this meeting having considered the correspondence between
the Home Office and the Honorary Secretary of the
Pawnbrokers' Defence Association, resolve that the
terms offered be accepted, and if the Exemption
Clause be maintained no opposition shall be offered
to the Stolen Goods Bill by this Association. (2)
That the report of the Executive Committee and
Treasurer's statement be received and approved."

The Treasurer's statement showed that no less
than £3,491 8s. had been collected from Guarantors
and Subscribers, and the expenditure had been £2,871,
leaving a balance in hand of £620, which was ultimately handed over to the Testimonial Committee.
The Defence Association was then formally dissolved,
but the Stolen Goods Bill never became an Act.
Thus ended one of the most important campaigns
ever commenced by, or on behalf of the Trade, and
a striking example of what may be achieved by
determination, tenacity, a knowledge of Parliamentary procedure, and the belief that the cause is
a just, fair and honourable one.

*   *   *   *   *

On the 3rd November, 1885, the most brilliant
function ever held in connection with the Trade took
place at the Holborn Restaurant, London. It was a
Banquet to celebrate the victory and distribute the
honourable awards to those who had fought and won
in the difficult and protracted struggle. The chair was
occupied by the late Mr. George Attenborough (Fleet-
street), and he was supported by the Right Hon.
Earl Beauchamp, Earl Fortescue, The Lord Mayor
of London (Sir Robert Fowler, M.P.), Sir David
Solomons, Bart., Hon. Francis Lawley, and Mr.
Alderman Hart. By a most unfortunate misunderstanding as to the date Earl Wemyss was not
present, as his Lordship had fixed the day in his
own mind as Wednesday, 4th, and appeared as he
thought to keep the appointment only to find the
festivities had taken place the evening before. Lord
Henniker, Baron Bramwell, Earl Pembroke, Baron
de Worms, and several members of the Commons
had been invited, all of whom returned most courteous replies excusing their absence.

Space will not permit more than to say that the
Banquet was a most successful one, over 200 guests being
present. The officers of the Defence Association were
the Hon. Sec., Messrs. J. A. Telfer, Richd. Attenborough,
Russell, Sprunt, Eaton and Grantham. The prizes
ranged from £1,000 and plate, to costly and tasteful
articles, selected according to the taste of each
recipient. The speeches, as we have already exceeded
the space allowed us, cannot be quoted here, but
it was especially pleasant to hear an English nobleman speaking of the Trade in these terms: " I am
very glad to meet the gentlemen around me and to
have given to their interests when the latter were
before the House of Lords my unflinching support.
I am also glad to take part in paying a just
tribute to the Parliamentary Committee of the

Defence Association. I have had the opportunity
of watching the many and distinguished services of
Mr. Hardaker throughout the manifold difficulties
he had to contend against—the promptness and
energy which he had displayed under the most
trying circumstances."

The Chairman performed his long and trying duties
with admirable tact and ability; the presentation
speeches being cleverly varied and eloquent. The
Hon. Secretaries of the Testimonial Fund—Mr. Alfred
George, London, and Mr. Wm. Guyler, of Liverpool
—elicited the highest praise and the most profound
gratitude of the recipients, for the devotion and
unceasing labours extending over 18 months, and the
magnificent results which they attained. They were
actuated by the most unselfish delight in their work,
and time, distance, comfort, or convenience were
never considered when the interests of those they
delighted to honour were to be promoted.

*　　*　　*　　*　　*

Nothing more remains to be chronicled in this
Brief History, for from 1885 to the present, the
period has been mainly uneventful. How long it may
so remain is doubtful. Two disquieting factors exist
—Mr. Howard Vincent and Sir Orr Ewing are still
members of Parliament. Trouble may not be now,
but it may be to come. What then the Trade have
to determine upon is to be ever on the alert and
prepared for the worst.

The motive which actuated the Author to compile
this little book, was principally, that the important
events in which he had personally taken part should
be collected and put on record while the memory
could retain the facts, and the hand had not lost its
cunning. There has been no attempt at brilliant

composition, and the Author is cognizant of many
defects and shortcomings; some of these were un-
avoidable under the exigencies of weekly publication,
therefore the indulgence of readers is entreated. It
may be objected that the latter chapters are strongly
flavoured with autobiography, but if such is thought
to be the case the cause is not to be attributed to
the Author, but rather to the prominent positions
to which he was relegated. If the facts which
the book contains are of value in the information
or instruction they convey, the labour of compilation will be amply repaid. It is hoped that
the History will be especially useful to the young
men of the Trade, who must be prepared to become
leaders when the present veterans are compelled to
lay down their arms, and if the perusal of the foregoing pages conduce to such victories as their elders
have achieved and are here narrated, the labour will
not be profitless.

THE END.

Printed by JACKSON, RUSTON & KEESON, *London*

www.ingramcontent.com/pod-product-compliance
Lightning Source LLC
Chambersburg PA
CBHW030906270326
41929CB00008B/602